Strengthening Families and Ending Abuse

The House of Prisca and Aquila

OUR MISSION AT THE HOUSE OF PRISCA AND AQUILA IS TO PRODUCE QUALITY books that expound accurately the word of God to empower women and men to minister together in a multicultural church. Our writers have a positive view of the Bible as God's revelation that affects both thoughts and words, so it is plenary, historically accurate, and consistent in itself; fully reliable; and authoritative as God's revelation. Because God is true, God's revelation is true, inclusive to men and women and speaking to a multicultural church, wherein all the diversity of the church is represented within the parameters of egalitarianism and inerrancy.

The word of God is what we are expounding, thereby empowering women and men to minister together in all levels of the church and home. The reason we say women and men together is because that is the model of Prisca and Aquila, ministering together to another member of the church—Apollos: "Having heard Apollos, Priscilla and Aquila took him aside and more accurately expounded to him the Way of God" (Acts 18:26). True exposition, like true religion, is by no means boring—it is fascinating. Books that reveal and expound God's true nature "burn within us" as they elucidate the Scripture and apply it to our lives.

This was the experience of the disciples who heard Jesus on the road to Emmaus: "Were not our hearts burning while Jesus was talking to us on the road, while he was opening the scriptures to us?" (Luke 24:32). We are hoping to create the classics of tomorrow: significant and accessible trade and academic books that "burn within us."

Our "house" is like the home to which Prisca and Aquila no doubt brought Apollos as they took him aside. It is like the home in Emmaus where Jesus stopped to break bread and reveal his presence. It is like the house built on the rock of obedience to Jesus (Matt 7:24). Our "house," as a euphemism for our publishing team, is a home where truth is shared and Jesus' Spirit breaks bread with us, nourishing all of us with his bounty of truth.

We are delighted to work together with Wipf and Stock in this series and welcome submissions on a wide variety of topics from an egalitarian inerrantist global perspective.

For more information, visit www.houseofpriscaandaquila.com.

Strengthening Families and Ending Abuse
Churches and Their Leaders Look to The Future

Edited by
NANCY NASON-CLARK
BARBARA FISHER-TOWNSEND
and
VICTORIA FAHLBERG

WIPF & STOCK · Eugene, Oregon

STRENGTHENING FAMILIES AND ENDING ABUSE
Churches and Their Leaders Look to The Future

Copyright © 2013 Wipf and Stock Publishers. All rights reserved. Except for brief quotations in critical publications or reviews, no part of this book may be reproduced in any manner without prior written permission from the publisher. Write: Permissions. Wipf and Stock Publishers, 199 W. 8th Ave., Suite 3, Eugene, OR 97401.

Wipf & Stock
An Imprint of Wipf and Stock Publishers
199 W. 8th Ave., Suite 3
Eugene, OR 97401

www.wipfandstock.com

ISBN 13: 978-1-62032-659-6

Manufactured in the U.S.A.

Contents

List of Contributors   vii

PART I: Strengthening Families

1. Introduction   3
   —Nancy Nason-Clark and Barbara Fisher-Townsend

2. A Woman After God's Own Heart: The Legacy of Catherine Clark Kroeger   6
   —Amy Rasmussen Buckley

3. Messiah Meets a Woman   15
   —Amy Rasmussen Buckley

4. The Effects of Love on Children   27
   —Juan Carlos Areán and Nancy Raines

5. Life Stories of Men who Act Abusively: Elements of the Coordinated Community Response   40
   —Nancy Nason-Clark, Barbara Fisher-Townsend, Steve McMullin and Catherine Holtmann

6. More Than a Simple List   65
   —David Horita

7. A Framework for Understanding Risk and Protective Factors of Intimate Partner Violence within a Larger Social Context   80
   —Victoria Fahlberg

PART II: Working to Strengthen Individuals within Family Life

8. Realizing the Potential of Second Stage Programming   99
   —Lorrie Wasyliw

9 Best Practices for Supporting Victims of Domestic Violence in Rural Communities   115
   —Julie A. Owens and Rhonda Encinas

10 From the Top: What Does It Mean When Catholic Bishops Speak Out on Issues of Family Violence?   139
    —Catherine Holtmann

11 Church Leaders and Family Violence: Understanding the Challenge   160
    —Victoria Fahlberg

PART III: Plan for Action

12 Clergy and the Pastoral Response to Domestic Violence: Understanding the Complexities   183
    —Steve McMullin

13 Preparing Congregations for Collaborative Work: The Role of the Mennonite Central Committee in Strengthening Families   200
    —Linda Gehman Peachey and Elsie Goerzen

14 Preparing Seminaries for Collaborative Work   220
    —Steve McMullin and Nancy Nason-Clark

15 Project Esther in New Zealand: The Challenge of Working with Women at Risk   242
    —Daphne Marsden

16 The Story of Restored   257
    —Mandy Marshall and Peter Grant

17 Caring for the Caregivers: The Efficacy of a Centred Meditation Practice within a Secular Setting   263
    —Irene Sevcik, Nancy Nason-Clark, Michael Rothery and Robert Pynn

18 The Dating Game: An Innovative Way to Engage Church Youth on Strengthening Relationships   287
    —Catherine Holtmann, Barbara Fisher-Townsend, Steve McMullin and Nancy Nason-Clark

19 Conclusion   309
    —Nancy Nason-Clark and Barbara Fisher-Townsend

Contributors

EDITORIAL TEAM

Nancy Nason-Clark, PhD, is the Chair of the Department of Sociology at the University of New Brunswick in Canada and Director of the RAVE Project. Her books include: *The Battered Wife: How Christians Confront Family Violence; No Place for Abuse: Biblical and Practical Resources to Counteract Domestic Violence* and *Refuse from Abuse: Healing and Hope for Abused Religious Women* (both with Catherine Clark Kroeger), *Partnering for Change* (co-edited) and *Feminist Narratives and the Sociology of Religion* (with M.J. Neitz).

Barbara Fisher-Townsend, PhD, works as a Contract Academic in the Department of Sociology at the University of New Brunswick, after having completed a post-doctoral fellowship with the RAVE project. She teaches family violence related courses in the Department of Sociology and for the Muriel McQueen Fergusson Centre for Family Violence Research certificate program in family violence. Her research focuses on the role of faith and hope in assisting men of faith who have acted abusively to move toward changed thinking and behavior. She is completing a book with Nancy Nason-Clark on the life stories of men who have acted abusively.

Victoria Fahlberg has a PhD in Clinical Psychology and a Master of Public Health in Population and International Health from Harvard University. From 1989 to 1997 she lived in Brazil where she founded ACODE, a social service/mental health clinic in a large *favela* (City of God) in Rio de Janeiro, initiated the first graduate program in Brazil in family violence at *Pontificia Universidade Catolica*, and directed a national research project on child abuse in Brazil. She returned to the US in 1997 and has been working with immigrants and refugees since

2001. She has worked as a consultant for UNICEF, was a member of the Governor's Commission for Domestic and Sexual Violence from 2003–2007, and was the Executive Director of One Lowell, a community-based organization in Lowell, Massachusetts from 2002–2010.

CHAPTER CONTRIBUTORS

Juan Carlos Areán, MM, is the director of the National Latin@ Network for Healthy Families and Communities. He is an active trainer who has led workshops and presentations on family violence prevention in the US and many other countries.

Rhonda Encinas is the Founder and Director of Priest River Ministries Advocates for Women and is author of *Healing Hearts: A Bible Study for Women*. She and her all-volunteer team provide free comprehensive faith-based services including a 24 hour hotline, confidential safe shelter, advocacy, support, education, legal assistance, jail ministry and Bible Study support groups for victims of domestic violence and their children in rural Idaho. Rhonda is a Biblical Counselor and member of the American Association of Christian Counselors. She earned a New Testament Degree from Moody Bible College.

Linda Gehman Peachey is a writer and editor from Lancaster, PA, who works with the Abuse Response and Prevention Network of Mennonite Central Committee Canada and US. She is married to Titus Peachey, has two adult daughters and is an active member at East Chestnut Mennonite Church.

Elsie Goerzen is the Coordinator of the Mennonite Central Committee BC, Abuse Response and Prevention Program. She has previously worked as a Registered Nurse, a child abuse prevention facilitator, a parenting educator, and Coordinator of a support program for single mothers with preschool age children. Elsie is married to Walt, her partner of 45 years and together they enjoy gardening and spending time with their five grandchildren.

Peter Grant is the Co-Founder and Co-Director of Restored. For the past five years he has been the International Director of Tearfund, with responsibility for Tearfund's worldwide work with partners and disaster response programmes in Haiti, Sudan, Congo and Afghanistan.

Prior to joining Tearfund, Peter worked for fifteen years with the UK's Department for International Development.

Catherine Holtmann, MDiv, MA, is a Catholic feminist interested in education and social justice. Her professional experiences involve pastoral ministry, music ministry, workshop facilitation, social movement organization and university teaching. She is a doctoral student in the Sociology Department of the University of New Brunswick and works with The RAVE Project team.

David Horita, MDiv serves one of the Fellowship of Evangelical Baptist Churches in British Columbia.

Daphne Marsden has been a member of a pastoral team at Spreydon Baptist Church in New Zealand for nearly 2 decades. Part of her ministry has been the establishment and leading of Project Esther, an arm of the local church relating to and serving women and their families facing difficulty.

Amanda Marshall is the co-founder and co-director of Restored, a Christian organization aimed at transforming relationships and ending violence against women. She previously worked for Tearfund as their Programme Development Advisor for Gender. Mandy has travelled extensively over the last 17 years and has run gender training across Africa, Central Asia, SE Asia & Latin America and the UK. In 2011, Mandy won a Deloitte Women Who Rock Award for her work on gender equality and ending violence against women.

Steve McMullin, MATS, PhD, is an Associate Professor at Acadia Divinity College in Nova Scotia, Canada and a member of the Religion and Violence Research team at the University of New Brunswick. He is a sociologist and an ordained Baptist pastor.

Julie Owens, BA, is a survivor of DV who has worked in the field of violence against women for 20 years. The daughter of a prominent pastor, her personal story of survival is featured in the documentaries, "Broken Vows" and "When Love Hurts." She trains faith leaders for the FaithTrust Institute and PASCH and was a site Coordinator for the RAVE Project. Julie has developed a hospital crisis team, counselor certification programs, and trauma research projects.

Robert Pynn is the Anglican Dean Emeritus of Calgary. Throughout his career he has inspired and helped found many social programs including HomeFront and FaithLink. He is the recipient of many awards and honors for his public service including the Alberta Centennial Award and the Queen's Diamond Jubilee Medal. His books of poetry include *Life Lines* and soon to be published *Writing the Wind*.

Nancy Raines, MDiv, MFA holds a Masters of Divinity degree from Harvard University. She worked for several years as a Staff Chaplain at Massachusetts General Hospital, and now works as a Spiritual Counselor for a hospice program.

Amy Rasmussen Buckley pursued a Master of Divinity at Gordon-Conwell Theological Seminary and George Fox Evangelical Seminary where she graduated in 2010. She has contributed to conferences and publications sponsored by Peace and Safety in the Christian Home, and she serves on the board of Life Together International. Amy lives in Palm Harbor, Florida with her husband and two adopted daughters.

Michael Rothery, PhD, is a professor emeritus, recently retired from the University of Calgary's Faculty of Social Work. Throughout his professional and academic career, Mike studied services to vulnerable families, with violence in adult intimate relationships having been an especially strong interest. He has, in recent years, devoted time and energy to understanding the relationship between religious and secular helping for people experiencing intimate partner violence.

Irene Sevcik, PhD, is a social worker whose career focused on services to children and families experiencing difficult circumstances, including those affected by intimate partner violence. Most recently her work has facilitated and researched the interface between religious/ethno-cultural communities and those providing secularly-based services to abused women. Irene holds a PhD from the Faculty of Social Work, University of Toronto.

Lorrie Wasyliw is the founder and Executive Director of WINGS [Women in Need Gaining Strength]. She serves as the President of the Fellowship of Evangelical Baptist Churches in British Columbia.

PART I
Strengthening Families

1

Introduction

Nancy Nason-Clark and Barbara Fisher-Townsend

IN SO MANY WAYS, this book represents a transitioning phase for us personally and for the work of PASCH—Peace and Safety in the Christian Home—an organization begun by the late Dr. Catherine Clark Kroeger in January of 2004. PASCH reflected the Jewish notion of Passover, the time of new beginnings. To its founder, our beloved Cathie, it drew its strength from the Biblical mandate to bring safety and respite, as well as practical and spiritual resources, to those who were suffering the impact of abuse in their family context.

We were Catherine's co-laborers in the vineyard of PASCH, as were those whose work is represented in the various chapters of *Strengthening Families and Ending Abuse*. By her enthusiasm and dogged determination, Dr. Kroeger drew in a wide circle of people to advance the cause of violence in families of faith. She wanted us to speak out against every form of violence and to use our prophetic voices to call religious leaders, ordained ministers, and those who faithfully attend congregational life to do likewise. She challenged us, and by her actions, enabled us to challenge others to offer a wide variety of services and resources to women, men, teens, and children who found themselves caught in the web of abuse.

Over the course of seven years, from its early days in 2004, until the year of her death in 2011, PASCH sponsored five major conferences. These were held in Newport Beach, California (2005), Boston, Massachusetts (2006), Portland, Oregon (2007), Washington, D.C.

(2008) and Abbotsford, British Columbia (2011). Based on several plenary sessions and workshops held at these first four events, two edited collections have been published under the titles, *Beyond Abuse in the Christian Home: Raising Voices for Change* (2008) and *Responding to Abuse in the Christian Home: A Challenge for Churches and their Leaders* (2011).

The current volume brings together many of the plenary sessions and workshops that were given at the conference held at ACTS Seminary, located in Abbotsford, not far from Vancouver, Canada. There was also a tribute to the life and work of Dr. Catherine Clark Kroeger, the founding President of PASCH, who until her death on February 14th, 2011 continued to serve as its president.

Often there is an element of sadness involved in transitions and to be sure we feel a degree of sadness as we write the introduction to this the third and last edited collection to be birthed by PASCH. In many ways, this book is a tribute to Cathie's legacy—her tireless energy and her passionate commitment to stopping abuse and teaching churches and pastors *what the Bible says about this horrific evil.*

At the 2011 Board of Directors meeting following her death, it was decided that the PASCH organization would continue its work until we had completed the edited collection to emerge from the Vancouver conference. With the publication of this volume, PASCH will no longer continue but the work and ministry of responding to the needs of victims, survivors, perpetrators, and their families goes on—in different forms, around the world, much of it having received some degree of support and encouragement from the life and work of Cathie.

We as an editorial team all served on the Board of Directors of PASCH and each of us worked with Cathie in a variety of capacities. We know first-hand of her warmth, her hospitality, her skill and intellect, her love of the Scriptures, and her dedication to those who suffered abuse in any of its ugly forms. Cathie had a passion for social justice, abounding energy, and the gift of hospitality. She had the capacity to speak many languages and to converse with scholars as well as the illiterate. We were amazed by her ability to think quickly, to translate and memorize the Scriptures, and to recall them on demand, and her extraordinary talent to tell the stories of the Bible with wit and tact.

She was a scholar-servant. The torch she carried for Christian equality and for the abused was sometimes misunderstood. We believe that the influence of her scholarship, her writing, and her compassion for people will continue to grow throughout the world, shining as a beacon of light.

It is our hope and desire that this book—one small piece of evidence of her enthusiasm and drive to support peace and safety in the Christian home—will be useful to pastors, advocates, victims, survivors, and men and women who love the church, and who have chosen to follow Jesus of Nazareth.

For the life of our beloved Dr. Catherine Clark Kroeger, wife, mother, grandmother, scholar, philanthropist, mentor, author, teacher, colleague, friend, and servant of the Lord Jesus Christ we give God thanks.

Additional word of thanks:

We are so grateful for the editorial assistance and suggestions of Jean Dimock of the House of Prisca and Aquila. Her attention to detail and helpful feedback have facilitated the editorial process and made our lives so much easier. It has been a pleasure to have three books published under the House of Prisca and Aquila imprint. Thanks are due to Aida Besancon Spencer and William David Spencer.

2

A Woman after God's Own Heart
The Legacy of Catherine Clark Kroeger

Amy Rasmussen Buckley

Dr. Catherine Clark Kroeger was an exemplary woman who gave much of her life to the struggle for justice for abused women. Her life's work reminds me of a parable that Jesus once told his disciples. It too concerned an exemplary woman who did not lose heart in the midst of a struggle for justice. The parable centers on a woman's relentless pleas for an unjust judge to respond justly. She is a widow struggling with an opponent. And although the unjust judge neither fears God, nor respects people, the widow tirelessly pursues a just verdict, demanding, "Grant me justice against my opponent." After continued rounds of refusals by the judge, and pleas by the widow, the unjust judge relents. It is not that the judge has come to fear God, or to respect anyone; rather, the widow's persistence has paid off! Jesus drives home the point: "Will not God grant justice to his chosen ones who cry out to him day and night? Will he delay long in helping them?" (Luke 18:1–8). At the close of the parable, Jesus informs his disciples of their need to pray always, have faith, and not lose heart: God will grant justice.

More than anyone I have known, Dr. Catherine Clark Kroeger demonstrated such faith, never losing heart as she communed with the One who desires to see peace and safety reflected in Christian homes. As Dr. Kroeger's student and academic assistant at Gordon-

Conwell Theological Seminary, I quickly came to see that the pleasant, twinkling-eyed lady was actually a force to reckon with! And it wasn't long before I noticed that Cathie (as she asked to be called) would not give up seeking justice and restoration for those who suffer any form of prejudice or abuse. Cathie often spoke of her desire to unite God's people to correct "a terrible evil" that affects so many Christian families.

For several years, I traveled to conferences with Dr. Kroeger to promote awareness about her newly founded organization, Peace and Safety in the Christian Home (PASCH). We conversed with hundreds of people who stopped by the PASCH booth, and Cathie tenaciously spoke of what so many Christians have refused to talk about for so long. She explained that PASCH was moving into an area where few Christians have been willing to go, and those who have experienced "alienation and shame" from church communities are finding "new pathways of faith and self-confidence." She smiled in the way she always did, and explained that this is a service we are "happy to provide."

The more time I spent with Cathie, the more I realized the depth of her concerns about domestic abuse and violence in Christian homes. To her, statistics were more than numbers—they pointed at real people who had suffered. Soberly, she explained one-on-one to those who asked, statistics and facts that had been researched and fully referenced in her books: One in three to four women have experienced domestic abuse; more women go to the emergency room due to abuse by an intimate partner than due to mugging, rape, or traffic accidents combined; fourteen to fifteen hundred women in the United States die each year at the hands of intimate partners, and the toll for children is even higher; and the United States Surgeon General has declared domestic violence to be the number one public health problem of women.

Cathie recognized that most Christian leaders do not mean for injustice to occur, or for harm to come to congregants. Rather, many well-meaning evangelical shepherds do not have enough training to recognize and appropriately respond to situations of abuse. She had grave concerns that our seminaries seldom offer biblical teaching, and practical training. Inadequate clergy responses may harm families and drive victims away from the very communities whom God calls to offer compassion and effective assistance. Drawing on materials, referenced in her books or in PASCH newsletters, Cathy would explain: As evangelicals, it is impossible for us to ignore what our Bibles say, and in the spirit of the prophets, we must—although unpopular—first point at evil and, second, bring God's word to bear upon it, and demand appropriate action. She pointed at over a hundred times in which the Bible says that abuse—whether physical, verbal, emotional or sexual—is wrong. She urged evangelical leaders not only to proclaim God's truth about domestic abuse but also to act on behalf of those experiencing it. She called attention to the prophet Ezekiel's words:

> But if the watchmen sees the sword coming and does not blow the trumpet to warn the people and the sword comes and takes the life of one of them, that man will be taken away because of his sin, but I will hold the watchman accountable for his blood. (Ez 33:6, NIV)

And to those who allow suffering to continue unchecked among God's people, she quoted the prophet Jeremiah:

> They have healed also the hurt of the daughter of my people slightly, saying 'Peace, peace' when there is no peace. (Jer 6:14, KJV)

It troubled Cathie that the unwillingness of many to face this reality results in denying, concealing, minimizing, or ignoring sinful injustice. Dr. Catherine Clark Kroeger intended for Peace and Safety in the Christian Home to sound a prophetic call for leaders to respond, biblically and practically to the prevalence of abuse and violence in Christian communities.

Cathie loved telling women the story of Hagar, the Egyptian slave, who escaped from the abuse of her mistress Sarai, wife of Abram. She explained that Abram and Sarai's abominable mistreatment of Hagar—forcing her to conceive, carry and deliver a baby for them—included sexual, emotional, mental, and physical abuse. Cathie explained the impossible circumstances that Hagar faced as she fled into the desert, sank at a well, and then discovered that she was not after all alone. Cathie loved pointing out that Hagar is the only person in all of Bible history who gives God a name and although others experienced the revelation of a divine name, Hagar alone discovered that God both *hears and sees* abused women.

Cathie helped victims see that they do not cause abuse any more than Hagar caused mistreatment by Sarai and Abram. Deeply moved, women listened as Cathie continued the story of God's intimate care for Hagar after a second experience of abuse by Sarai and eviction, by Abram, to the wilderness. She would note how God commands Hagar to stand up and take her child by the hand. Rather than sinking in self-pity, and helplessness, God wants Hagar to learn survival in the desert. In that moment God opens her eyes and she sees a well of water that she has not seen before (Gen 21:19). Smiling, Cathie would point out the hopeful future ahead—Hagar sends to Egypt for a bride for her son, exercising newfound freedom while living in alliance with the One whose goodness and love she deeply knows (Gen 21:21).

Ministering to victims of abuse, Cathie offered respite where they might encounter the *God Who Sees*. Cathie did not hesitate to recommend that women in need turn to shelters that are generally better equipped to handle their immediate needs than churches. At the same time, she urged women never to forget the value of prayer support, loving fellowship, and spiritual guidance that so many churches have to offer. Cathie never gave up believing that God can restore any circumstances. If a woman expressed regret after multiple times leaving and returning to an abusive husband, Cathie listened. She offered assurance that, although painful, the journey had to have challenged the woman's growth while leading her to deeper knowledge of God's continuing love and care. Cathie offered material assistance to women, usually secretly, believing that the greatest gift to them was the reflection of God's care for their souls. In doing so, she incarnated God's word in practical ways: "Share the sorrow of those being mistreated as if you feel their pain in your own bodies" (Heb 13:3, NLT) and "Never get tired of doing good (2 Thess 3:13, NLT)."

The year I volunteered as the PASCH intern, Cathie and I responded to telephone calls from many individuals requesting biblical and practical resources—clergy, health care providers, rescue teams, shelter personnel, social workers, therapists, counselors, concerned friends, and family members. Victims also contacted PASCH. Their stories provided a glimpse behind a veil that so often hides the wounds of our Christian communities. I had known the wounds existed but I had never realized the numbers of women, children, and even men, who suffer secretly behind closed doors.

Victims requested help with basic needs (food, clothing, shelter). Many feared for their safety and for that of their children. Others struggled, sorting out desires to leave and return to abusive partners, multiple times, when help networks had given up. Many needed assistance with judicial arms of government that handle restraining orders, separate support, divorce proceedings, child custody, and prosecution. Most struggled with affordable housing, reentry into the workforce, childcare, health insurance, and making ends meet through expensive litigation proceedings. Healthcare issues arose. Some had physical ailments such as broken bones and damaged eardrums. Others had mental and emotional struggles such as PTSD, depression, and suicidal impulses. Issues involving the rehabilitation of abusers also arose. Many victims felt hurt by church leaders; most struggled with their relationships with God; many no longer wanted anything to do with churches or God. More than ever, I realized the sobering realities that shaped Cathie's vision for PASCH. I came also to recognize a large population of people who need biblical and practical resources if peace and safety is to become a reality for much of Christ's body. Cathie and I worked hard to connect callers with resources. And I must admit that the obstacles seemed overwhelming when so few resources existed to service so many needs, big needs. I know that weighed on Cathie, too.

In the midst of numerous activities and projects, Cathie never lost her winsome spirit. And she never gave up promoting peace and safety in Christian communities. Maintaining connections with numerous people all over the world, Cathie sought to connect those she knew for mutual encouragement, collaboration, service to others, and ultimately God. Goran Kojchev, who worked as Cathie's teaching assistant a few years later, noted her great ability to juggle correspondence and everyday tasks. At age eighty-five, she maintained connections with hundreds of people while writing articles, answering phone calls, teaching classes, and drafting a manuscript for a new book. Cathie perceived others as unique strands twining into a fabric of God's purposes. Cathie believed that each member of Christ's body holds an important key to solving the problem of domestic abuse and violence. But ultimately Christ holds all the keys to creating peace and safety in Christian homes as members of his body bear his presence and purposes to the world. This thinking propelled Cathie's vision for Peace and Safety in the Christian Home to become an international network sharing biblical and theological insights, research, training, and safety information. Cathie envisioned a threefold goal: first to demonstrate the reality of the problem within evangelical homes, second to lay out the biblical imperatives that demand a response, and third to offer credible resources to bring about safety and healing to Christian communities. She believed the work possible because God's Word promises new life for the suffering: "I will lie down and sleep in peace, for You alone, O Lord, make me dwell in safety" (Ps 4:8)."

To her students at Gordon-Conwell Theological Seminary, Dr. Catherine Clark Kroeger demonstrated that domestic abuse is more than social injustice; it is sin. And the remedy for sin involves right thinking and responses to God's Word. She pointed at some hundred biblical passages addressing battering, violence, rape, incest, stalking, lying in wait, twisting the words of another, threats, and intimidation (all forms of abuse). "If this is what the word of God says, then we must be faithful in proclaiming it" she would say. She urged Christian leaders to remember that what they teach permeates society far beyond the walls of the church.

Dr. Kroeger urged church leaders to proclaim from the pulpit that domestic abuse is sinful, expound it in Bible studies, and discuss it in small groups. However, she pointed out that preaching and teaching against domestic abuse is not enough. She would remind us that Scripture forbids leadership to those who mistreat their families (1 Tim 3:3, Titus 1:7). Churches must uphold discipline and keep those who have been victimized safe (Gal 6:1; Matt 18:15; 1 Thess 5, 11–14; James 5:20). She once explained to a class, "It is not in the best interests of a man's soul for a church to cover his sinful actions." Rather, she went on to argue, it is imperative to hold an offender accountable so he may repent and take responsibility for the lengthy process of rebuilding trust necessary for relating to his wife and children in healthy ways.

In an article entitled "Are the Shepherds Safeguarding the lives of the Sheep?" Dr. Kroeger called Christian leaders to accountability. She emphasized that we must teach pastors that it takes great courage for a woman to disclose the humiliating truth that she is a victim of abuse and the danger for women and children is real. Pastors must realize that abused women struggle with shame and with fear; fear that she will not be believed; and fear that it may go worse for her at home behind closed doors once she has disclosed the truth. In this article, Cathie goes on to explain that abusers may seem very pious, very self-controlled, or even very repentant, but they may also be very dangerous. Even the most convincing statements may not guarantee safe behavior behind closed doors.

With regard to the prevalence of abuse in Christian communities, Dr. Kroeger told her students, "We have not loved each other as we ought." She wrote of these concerns in an article entitled "The Abused Bride of Christ," published in "PRISM Magazine" (May/June 2004):

> Evangelicalism has been effective in proclaiming the redemptive and reconciling love of God to a world in desperate need. In the last half-century, it has gained in both numbers and influence throughout the globe. Believers can point to many accomplishments and ministries through which they have sought to bring glory to God and healing balm to those in need. There has been recognition that we must be doers of the word and not hearers only. In at least one area, however, evangelicals have lagged far behind others involved in humanitarian endeavors. We have failed to address the issue of domestic abuse in any significant way. In actuality, our leaders have been caught in a dilemma that leaves them with a high degree of discomfort even to acknowledge the problem.

Although uncomfortable, Dr. Kroeger insisted that evangelicals re-examine their attitudes and actions in light of the biblical mandates. "Whoever winks the eye causes trouble, but the one who rebukes boldly makes peace. The mouth of the righteous is a fountain of life, but the mouth of the wicked conceals violence." (Prov 10:10–11, NRSV)

A passionate evangelical, Catherine Clark Kroeger never gave up unveiling God's intended purposes for the written Word. She shared increasing archeological evidence that the Greek meaning of the word head (*kephale*) is akin to that of a head of a fountain or a river. According to Scripture, Christ—the *head* of the church—is the source of all life similar to the head of a fountain, or river, serving as the starting point (the source) of life-giving waters. Cathie would quote Ephesians 4:15–16:

> We must no longer be children, tossed to and fro and blown about by every wind of doctrine. . . . But speaking the truth in love, we must grow up in every way into him who is the head, into Christ, from whom the whole body, joined and knit together by every ligament with which it is equipped, as each part is working properly, promotes the body's growth in building

itself up in love." (Women's Study New Testament, Based on the NRSV)

Christ, who is the *head* of the Church, is the *Source* of all life and goodness. And when the metaphor of *head* is used for husbands, it does not mean they are to be the bosses, but they are to empower their wives toward fullness of life in Christ. This entire teaching is presented within the context of mutually submitting to one another (*hupotasso*) as members of Christ's body (Eph 5:21). Dr. Kroeger's scholarship reveals the beauty contrasting what some have twisted. This is what God intends not just for marriage but also for the community of the Church.

Shortly after Dr. Catherine Clark Kroeger's passing, Dr. Frank James, Provost at Gordon-Conwell Theological Seminary, spoke of her legacy: "She will be remembered as one of the most respected Bible scholars of our day, a champion of the equality of women and a staunch opponent of domestic violence. It was just a few short weeks ago that she was reminding me, with a twinkle in her eye, that we needed to devote a chapel service to encouraging women. She will be greatly missed by our community, but we are confident she will brighten the halls of heaven." Catherine Clark Kroeger's teaching affected countless Christian leaders who continue carrying the good news of God's good purposes to the ends of the earth.

In her book *100 Christian Women Who Changed the 20th Century*, Helen Kooiman Hosier celebrated the lives of women whose work has significantly impacted the world. It wasn't until I had known Cathie for five years that I realized she was among those whom Hosier had honored. Catherine Clark Kroeger never set out to be great. Rather, she looked for waters in which the Spirit was stirring, and she dove in. Whether those waters involved teaching, writing books, speaking with dignitaries, ministering to women and children, or folding PASCH newsletters, Cathie swam full force. And she encouraged countless others to swim with her. More than that, she urged them—she urged us—to swim with the One whose Presence we bear. She never gave up believing that the Father, Son, and Spirit promise to recreate our otherwise hopeless world. Knowing the waters are deep, she urged us to never give up. Collating newsletters, one time, I noticed a tiny note next to a recipient's name and address: "Love from Cathie." Beside that she had drawn a heart.

Like so many, I am indebted to Catherine Clark Kroeger for being my teacher, mentor, and beloved friend. I am indebted even more to God for allowing me to know such an amazing woman. As we celebrate Catherine's life, I pray that we discern the waters in which the Spirit is stirring, and dive in. I pray that we never stop swimming with the One whose Presence, through us, promises to usher peace and safety in Christian homes. As we move forward, I can't help but wonder if Cathie is standing with a cloud of witnesses, high-fiving angels, and scoring a big win for Heaven! And I can't help but wonder if she is standing next to Jesus urging us to never give up.

(This tribute is based upon words shared during the memorial service, honoring Catherine Clark Kroeger, at the PASCH 2011 Conference in Abbotsford, British Columbia.)

3

Messiah Meets a Woman

Amy Rasmussen Buckley

STORY OF A SAMARITAN OUTCAST

The woman didn't mind coming to the well in the middle of the day. It mattered little that the sun burned like a hot coal in the sky. Other women came at the end of day when it was cooler. She figured that coming in the middle of the day was better than enduring the cold stares of the pious women who waited turns to lower their buckets into the deep waters of Jacob's well. Not even a cool pot of water in the middle of the desert was worth their silence and condescending eyes.

As the Samaritan woman approached the well, she thought of her ancestor Jacob seeing Rebecca for the first time. She liked imagining his giddy stare as he watched Rebecca lower and raise her bucket of water. She liked thinking that a man could love a woman so much that he would want her to be bone of his bone and flesh of his flesh.

Mount Gerizim rose in the distance. Moving toward the well, she noticed a Jewish man resting. Thoughts stirred in her mind: Why was a Jewish man traveling through Samaria when other Jews traveled around it? Why was he lingering at the well when everybody knew that only morally reprehensible women drew water in the middle of the day? Tentatively she approached the stone mouth of the well. She suspended the pot over the dark hole, and pretended not to notice the man watching as she extended the rope from one hand through the other.

"Give me a drink," the man said.

She caught her breath and looked up. Beads of sweat ran down his face and neck. Astounded, she wondered why a Jewish man was speaking to her. Surely he knew the rule—that Jews do not share things, including water pots, with Samaritans. The woman shifted from one foot to the other due to the weight of the bucket and her own discomfort. "How is it that you, a Jew, ask a drink of me, a woman of Samaria?" She braced herself for his answer and wondered *what he would want* after she gave him a drink.

Messiah meets a woman (John 4: 4–26)

The Samaritan woman who Jesus met at the well was thirsty. We know this because she carried an empty water pot from the village of Sychar to Jacob's well (over a half mile). We know this because she went for water during the hottest time of day—when social outcasts likely avoided confrontations with pious women[1] who drew water during the cooler late afternoon.[2] We know the Samaritan woman was thirsty because Jesus said to her, "If you knew the gift of God and who it is that is saying to you, 'give me a drink,' you would have asked him, and he would have given you living water" (v. 10). Jesus pointed at a thirst that Jacob's well could never satisfy. Intrigued, the woman had to have wondered where Jesus would get that living water, especially when he had no bucket and the well was deep. Was it possible the man standing before her was greater than her ancestor Jacob who had built the well?

Speaking with the Samaritan woman, Jesus acted unconventionally. A Jew who addressed a Samaritan might as well have exposed himself to a communicable disease. Jews considered Samaritans to be hopelessly unclean. For one, Samaritans did not pay homage to all the Jewish writings. They only followed the Pentateuch, the first five books that Moses wrote.[3] Samaritans also worshiped at Mt. Gerizim instead of the temple in Jerusalem.[4] Generally, Jews and Samaritans did not get along. And Jews did not share things, including water pots, with Samaritans. When Jesus asked the woman at the well for a drink he invited religious contamination. Pious Jewish men were not to speak

---

1. Kroeger and Evans, "Study Bible," 1995, 188.
2. Kroeger, lecture from "Women in the Early Church," 2005.
3. *NIV Archeological Study Bible*, 1727.
4. Ibid.

with women outside their families.[5] Carrying on a religious conversation with a woman was tantamount to trampling Yahweh's Word in the dirt![6] Most outrageously, Jesus addressed the outcast Samaritan woman after his colleagues went on an errand in town. Such behavior in first century Palestine had the appearance of a sexual proposition.[7]

The woman responded enthusiastically to Jesus' offer of a spring of water gushing up to eternal life. "Sir, give me this water so that I may never be thirsty or have to keep coming here to draw water" (v. 15). The woman grasped the possibility of no longer having to thirst.

"Go call your husband," Jesus said, "and come back."

Painful memories had to have called attention to her soul's thirst as the woman admitted to having no husband (vv. 16–17). Gently, Jesus expressed knowledge that she'd had five husbands and the man she was with was not her husband.

"What you have said is true!" It shocked the woman that he knew so much about her life.

The apostle John does not give many details about the Samaritan woman's story. However, the culture of her day can tell us some things. The surrounding community would have tolerated two, or maybe three, divorces.[8] Five marriages amounted to a disaster! Notably, Jesus refers to the woman's illicit relationship with a man (not prostitution as many assume beyond the actual text). In this case, the woman was committing adultery against her fifth husband.[9] By Jewish and Samaritan standards, we know this woman's life was outrageously immoral. No doubt, her choices had contributed to her lack of status in the community. Yet, in fairness, we have to consider–Was there more to her story? What other factors may have precipitated the end of her former marriages? Did she deserve such judgment from the religious establishment? Was she worthy of being ostracized by her community?

A law in the Pentateuch allowed a husband to divorce his wife for "some uncleanness." The term was ambiguous and sometimes misapplied. Rabbinical literature (not part of the Old Testament) also considered burnt food as grounds for divorce. Was it possible the Samaritan

5. Kroeger and Evans, *IVP Bible Commentary*, 2002, 597.
6. Kroeger and Evans, *Study Bible*, 1995, 187.
7. Kroeger, lecture from "Women in the Early Church," 2005.
8. Ibid.
9. Ibid.

woman might not have been a first century Martha Stewart? Had she, on certain occasions, burned too many pieces of meat?! A former husband might also have found an excuse to divorce his wife for a younger, more fertile wife. If a husband built a convincing enough case against a wife, he could keep her dowry and cast her into the streets. And without a dowry, or an official divorce certificate, a woman could not remarry.[10] Injustices were possible because of loopholes in the system, resulting in grave mistreatment, social stigma, and few options. Questioning how else to survive, the woman may have chosen to cohabitate with a man instead of living without protection on the streets. Aside from these possibilities, we must consider that one or more of the woman's husbands had died. Prior to falling into disgrace, the Samaritan woman had experienced a string of painful losses. Nevertheless, Jesus gently calls attention to her history of having five husbands while the man she with was not her husband. God's Word does not include any more details about her sins. But we have enough information to know that the Samaritan woman had a painful, immoral past that resulted in her becoming ostracized by her community.

Far from ostracizing the Samaritan woman, Jesus invites her to drink water that promises to quench her deepest longings. He explains, "everyone who drinks of this water will be thirsty again, but those who drink of the water that I give them will never be thirsty. The water that I give them will become a spring of water welling up to eternal life" (v. 13). Jesus built upon the woman's understanding of physical water—that it has life giving properties. The woman knew that humans, and animals, do not last long in the desert without water. She understood her need for water on scorching hot days when she felt thirsty. Clearly Jesus wanted her to realize her deepest need and do something about it. "But those who drink of the water I give them," Jesus told her, "will become a spring of water welling up to eternal life." Here Jesus addressed the human need for spiritual water. He wanted the woman to recognize her thirst in the desert of disappointment, shame, anger, loneliness, and pain. More than that, he wanted her to receive the drink he offered—from the spring of living water welling up to eternal life.

No doubt the Samaritan woman felt her soul's thirst as she reflected upon her life. The man standing before her was obviously some kind of prophet. How else would he understand so much about her

10. Ibid.

when others misunderstood? "Sir, I see you are a prophet," she said. "Our ancestors worshiped on this mountain, but you say that the place where people must worship is Jerusalem" (vv. 19–20). The woman may have felt flustered that Jesus knew so much about her. Obviously, she considered the true place of God's temple a worthy subject of discussion with Him.[11]

Jesus responded, "Woman, believe me, a time is coming when you will worship the Father neither on this mountain nor in Jerusalem. You worship what you do not know; we worship what we know, for salvation is from the Jews" (vv. 21–22). Jesus clarified to the Samaritan women that salvation would arrive through the lineage of the Jews. And although the Samaritans had some grasp of God's truth, they did not fully comprehend it. Most surprising, perhaps, is Jesus' statement that she would worship neither on Mt. Gerizim, nor in Jerusalem. Here the apostle John marks a shift in the New Testament: Being a worshiper in spirit and truth involves something different than making pilgrimages to Jerusalem or Mt. Gerizim. The woman had to have wondered, "So where do we go? Where is a true worshipper to go?"

Jesus went on: "But the hour is coming, and is now here, when the true worshipers will worship the Father in spirit and in truth, for the Father seeks such as these to worship him. God is spirit, and those who worship him must worship in spirit and truth" (v. 24). Jesus told the woman that God is spirit and God longs to commune with human spirits. He wanted her to know that true worship takes place through a relationship with the Father. He wanted the Samaritan woman to understand that—through a relationship with Him—she would become part of God's temple.[12]

A light flashed through her mind—"I know that Messiah is coming" (who is called Christ). When he comes, he will proclaim all things to us" (v. 25).

"I am he," Jesus answered, "the one who is speaking to you" (v. 26).

---

11. Wenham et al., *New Bible Commentary*, 1994, 1034.

12. God establishes the eternal Temple of Christ's Body as believers receive Messiah—their Source of living water welling up to eternal life. Members of Christ's Body embody His Temple on earth, individually and corporately, through the local and worldwide Church. Eph 2:21; John 2:19–21; 1 Cor 3:16–17, 6:17; Rev 3:12.

Story of a new temple

The Samaritan woman set her water pot on the ground, stunned. It mattered little that Jesus' colleagues were returning from town, carrying sacks of grain, fish and fruit. She hardly noticed their surprise at the sight of their leader talking to a Samaritan woman. For an instant, she expected someone to reprimand her for violating the unspoken divide between Jews and Samaritans, men and women, the pious and the not so pious. But their eyes did not condemn her. Turning, she left her water jar on the ground and quickly started toward Sychar. As she moved across the hot sand, her mind raced. Could the man by the well really be Messiah? Did Yahweh really want a temple somewhere besides Jerusalem or Mt. Gerizim? If so, then were her legs carrying a temple?! Arriving in town, she proclaimed to everyone: "Come see a man who told me everything I ever did. Could this be the Christ?!" Stunned, by her testimony, many of those who once ostracized the Samaritan woman followed her to Jacob's well to meet Messiah.

The Samaritan woman among us

If the Samaritan woman lived today, she would slip into a back row of our sanctuaries late, and leave early, because she would rather not discuss her story with some who have *wrongfully judged* and *marginalized* her. She would be a reclusive, middle-aged woman whose pastor has told her to keep praying after two decades of asking God to stop her husband from isolating and belittling her. She would be a separated mother who refuses a physically abusive husband contact with the children as her church withholds support until she stops "breaking up the family." She would be a seventeen-year-old high school student whose youth pastor has rebuked her for putting up with a boyfriend who routinely calls her names, and forcibly pursues sex. She would be a woman, in a rural community, who has been told to stop "stirring up trouble" by asking the elder board to confront her elder husband's jealous, violent outbursts. She would be a newly married woman who has received advice, from a women's ministry coordinator, to win her pornography-addicted husband to Christ through "submitting more" and "giving him better sex." Her story would parallel that of a newly divorced man whose small group leader has asked if his "lack of affection" drove his former wife to sleep with a string of men she met via Internet chat-rooms. Of course, such wrongful reactions occur in situations beyond abuse and violence. And, indeed, God's Word calls communities to enact proper confrontation of sin where it is due (Matt 18:15–20). The point is that, like the Samaritan Woman, some victims of abuse experience *ungodly judgments*, and *marginalizing*, from the very communities whom God calls to minister the Presence of Christ to them.

Messiah meets victims of abuse

How many souls avoid uncomfortable, hurtful responses from members of their faith communities? Heartbreakingly, the occurrence of family abuse within church communities is just as prevalent as in secular society.[13] According to current statistics, one in three to four women experience domestic abuse and violence.[14] Approximately 11.5 percent of adult men experience intimate partner violence victimization.[15] Tragically, 65 percent of children are impacted by domestic abuse. One in five female high school students report being physically and/or sexually abused by a dating partner.[16] Additionally, victims testify that responses of religious people frequently add to their suffering,[17] making it difficult for their souls to acquire life-giving water at church. Although such sobering realities exist, God's Word promises new possibilities. Jesus' relationship with the Samaritan woman offers a portrait of God's care for *wrongfully judged* and *marginalized* people. He leaves a number of footprints for us to follow as we minister His Presence to hurting, broken people including victims of abuse:

1. Jesus enters the uncomfortable, upside-down world of the Samaritan woman.

On a scorching afternoon, Jesus ventures into the desert where the Samaritan woman draws water. Sitting by Jacob's well, He embraces human thirst. In doing so, He identifies with a difficult aspect of the woman's situation—meeting her need for physical water in the midst of community scorn. Jesus acknowledges the added burden of her pun-

13. Wilson, *When Violence Begins at Home*, 179.
14. Kroeger and Nason-Clark, *No Place for Abuse*, 2001, 19.
15. *CDC Adverse Health Conditions*, 2005.
16. Silverman et al., "Dating Violence," 2004.
17. Kroeger and Nason-Clark, *No Place For Abuse*, 2001, 17–19.

ishment by the community—acquiring water alone in the baking sun. In contrast to the Samaritan religious establishment, Jesus seeks her company. God in the flesh establishes a relationship with the Samaritan woman, rendering it possible for the waters of God's Realm to spill into her parched soul. Following in Jesus' footsteps, God's Word exhorts us to cultivate non-judgmental relationships with those who suffer abuse, opening the way for them to drink from the well of water promising new life.

  2. Jesus values God's purposes over religious, political, and social agendas.

Jesus ministers to the Samaritan woman in a world full of divides—Jews versus Samaritans, the clean versus the unclean, men versus women, the pious versus the not so pious, those who belong versus those who are outcasts. Remarkably, Jesus defies traditional Jewish standards—seeking a relationship with a Samaritan who does not believe "correctly" about Yahweh's Word and the true place of Yahweh's temple. Even more shocking, Jesus relates to a woman whom the surrounding Samaritan community has labeled "unclean, hopeless, and useless." Religious, political, and social correctness does not stop Jesus from pursuing a relationship with the Samaritan woman before he reveals his identity—as Messiah—to her. Jesus' footsteps call us to fulfill God's purposes, in ministry to victims of abuse, even when those clash with cherished religious, political and social agendas.

  3. Jesus risks His reputation to embody God's Word to the woman.

Although an occupational hazard, Jesus converses with an unclean person whose presence equates with exposure to a communicable disease. He does not maintain distance for fear of becoming "defiled," rendering Him "unfit" as a Jewish religious leader (according to Jewish law). In doing so, Jesus risks the reputation of His ministry. He risks His reputation, also, by conversing with a woman—tantamount to "trampling Yahweh's Word in the dirt." In truth, Jesus embodies the Good News of God's Word to the woman. Notably, His ministry actually becomes more fruitful—when the woman's testimony about Messiah brings many from the Samaritan community to God's Realm. Obviously, He knows what He is doing! Jesus' footprints challenge us to be willing to risk our reputations as the Presence of Christ breaks down ministry barriers.

4. Jesus affirms the woman's value, dissolving gender divides.

Within a culture that prohibits conversations between men and women who are unrelated, Jesus does not hesitate to speak with a woman whose soul desperately thirsts for living water. Doing so, He conveys her great value to God and the community He is building. Jesus engages in a profound theological discussion unlike any, thus far, in His ministry. He reveals his identity as "Messiah," first, to her. Jesus treats the woman as someone special whom God is calling to play a unique part in the establishment of God's Realm.

Within a culture that perceives such actions as "sexually" motivated, Jesus models the potential for healthy inter-gender relationships. If Jesus had treated the Samaritan woman according to cultural gender prescriptions, she might never have found reason to turn from her hurtful, illicit relationship. More than that, she and many from her community might never have come to Christ. Following in Jesus' footsteps, it is necessary to teach and model healthy inter-gender relationships, freeing the way for Christ's Presence to minister new life to victims of abuse.

5. Jesus counted the costs of ministering to the woman while trusting the Father for the future.

Very soon, Jesus and His disciples would travel to other areas of Palestine, making known God's Realm breaking into the world. No doubt, news of Jesus' conversation with the Samaritan woman would follow. And while some would rejoice over Yahweh's great goodness, others would criticize Jesus' unorthodox and politically and socially incorrect behaviors. Similar to today, support would ebb and flow among those who agreed, or disagreed, with Jesus' means of ministering to people. More than that, many of His own people would consider His message heretical, resulting in further investigations, and grilling, by Jewish religious leaders. Ultimately the truth of His identity—as Messiah—would lead to His death. Jesus reveals His identity to the fallen, outcast Samaritan woman. Counting the costs, Jesus entrusts her with the most important news of His entire ministry. Following in Jesus' footsteps, God's Word requires us to minister to victims of abuse, ever trusting that God will provide for the future despite the costs.

6. Jesus confronts the woman's legitimate sin, gently, and offers her the promise of new life.

Jesus gently segues into the topic of the woman's sin: "Go call your husband and come back." As painful memories heighten awareness of her soul's thirst, she admits to having no husband; Jesus expresses knowledge of her five husbands. Assuming nothing false about the reasons for her failed marriages, Jesus plainly communicates understanding that the man she is with is not her husband. No assumptions. No accusations. No judgmental comments. Not even Jesus judges and condemns her. Following in Jesus' footsteps requires that we assume nothing about the reasons behind a victim's failed relationship(s). Jesus' actions entail no hollow accusations or ungodly judgments, to a broken, marginalized soul. Rather, Jesus confronts legitimate sin gently and offers the promise of a spring of water welling up to a new life.

7. Jesus invites the women to contribute to his life and ministry.

Stepping into the remote, burning desert, where the Samaritan woman fetches water, Jesus makes a shocking request. Aside from the fact that Jews do not share things like water pots with Samaritans, Jesus places Himself in a genuine position of need. Once again breaking religious and social mores, the Son of God asks for "unclean" water contained in an "unclean" Samaritan pot delivered by the hands of an "unclean" Samaritan woman. Jesus' request communicates profound *value* of what the woman has to offer. In a physical sense, Jesus invites her to tend to Him, putting her in a position of power to meet His need (or not). In doing so, Jesus offers her dignity.

How shocking is it that Jesus then offers the woman a drink from a spring of water welling up to eternal life? Enthusiastically, she expresses a desire to know more: "Sir, give me this water so that I may never be thirsty or have to keep coming here to draw water." His invitation to the woman reciprocates hospitality, cultivating a personal relationship. Jesus' treatment of the Samaritan woman powerfully contrasts treatment by those in the religious community who have no regard for her spiritual needs, wellbeing, and value to God. Following in Jesus' footsteps entails cultivating mutual relationships with victims of abuse. We offer them Christ's life-giving water as well as opportunities to contribute to the Body of Christ (our communities).

Envisioning new temples

What does it look like to minister the Presence of Jesus to victims of abuse and violence? On Sunday morning, we venture to a back row of our sanctuaries to sit beside those who arrive late and leave early. We greet them warmly. We learn and worship and pray beside them. We share our lives and listen to their stories (as they choose to share). We make no assumptions and no accusations. We refrain from asking questions or making comments about what we think a victim may have done to bring abuse upon herself/himself. We withhold comments about assumed reasons behind failed/failing relationship(s). We bring the eyes, and hands, and encouraging Presence of Jesus to them.

We follow Jesus' footprints, allowing no human agendas to stand in the way of God's purposes. Religious, political, and social correctness do not stop us from pursuing ministry relationships with victims of abuse. We stand up for those who have been mistreated according to labels that divide—*sinners* versus *saints, weak* versus *strong, faithful* versus *faithless, married* versus *divorced, men* versus *women, insiders* versus *outsiders*. We do so knowing that some will rejoice while others will criticize what they consider unorthodox, politically and socially, incorrect ministry. Despite the ebb and flow of human opinions and support, we trust our Heavenly Father for the future without becoming caught up in the costs or our reputations. We allow no human agendas—whether religious, political, or social—to stand in the way of confronting *legitimate* sin where it is due. We confront the *legitimate* sins of those who commit abuse according to Matt. 18:15-20 (church discipline). We gently confront *legitimate* sins of victims—as with all hurting, broken people in search of life-giving waters. We open ways for them to drink from Jesus' spring of water welling up to new life.

We bind ourselves to the standards of God's Word including over one hundred Scriptures that condemn all forms of abuse and violence. We write them on the tablets of our hearts. We write church policies that clearly outline biblical and practical responses to situations of abuse and violence. We teach and model the potential for healthy inter-gender relationships, creating a category of friendship in Christ that is not sexually motivated. Within that context, we speak to women and men whose souls desperately thirst for living water. In doing so, we affirm their great value to God and the community. We invite them to contribute their talents and gifts to the community (teaching Sunday school, singing in choir, helping with VBS, serving as a deacon . . .) We offer them dignity. We invite opportunities for them to share their testimonies, bolstering our own faith in Christ. We share our lives with them as they share their lives with us. We drink continuously from Jesus' spring of living water, welling up to eternal life. We embody the good news of God's Word to victims of abuse and violence, welcoming them with the arms of Christ.

We do not forget that everyone faces deserts of disappointment, shame, anger, loneliness, and pain. Externally we may or may not show it. Socially we may or may not pay a price. Others may not know the twists and turns that have led us to hardships and fallen choices. But the One who met the Samaritan woman at Jacob's well, the One who knew her so well, is the same One offering to satisfy our every thirst. God promises a spring of living water, welling up to new lives and God-honoring communities. "If the spirit of him who raised Jesus from the dead dwells in you, he who raised Christ from the dead will give life to your mortal bodies also through his spirit that dwells in you" (Rom 8:11).

BIBLIOGRAPHY

"CDC Adverse Health Conditions and Health Risk Behaviors Associated with Intimate Partner Violence–United States 2005." Quoted on-line: http://www.thehotline.org/get-educated/abuse-in-america/.

Kroeger, C. Clark. Lecture from seminary course "Women in the Early Church," South Hamilton, MA: Gordon-Conwell Theological Seminary, Spring, 2005.

Kroeger, C. Clark, and M. J. Evans. *The IVP Women's Bible Commentary, An Indispensible Resource for All Who Want to View Scripture Through Different Eyes,* Downers Grove: InterVarsity Press, 2002.

———. *Study Bible for Women, the New Testament,* Grand Rapids: Baker Books, 1995.

Kroeger, C. Clark, and N.Nason-Clark. *No Place For Abuse, Biblical and Practical Resources to Counteract Domestic Violence,* Downer's Grove: InterVarsity Press, 2001.

New International Version Archeological Study Bible, An Illustrated Walk Through Biblical History and Culture, Grand Rapids: Zondervan, 2005.

Silverman, J. G., A. Raj, and K. Clements. "Dating violence against adolescent girls and associated substance use, unhealthy weight control, sexual risk behavior, pregnancy, and suicidality," *Pediatrics,* August 2004. http://www.thehotline.org/get-educated/abuse-in-america/.

Wenham, G.J., J.A. Motyer, D.A. Carson, R.T. France. *New Bible Commentary, 21ST Century Edition,* Downers Grove: InterVarsity Press, 1994.

Wilson, K. J. *When Violence Begins at Home, A Comprehensive Guide to Understanding and Ending Domestic Abuse,* Alameda: Hunter House Inc. Publishers, 1997.

4

The Effects of Love on Children

Juan Carlos Areán and Nancy Raines

> [Love] always protects, always trusts, always hopes, always perseveres. 1 Cor 13:7

INTRODUCTION

Bobby was a teenager in a very dark place. A number of adverse factors were at play in his sadness, including having experienced violence at home. He went from being a happy and charming little boy to an angry and despairing adolescent, engaging in unsafe behaviors and generally acting cynical and miserable. His distraught parents tried many avenues recommended to them including psychological and behavioral therapy for Bobby and for the whole family. Nothing seemed to get through to him and they family was frightened for his ultimate safety.

It was not until his parents found a way to engage him spiritually that Bobby's life turned around. This was a process that developed over more than a year's time, as they "swooped in," showing him how much he was loved, helped him correct negative thinking, and then guided him in feeling the love of God and power of the Holy Spirit[1].

Today Bobby is a blooming, engaging, and joyful young man. His parents report that his smile is back and his loving heart is once more

---

1. While this is couched here in Christian terms, we recognize the Divine as encompassing all peoples and faiths.

open and hopeful. Bobby attests that what brought him out of the darkness was a spiritual awakening. What was this process, and how did it help this young man heal from trauma?

In this article, we will look at the definition and scope of the problem of childhood exposure to violence; we will review the research on the effects and symptoms of abuse and trauma on children; we will propose a shift on the field's focus, from primarily centering on the bad news (exposure to domestic violence can have a devastating impact on children's lives), to emphasizing the good news (many of these children can grow up to have healthy and productive lives); we will explore the research on resilience to trauma and violence to better understand what can help traumatized children heal; and emphasize spirituality as a protective factor and means to heal from the effects of abuse.

We hope this will be helpful to clergy and communities of faith, who are in a unique and ideal position to foster the spiritual feelings of children, and to show them the way out of grief, the way out of despair, and the way to God.

CHILDHOOD EXPOSURE TO VIOLENCE: SCOPE AND DEFINITION OF THE PROBLEM

Exposure to domestic violence and other traumatic experiences is often very damaging for children, and the effects of this exposure often pursue the child into adulthood. In fact, researchers have demonstrated that being exposed to violence and trauma can be as harmful to children as experiencing the violence directly. The effects and symptoms of child abuse and exposure to violence are virtually undistinguishable.[2]

The definition of exposure to violence has recently been expanded. Previously, it was thought that the primary means that children experienced adult violence was by directly witnessing or hearing the incidents of abuse. New research has enlarged this definition by adding listening to threats of physical harm and other emotional abuse, feeling the tension building prior to an assault, seeing the aftermath of violent incidents, experiencing the undermining of the relationship with the non-abusive parent, and being enlisted by the violent parent to align against the other parent.[3]

---

2. Jaffe et al., "Similarities."
3. Fantuzzo and Mohr, "Prevalence."

This new definition has helped researchers better estimate the epidemic proportion of childhood exposure to domestic violence. In a recent study, Jouriles, McDonald and colleagues calculated that every year in the United States, 15.5 million children are exposed to domestic violence.[4] That means that in a single year, almost one in five American children suffer the consequences of living with domestic violence.

The bad news: The impact of exposure to violence on children

For this article, we will consider the effects of violence and trauma in three categories, with the understanding that there is some overlap among them: the impact on the heart, the mind, and the spirit. We will not address a fourth category, the impact of violence on the body and the brain, but will point out that there can be many devastating health consequences and actual and psychosomatic physical symptoms due to exposure to trauma.[5]

Heart

We are calling the effects of violence on the heart those that directly damage the emotional self. Children exposed to abuse and trauma might experience one or more of the following feelings: despair, hopelessness, guilt, shame, powerlessness, helplessness, terror, insecurity, low self-esteem, self-hatred, humiliation, inferiority, resentfulness, worthlessness, loneliness, rejection, confusion, insecurity, rage. Violence within a family constitutes the betrayal of our apparently closest bonds. This can be devastating to a child's sense of connection and loyalty.

Mind

The impact of violence and trauma on the mind can lead children to incorrect thinking about themselves and the world around them. For instance, children often blame themselves for the violence, and conclude that they are bad, or that they don't deserve to be loved. They may think that violence is normal in families, and that the world is unsafe and that they cannot trust anyone. Children might determine that they are insignificant, unimportant and/or unwanted, or that no one under-

---

4. Jouriles et al., "Documenting."
5. Campbell, "Health Consequences."

stands them. They might lose their ability to hope for a better future, either for themselves or for their family.

Spirit

The spiritual impact of childhood exposure to violence and trauma has not been well researched to our knowledge, even though it could potentially be the most devastating. It is probably safe to assume that being exposed to violence could create a form of spiritual distress such as loss of faith, spiritual isolation, feelings of betrayal and abandonment by God, anger at God, and an overall sense of not being loved by God or not being worthy of that love. If God represents the ultimate safety net for a child in an unstable home, the loss of that connection can be very damaging.

We are including in this article a list of common symptoms and behaviors seen in children exposed to violence or trauma (See Box One). They comprise both internalized and externalized symptoms. Internalized symptoms are self-destructive behaviors, such as cutting or eating disorders and are more commonly found in girls. Externalized symptoms are behaviors directed at others, such as aggression, and tend to be displayed more often by boys.

It is imperative to point out that some of these behaviors and effects may be seen in children who have not been exposed to violence or trauma. There are many potential stressors and life circumstances, which could impact a child's mind, heart, or spirit in these ways. However, given the prevalence of exposure to domestic violence, when we observe a child displaying multiple negative behaviors, feelings or thoughts, it is important not to discount the possibility of trauma or exposure to abuse.

BOX ONE—SYMPTOMS OF VIOLENCE AND TRAUMA ON CHILDREN CLASSIFIED BY AGE[6]

Infants/toddlers/young children (0–6)

Low birth weight	Difficulty attaching to caregiver
Extreme irritability/tantrums	Hyper-vigilance
Exaggerated startle response	Eating problems
Regression in toileting or language	Extreme separation anxiety or clinging to care giver
Sleep disturbances	

School-aged children (7–12)

Difficulty paying attention	Wanting to be left alone
Becoming quiet, upset, and withdrawn	Eating more or less than usual
Being tearful and sad and talk about scary feelings and ideas	Getting into trouble at home or school
	Low self esteem
Fighting with peers or adults	Self blame
Changes in school performance	

Adolescents (13–18)

Experiencing frequent nightmares	Increasing aggressive behaviors
Sleeping more or less than usual	Eating disorders
Complaining of being tired all the time	"Cutting" or suicidality
Refusing to follow rules or talk back with greater frequency	Using violence in their own intimate relationships
Wanting to be alone, not even wanting to spend time with friends	Using drugs or alcohol, running away from home, or getting into trouble with the law
Engaging in risky behaviors	

SHIFTING THE FOCUS

As important as it is to know that exposure to domestic violence and other traumatic experiences can be devastating for children, it is also essential to understand that not all children are affected in the same way, and that many children can heal from these traumas and lead happy, wholesome lives.

Recent research has shown that there are many variables that influence how children react to exposure to violence and trauma. These include the age and developmental stage of the child when the violence happens, their role in the family, and their personal characteristics.

---

6. Adapted from Safe Start Center, "Healing."

Other variables identified are gender, intellectual ability, socioeconomic status, and access to social support. Some children seem to be minimally affected, whereas others exhibit many symptoms of trauma.[7]

It has often been the case, in both research and practice, that mainly the negative aspects of exposure to violence are discussed, leaving out critical information on how the impact of violence can be diminished and reversed. For instance, there are more than two hundred studies looking at the effects of exposure to abuse on children,[8] whereas there are only a few that explore resilience and protective factors from that abuse.

One striking example of undue emphasis on the negative is the fact that, contrary to what many people think, most boys who grow up in abusive households do not become abusers themselves.[9] That is, even with the modeling of abusive treatment of women, most boys do not repeat the violence they experienced as children. This is a profound and important truth not to be overlooked. It is very hopeful information for victims and practitioners alike and, as such, serious research dollars should be invested to determine the protective factors behind this evidence.

Moreover, there have been adverse, unintended consequences to victims of domestic violence and their children due to the unbalanced nature of the information available. When the non-abusive parent hears only about the impact of violence and not about resilience and protective factors, the little hope that they might have for their children's wellbeing can be crushed. How beneficial then for parents of children exposed to violence to both understand that healing is possible and the key role that they themselves might play in helping their children overcome negative experiences!

An even more destructive unintended consequence of focusing only on the negative has been the Child Protection Services' practice of removing traumatized children from their non-abusive parent, because of that parent's alleged "neglect" or "failure to protect." The prevalence of this widespread and devastating intervention may be partially due to the lack of information on resilience available to child protection

---

7. Kolbo, "Risk and resilience."
8. Overlien, "Children exposed."
9. Egeland et al., "The long term;" Rogosch et al., "The role."

workers. As the research indicates, a child's connection to his or her non-abusive parent can be an essential catalyst for the child's recovery.[10]

Using the word love instead of violence or trauma in the title of this article is an intentional way to shift the focus onto the solution rather than the problem. We will make the case that while being exposed to violence and experiencing trauma can gravely affect children, love can help them heal. We will look at current literature supporting this view, as well as sharing something of our own journey. It is our firm belief that love is more powerful than violence, and that the combination of human and Divine Love can heal trauma.

THE GOOD NEWS: THE POWER OF RESILIENCE

> "But the fruit of the Spirit is love, joy, peace, patience, kindness, goodness...." Gal 5:22

Even though the research on resilience is in its infancy, there is a growing body of studies exploring the factors that help children heal from traumatic experiences. Steel concludes that the number one protective factor is the "development of empathy for the self and others through caring relationships with friends, intimate partners, family members, or professional therapists or counselors."[11] Margolin states that "children's resilience to trauma is linked to the presence of a healthy parent or adult in their lives."[12] Osofsky argues that "the most important protective resource to enable a child to cope with exposure to violence is a strong relationship with a competent, caring, positive adult, most often a parent."[13] And Bancroft and Silverman determine that "children's emotional recovery from exposure to domestic violence depends more on the quality of their relationship with the non-battering parent than any other single factor."[14]

Without actually using the word love, these and other studies indicate that a traumatized child's bond to a loving adult is central to resilience and recovery from violence. The researchers use words like "caring relationships," "strong relationships," and "the quality of rela-

10. See notes 14–16.
11. Center for the Study of Social Policy, "Strengthening," 1–8.
12. Margolin, "Effects."
13. Osofsky, "The Impact," 38.
14. Bancroft and Silverman, "The Batterer."

tionships," but what they are really talking about is loving relationships: the power of love in an adult-child relationship to heal trauma and violence.

One author who does directly name love as a resilience factor is Gina O'Connell Higgins in her remarkable book Resilient Adults; Overcoming a Cruel Past.[15] The book tells the stories of forty men and women who suffered extreme abuse as children and yet were able to develop into healthy, functional adults. The author identifies the presence of "surrogate love"[16] as a key element in recovery and healing in the great majority of the cases: "all but four out of forty subjects recalled at least one person who was a focal and intense source of sustenance in infancy and early childhood."[17] "For some . . . the initial promise [of healing] was a parent. . . . For others, it was an extended family member. . . . Many were loved well by hired help, strangers, peers, parents of friends, or even pets."[18]

This research validates what we have observed both in our professional lives. When working with clients and patients we have heard many stories of recovery and healing; almost universally, the narrator has identified a person or persons who "rescued" them by offering love, caring and attention, helping them to feel worthy of being loved again.

Heart

As we considered the impact of violence and trauma in the three categories of heart, mind, and spirit, we will use the same framework in considering the possibility for healing from abuse. The above-mentioned studies on resilience clearly illustrate the healing of the heart. The love of a single adult can reverse feelings of guilt or shame, feelings of unworthiness, self-hatred or loneliness that might develop in traumatized children. A loving grown-up can help a distressed child feel lovable again and can transform a child's despair into hope.

---

15. O'Connell Higgins, "Resilient."

16. Surrogate love refers to the love that should have come from the abuser, but instead comes from someone else.

17. O'Connell Higgins, "Resilient," 75.

18. Idem, 77.

Mind

The resilience research also addresses the healing of the mind. Words like "empathy," "healthy parents," and "competent, positive adults" are code for role models who help correct a child's negative thinking. Positive adults heal with their love and teach with their words and their actions. They provide a living example of loving relationship; they demonstrate to the child that violence is not a normal way of coping or communicating. They help the child understand that the abuse is not their fault and that the child is deserving of love. When children are able to shift these negative assumptions about themselves they can begin to imagine a better life for themselves: a life without constant fear, a life filled with happy and loving relationships.

Spirit

If human love is a powerful influence for healing, how much more powerful is God's love to heal? If human love can help us recover our sense of worth and dignity, God's love can help us feel that we are part of the Divine web, made in His image, created in love, never abandoned, never forsaken, precious. Divine love teaches us that our lives matter and have purpose.

There is one story in *Resilient Adults* that beautifully illustrates the power of spirituality in resilience. A man named Robert "found surrogacy[19] in Christ, including the loadstone of resilient love, unconditional acceptance."[20] It was not a loving adult that countered his feelings of shame and unworthiness, but rather the presence of Jesus that was the antidote to his despair. Robert is quoted as saying: "I'm describing to you a feeling that Christ was closer than you and I are sitting right now. I could have touched Him if I wanted to. He was that real."[21] What a powerful endorsement of Robert's worth as a person!

Another compelling example of resilience through spirituality (as well as heart and mind) is found in Olga Trujillo's engaging memoir, *The Sum of My Parts: A Survivor Story of Dissociative Identity Disorder.*[22] Trujillo writes about enduring cruel and pervasive physical and sexual

---

19. See supra note 18.
20. O'Connell Higgins, "Resilient," 199.
21. Idem, 199.
22. Trujillo, "The Sum."

abuse at the hands of her father, her brother, and other men. She clearly identifies the love of non-family members as her only lifeline in an otherwise desolate childhood. She particularly remembers her first babysitter, Doña Graciela, as the foundation upon which she started to build resilience. Doña Graciela was a devout Catholic who knew that the four-year old Olga and her brothers were being abused. She directly referred to the abuse by telling Olga that it wasn't her fault, and that God loved her.[23]

She also gave her a rosary and taught her to pray the Hail Mary when she was feeling scared. Trujillo writes: "I took Doña Graciela with me when I returned home each night. . . . I whispered her words, 'God loves you, Olguita,' into my hand, then closed my fist as if to trap her calm, steady voice and hold her words with me. . . . At night I could put my fist up to my ear, slightly open it, and imagine Doña Graciela's voice saying to me, 'It's not your fault.'"[24]

The power of this kind woman's love and her teachings about God's love were so seminal for Trujillo that she dedicated the book to her and other adults who gave her similar gifts: "For Doña Graciela, my next door neighbor, and all those who came after her: youth directors, teachers, coaches, mentors, and parents of friends. Your seemingly small kindnesses and ordinary encouragement helped me to survive and made me who I am today." What a beautiful testament to the power of love to heal!

We believe that everyone is deeply and unconditionally loved by God. This Divine love accompanied by human love constitutes a powerful antidote to despair and hopelessness. There is a lovely analogy about God that imagines the Divine as a mountain. There are many paths to get to the top. In this way, we understand that there are many ways to feel the power of God's love and trust that God is always working in our live. God is available to all, and we will each have our own way to feel and experience the Divine.

CONCLUSION

> O LORD my God, I cried unto thee, and thou hast healed me.
> Ps 30:2

---

23. Idem, 15.
24. Idem, 16–17.

Childhood exposure to domestic violence and other traumatic events can be a devastating experience, and yet there are many children who recover from these incidents and lead happy, fulfilling lives. The resilience research demonstrates that a key factor in helping traumatized children heal and thrive is the love of one or several adults. These loving adults can be family members, family friends, teachers, mentors, coaches, clergy, or members of a faith community.

In the last few years, programs have been developed to encourage adults (especially men) to support children (especially boys) concerning issues of domestic violence. These programs are designed not only to invite adults into the lives of troubled children, but to train them to make a difference in every child's life, by learning about the issue, talking to children about it, and modeling positive behaviors.

One such program, *Coaching Boys into Men*, created by Futures Without Violence,[25] targets high-school athletic coaches, since they have excellent access to student athletes and are genuine role models to them. Another one, *It Starts With You, It Stays With Him*, developed by the White Ribbon Campaign in Canada,[26] has a broader audience, including fathers, educators, coaches and leaders. Either of these models could be easily adapted to educate, train and mobilize members of a congregation, including pastors and youth leaders to work with children.

Many of us who lead busy lives cannot imagine having the time or energy to devote to a troubled child. What we must realize, however, is that we can powerfully touch another human being with even the smallest of gestures or "kindnesses" as Trujillo wrote in her dedication. Looking a child in the eye, speaking a few words and showing an interest in him, treating a child with respect, asking her opinion on something, are ways that we acknowledge and affirm a child's self-worth. Time and again in stories of resilience we hear how adults made a difference in a child's life by interceding at crucial moments in their lives, standing up for them at a critical time, believing in them when everyone else lost hope. These are the ways, the very small ways that regular human

---

25. Full disclosure: Mr. Areán was one of the developers of this program. For more information, go to http://www.futureswithoutviolence.org/section/our_work/men_and_boys/_coaching_leadership/

26. For more information, go to http://www.itstartswithyou.ca/index.cfm?pagepath=EXPLORE_SHARE/Make_a_Move_/Pass_it_on&id=34260

beings change the world. We are powerful beyond our knowledge, and our power lies in our kindness, in our "ordinary encouragement," in our love and respect, generously given.

As clergy and members of faith communities we have a great opportunity to be on the watch for children who are falling between the cracks, kids who seem silent or withdrawn, teens that are acting out or using drugs. Whatever that child is going through, we can make it our responsibility and privilege to show kindness and to model love and respect to them. Look a child in the eyes, ask her what she needs, what she wants for her life, what his hopes are, and then smile into those eyes and let that child know that they are respected, honored, and loved. A small but extraordinarily powerful gesture! Of such as these will come the healing of the world!

BIBLIOGRAPHY

Bancroft, L. and J. Silverman. *The Batterer as Parent: Addressing the Impact of Domestic Violence on Family Dynamics*, Thousand Oaks, CA, Sage Publications, 2002.

Campbell, J. C. "Health consequences of intimate partner violence," *Lancet* 359 (2002) 1331–6.

Center for the Study of Social Policy. *Strengthening Families: A Guidebook for Early Childhood Programs, Revised Second Edition*, Washington DC, 2007.

Egeland, B., T. Yates, K. Appleyard and M.van Dulmen. "The long term consequences of maltreatment in the early years: A developmental pathway model to antisocial behavior," *Children's Services: Social Policy, Research and Practice* 5 (2002) 249–260.

Fantuzzo, J.W. and W. K. Mohr. "Prevalence and effects of child exposure to domestic violence," *The Future of Children* 9 (1999) 21–32.

Jaffe, P. G., D. Wolfe, S. Wilson and L. Zak. "Similarities in behavioral and social maladjustment among child victims and witnesses to family violence," *American Journal of Orthopsychiatry* 56(1) (1986) 142–5.

Jouriles, E. N., R. McDonald, W. D. Norwood and E. Ezell. "Issues and controversies in documenting the prevalence of children's exposure to domestic violence," in S. A. Graham-Bermann and Edleson, J. L. (Eds.), *Domestic Violence in the Lives of Children: The Future of Research, Intervention, and Social Policy*, 13–34, Washington DC, American Psychological Association, 2001.

Kolbo, J. R. "Risk and resilience among children exposed to family violence," *Violence and Victims* 11 (1996) 113–28.

Margolin G. "Effects of domestic violence on children," in P. K. Trickett and Schellenbach C. J., (Eds.) *Violence Against Children in the Family and the Community*, 57–101, Washington, DC: American Psychological Association, 1998.

O' Connell Higgins, G. *Resilient Adults: Overcoming a Cruel Past*, San Francisco, CA, Jossey-Bass, 1994.

Osofsky, J. D. "The Impact of Violence on Children," *The Future of Children* 9 (1999) 33–49.

Overlien, C. "Children exposed to domestic violence: Conclusions from the literature and challenges ahead," *Journal of Social Work* 10 (1) (2010) 80–97.

Rogoscha F. A., D. Cicchettia and J. L. Abera. "The Role of Child Maltreatment in Early Deviations in Cognitive and Affective Processing Abilities and Later Peer Relationship Problems," *Development and Psychopathology* 7 (1995) 591–601.

Safe Start Center. *Healing the Invisible Wounds: Children's Exposure to Violence. A Guide for Families*. North Bethesda, MD. 2009.

On-line: http://www.safestartcenter.org/pdf/caregiver.pdf

Trujillo, O. *The Sum of my Parts: A Survivor's Story of Dissociative Identity Disorder*, Oakland, CA, New Harbinger Publications, 2011.

5

Life Stories of Men Who Act Abusively
Elements of the Coordinated Community Response

Nancy Nason-Clark, Barbara Fisher-Townsend, Steve McMullin and Catherine Holtmann

R ELIGIOUS WOMEN WHO HAVE experienced domestic violence often believe that if only their partners had received help, the violence would have ceased and the marriage would have survived. This enthusiasm for various kinds of intervention in the life of a man who has acted abusively prompted us to begin research several years ago to see if there was any evidence of changed behavior amongst religious men who had been participants in a faith-based, state-certified program for violent men. We have completed case file analysis on almost 1,200 men in one agency as well as personal and/or focus group interviews with over 100 men in another agency—many of them every six months for a four year period.

In order to highlight some features of that work, we introduce three different men who were seeking help in the faith-based agency we were studying.[1] When this was presented at the 2011 PASCH Conference, we spoke the different parts. Here, of course, it appears in print. Each

---

1. Adapted from work in progress on *Men who Batter*, a book manuscript co-authored by N. Nason-Clark and B. Fisher-Townsend, under contract with Oxford University Press; for a fuller explanation of our ongoing research on abusive men, see Fisher-Townsend, et al., 2008.

story has a narrator, the man himself, a religious leader, and a domestic violence advocate. The narrated story and the man's words come directly from our research—his words, presented in italics, are verbatim from our interview scripts; the voices of the religious leader and the domestic violence advocate are based on the story—as told to us by the man himself—but have been crafted by our research team based upon our extensive experience in working with domestic violence advocates and religious leaders over the last twenty years.

NED'S STORY

Overview:

Many of the men whose lives we have attempted to understand are replete with layers of failed dreams, tragic life circumstances beginning in childhood, unrealistic expectations for current relationships and a desire to erase—or at the very least minimize—the long term impact of the incredible abuse they have meted out to others. There is often a persistent inability or unwillingness to take responsibility for past actions. Many show little empathy for their victims. Sometimes they see the church, or the pastor, as a "quick fix" to the multiple emotional and interpersonal problems they face. Ned's story illustrates many of these complicated dynamics. It reveals the difficult and delicate situation of a pastor attempting to minister to someone like Ned, especially if there is no specific training or understanding of domestic violence. It also highlights the compromised safety of church people who might reach out "in the name of God's love." At the end of the chapter, we offer some reflections for working with men who have acted abusively, but first we tell some of their stories. Without a true appreciation for the way that such stories unfold, it would be unwise—and potentially dangerous—to intervene.

Narrator: Ned has been a scrapper for most of his life. He has been in prison on many occasions, most recently for a ten year period because of *manufacturing*—his fourth or fifth time for selling illegal substances. In prison, he connected with God and since his release three years ago, Ned has been trying to live in a way that would keep him on the "straight and narrow." Despite this, however, he received a misdemeanor assault several months ago—for pushing an ex-girlfriend—

that resulted in a mandate to attend an intervention group for domestic violence. This is how he found his way to the program we were studying. Ned lives and breathes the biking world, and as an occupation, he works on bikes.

Ned: *I have been riding motorcycles for 38–39 years. . . . I am still a Harley Davidson mechanic and I really like my work.*

Narrator: Intertwined throughout his life has been contact with the law.

Ned: *I was brought up in a really, really harsh environment.*

Narrator: From about the age of five, Ned had contact with the police and youth detention, followed by jail time, and then eventually prison.

Ned: *I was very, very young and I hung with older kids—they used to drop me down air conditioning chutes in stores at night when they were closed, tie a rope around my waist. I did that for a long time, always getting in trouble, took off with my grandfather's rifle from the service when I was like 5,6,7.*

Narrator: How much time had Ned spent behind bars?

Ned: *In my whole life? I started my real time in 1968—I was probably about 15. . .I know how to do jail but I don't like it now. I'm going to be 54. You know I have missed a lot of my children growing up. . . .*

Narrator: The difficult and rough childhood he experienced cannot be denied: neither can the difficult and rough childhood he offered his own kids. As a child Ned was moved from city to city as his mother moved in and out of relationship with various men. She married his father, who was 25, before her 15th birthday, had Ned at 15, and left when the relationship turned violent. In all, she married 5 times—twice to the same man. As a young boy, it did not occur to Ned to call 911 when his mother endured abused—precisely because the police were people to be avoided, at all cost.

Ned: *. . . I want to say since 1960 I have been getting into trouble off and on. . .'53 is when I was born and I was brought up in a really harsh, harsh environment.*

Narrator: It never took long for Ned to connect with older youth intent on breaking the law. As an adult, he began his longest prison sentence two weeks after his wife gave birth to their daughter, and they were divorced shortly after he completed his time.

Ned: *We were divorced, she divorced me and I was the one who had changed. She grew weary and she just fell out of love and this time I just let her go.*

Narrator: Life in prison took its toll on his family.

Ned: *I have a biological girl with her and my stepson—he was very young when I hooked up with her. He is my son too so. And so he is in jail right now since he was like, for the last 2 and one-half to three years, he's been in jail for molesting my daughter when I was gone. . . . I should not have been dealing drugs. I should have been a father and a husband and all that, so all those years I went away I left them to fend for themselves and she sold one of my Harley Davidson's and just about everything else I owned to take care of her and the kids and I was pretty mad about that for years.*

Advocate: When I first met Ned's wife, Suzanne, she was in dire straits. She had endured years of horrible abuse from Ned when he was around and when he was in jail, she and her kids lived in extreme poverty. I was the one who encouraged her to sell Ned's motorcycle. She started telling me about his obsession with his Harley, and I explained to her that by selling the bike, she could buy groceries, get school supplies for the kids — all sorts of necessities. Ned's abuse was not only physical and sexual, it was emotional and financial. She was so scared about selling the motorcycle — but for her it was the first step towards getting her life back.

Ned: *But really God had been really good to me. I have got everything that I had back then, a hundred times better. A nicer motorcycle and nicer set of tools, whatever.*

Pastor: It concerns me that Ned always talks about God when he needs to excuse his past behavior or his current attitudes. In his mind, God is Ned's servant, doing the things Ned wants him to do as proof that Ned has changed and Ned is good and Ned needs to take no responsibility for his past. By convincing himself that he is okay with God, Ned avoids the kinds of changes in his life that he needs to make.

Narrator: What about contact with his family now?

Ned: *And my wife and I haven't talked in a little over two years. . . . I haven't seen my kids in that long. Now it's hard because I know that I have a lot to offer my children you know. I am a pretty good person.*

Pastor: Yet he has hurt his children in terrible ways, and his unwillingness to change is obvious in his assessment of himself as "a pretty good person."

Narrator: At present Ned is connected to a large Four Square church, he is a regular attender of Sunday services and their midweek meeting. He loves the music, the many programs, and when needed, he is able to avail himself of the counsel of one of the many associate pastors—something he did shortly after his release from prison.

Ned: *. . . me and my wife were together for like 10, 11, 12 months.*

Pastor: Ned is the kind of person that scares me as a pastor—his church activity and attendance make him appear to be very committed and devout, but I believe that he uses his outward church activity to avoid dealing with the many problems on the inside. More than that, I fear that Ned thinks the church will be a good place for him to meet potential girlfriends who will be caring and forgiving. I worry about who his next victim will be.

Narrator: Was the pastor helpful?

Ned: *He did his best, he listened a lot, he listened to a lot of venting. Now I am at a place where I have met a school teacher.*

Advocate: (frustrated) And the story begins again. . . .

Pastor: Just as I feared. . . .

Narrator: Five months later when we interview Ned again, the school teacher is gone and she is replaced by two women Ned is

Life Stories of Men Who Act Abusively 45

seeing: Sue, a mother, with four difficult children, and the other woman, Helen, who works in a dentist's office. As he is describing these emerging relationships, Ned notes along the way an altercation he has had already with Sue's teenage son—and by extension his father, a man not yet divorced from Sue. For Ned, new relationships bring enormous new challenges.

Pastor: And it seems he is always in a new relationship. How do I, as a pastor, protect women in the congregation who are made vulnerable by feeling sorry for Ned and end up being victimized by his controlling behavior?

Narrator: These are issues Ned can—and does—discuss in the batterer intervention group. Here the facilitators and the other men attempt to assist him to gain control over his emotions, challenge his erroneous ideation, and see and live the world in a different way than he has in the past. But these challenges should never be underestimated!

Ned's story offers us, as pastors, advocates, and those who want to make the world a safer place for women, men and children a lot to think about. We need to be mindful of his strategies for harnessing religious support without any deliberate intention or plan to follow through with personal responsibility for changed thinking and behavior.

CHRIS' STORY[2]

Overview

While Ned's story helps us to understand some of the longer term consequences to a violent past, and its intergenerational character, the life of Chris Holland points out the dangers of the misinterpretation of the Biblical passages about family life. His speech is infused with religious language at every turn. He grew up in a very strict home, one that he attempted to replicate many years later in his own marriage. Chris employs the words of the Bible, twisting them to support his desire for ulti-

---

2. Portions of this story have been told in our 2010 book, *No Place for Abuse: Biblical and Practical Resources to Counteract Domestic Violence* (Downers Grove, IL: InterVarsity Press), authored by C. Clark Kroeger and N. Nason-Clark.

mate control over all of his family members. Perhaps more clearly than any other man we interviewed, but certainly a pattern that could be observed in others as well, Christopher retreated to what he claimed to be the Scriptural message about harmonious relations between marital partners—where the man laid down the rules and everyone else in the household followed his leadership. When the plan did not materialize for Chris, things turned ugly.

Narrator: Chris Holland has just switched careers and recently changed marriage partners. He is about to turn 40, teaches science to students in their early teens, and lives under the same roof as his seven children in a blended family situation. In the aftermath of a violent incident, Chris sought help in a faith-based batterer intervention program because his wife was unwilling to allow him to return home unless he agreed to go to classes.

Chris: *[P]ersonally I think that she is the abusive one. . . . I agreed to go through this so it was like, okay, fine, I will do anything to get back into the house. . . .*

Narrator: His wife, employed as a physiotherapist, learns of the agency through her Christian friends. Desperate, Chris is willing to do anything that would get him back in the house. From his perspective, he is better than other men in the program, many who have been mandated by the courts to attend.

Chris: *No big deal, I guess the other part is I always think I am better than everybody else in the sense that okay if Joseph can handle seven years in prison for something he didn't do, I can handle this ninety days. If Peter can be crucified upside down, okay I can do this.*

Narrator: Often in conversation Chris uses religious language and Scriptural references.

Pastor: As a pastor, it continually amazes me to see the way that abusers can refer to and manipulate Scripture to make them seem like model Christians.

Narrator: He wants to intimidate, but since the facilitators at the program know this language too, this dismantles his power. Chris talks about being unequally yoked with his wife, a reference to the Biblical notion that they do not share the same worldview or theological beliefs. But this is not exactly how Chris is using the term. Rather, he is referring to the fact that his wife called 911, involved the police and the courts, and is now considering divorce, something from his perspective that Christians should never do. He does not deny that she is a Christian—but he firmly believes that she is not living the way he feels a Christian should live.

Chris: *I wished that I did not marry somebody who didn't have the same religious beliefs I have. . . . I would prefer that my children marry somebody who will, has already agreed that the Bible is how they are going to live and that court is not going to be, you know, divorce is not going to be an option. . . .*

Narrator: In Chris' world, everything is either right, or it is wrong.

Chris: *I went to Bible College for a year and a half but dropped out because I didn't agree with the theology.*

Advocate: This was a really challenging case, for me. Chris and his wife Rita are highly religious and extremely conservative. I find it difficult trying to understand the language that they use to describe their relationship. Chris seems much more rigid in his beliefs than Rita yet she often doubts herself. I don't feel I have an adequate understanding of her beliefs or of Christianity in general to support her spiritually. I do affirm the decisions she has made for the safety of her children and for herself. I don't know if these are spiritual decisions, but they are moving her in the right direction.

Pastor: It is very hard to know how to help Chris. As far as he is concerned, he is always right—especially in spiritual matters. Even though I am a seminary-trained pastor, there is no way to convince Chris to listen to what I might say from a spiritual point of view. If he disagrees with me, he will just convince himself that I am not as spiritually mature as he is. Chris can always excuse his behavior and controlling attitudes by appealing to his sense of spiritual superiority—when others disagree with him, he thinks it is because they are not his spiritual equals.

Narrator: Before he began attending classes at the intervention program, the Hollands sought help at their church. But Chris was not happy with the pastoral counsel they received.

Chris: *I just feel like they are incapable of dispensing good advice.*

Pastor: See what I mean?

Narrator: When Chris and his first wife sought marital counsel from their pastor, Chris wanted their minister to invoke church discipline against his wife and make public their marital woes.

Pastor: Chris not only wants to maintain control of his wife and family, he wants to control me and the church also. He actually wanted us to discipline his wife for seeking help from his abuse.

Narrator: Chris reflects on what he said to the minister...

Chris: *I want you to follow the church discipline procedure, where you talk to her and if she doesn't listen to you, you bring her in front of the church or tell the church that we have a person here who has chosen not to be a part of this faith and is doing something that we have all agreed that will not happen.*

Narrator: When the pastor would not collaborate with this plan, Chris left the church.

Chris: *I am finding, many of the churches that I have recently gone to, pastors just don't want to be involved in anything to do with the family.*

Pastor: On the one hand, I was very relieved when Chris angrily left our church. His controlling behavior was a major problem in our congregation. Yet I worry about where he is worshipping now—what problems will he cause in that congregation? And I continue to be very concerned about his wife and family.

Narrator: Interestingly, Chris Holland credits the faith-based program and its staff for their humility, but he criticizes it for not being religious enough. According to him, staff should simply tell pastors what to do and when they see pastors making errors of judgment in terms of counseling, they should reprimand them.

Chris: *So, for instance, if I were running the show, I would call the pastors and say, "You are doing something wrong, and we are going to get it straightened out right now, because this is Christian-based and I just found out that a church is doing something, allowing something to happen within their church that is clearly against what the Bible teaches."*

Narrator: Coming from a very conservative Protestant tradition, Chris feels fully empowered as a lay person to interpret the Scriptures without any particular guidance from the ordained leadership. With his father serving as a pastor, Chris grew up in a household that he claims was very strict and orderly.

Pastor: It makes me wonder what kind of abuse Chris and his mother and siblings may have endured when he was growing up. Is Chris following the behavior that he learned from an abusive father? Has he confused *discipline* with *control*? And because his father was a pastor, has sincere religious devotion become entangled in his mind with rigid religious rules?

Narrator: He laments that this is not the case in his own household.

Chris: *I am a disciplinarian....*

Narrator: As he speaks about family life, it appears that there is excessive rigidity and very little fun.

Advocate: Rita spoke to me about how, before she married Chris, her faith had given her a deep sense of joy and peace. After she married Chris things changed. His brand of religion was all fire and brimstone, spare the rod and spoil the child, and an angry God of judgment. I encouraged Rita to rely on the support of her church community and pastor—who seemed to be able to hold his ground against her husband's dogmatic religious views. Having survivors connected to a community support system is important.

Narrator: When we return to interview Chris for a third time, he has left the program.

While it was disappointing that Chris was unwilling to stay in the program until he had completed the 52 week curriculum, it was not surprising. Not unlike others who have acted abusively towards their intimate partners, Chris was unrepentant of his violent actions, blaming his wife for all their marital woes—all the while employing religious injunctions to support his views and behavior. From his perspective, he was not at fault. It was everyone else that needed help to change. Pastors are frequently confronted by men whose circumstances bare a resemblance to the story of Chris, while the advocates at shelters attempt to help the partners they have abused. For women like Rita, a central part of the journey towards healing and wholeness is support that has a spiritual dimension—offered by a minister, or a counselor who is a person of faith themselves. Men, like Chris, are not interested in help to change.

PABLO'S STORY[3]

Overview

Our next story involves a couple who were eager to have assistance from their church community. They recognized at least some of the challenges with which they were faced and they wanted to alter the circumstances that brought them into contact with law enforcement. As we shall see, they were the recipients of tremendous church support. In fact, the church leadership—the pastor and other lay leaders—seemed to do everything they could to offer practical, emotional and spiritual help to this young couple and to their child. But, as is so often the case, there were enormous obstacles to be overcome—including the abuse of alcohol, and a past where violence was glorified.

Narrator: Pablo and Nala begin to look for help when the Department of Human Services (DHS) take their little girl from their home and place her in foster care. In the tailspin that fol-

---

3. Portions of this story have been told in N. Nason-Clark's chapter, "Strong Spirits, Abused Bodies: Social, Political and Theological Reflections" in a forthcoming collection edited by P. Dickey Young to be published by the University of British Columbia Press.

lowed, Nala received information about the faith-based program for families experiencing domestic violence from her DHS worker. She acted on the referral suggestion right away.

Pablo: [w]*e decided that we don't want this to, I guess, continue . . . dv in our relationship because I am not a woman beater and she is not a man beater and we had a very unfortunate incident happen in our house and we wanted to correct that.*

Narrator: The incident to which Pablo alluded was witnessed by their 18 month old daughter and when the police were called DHS became involved because there was evidence of blood on the child's head. Automatically they suspected the couple of child abuse and she was removed from their care. Adamant that they were not guilty of child abuse, but clear that they had been involved in domestic violence as a couple, Pablo and Nala were on a mission to get their child back. They were young—still in their twenties. They were vulnerable—as working poor Latinos in a region of the US that was not very diverse ethnically. They were very, very scared.

Advocate: Nala was one tough lady! She had to learn from a very young age to protect herself from the men in her family—her father, uncles, brothers. She's been subject to violence and abuse all of her life and her relationship with Pablo is just a continuation of that. She fights back. I don't think she realized the consequences of a violent home until she had a baby. Becoming a mother was a real game-changer. This incident with the DHS has really opened her eyes too. Now she's thinking about the future of her child and she doesn't want history to repeat itself.

Pablo: *So me and my wife decided we are going to try to satisfy DHS, enroll ourselves, get help for what happened way back then and just continue this course of bettering ourselves. . . . So I am here mainly to try to get my daughter back. We know nobody hurt our child, but they don't, so they want us to attend these classes.*

Narrator: Simultaneous to their involvement with the intervention programs and personal counseling at the faith-based agency, Nala sought help from her pastor for all their troubles: Pablo accompanied her to pastoral counseling and information training related to the family.

Pastor: I was glad when Nala called to make an appointment to talk with me about her home situation; I had been very concerned about the relationship between her and Pablo, but I was taken by surprise when Pablo showed up with her for the appointment. In retrospect, I fear that instead of coming for help, Pablo really came to make sure Nada didn't tell me anything he didn't want her to say. During that visit in my office, I was afraid for Nala—I feared that if she really opened up to me about the problems at home, she would be punished later. I have decided that in the future, I will be glad to talk with Pablo also, but only if he comes separately from Nala. I will not talk to both of them together about their family problems.

Narrator: Pablo's background had been difficult. His father was an alcoholic who made extra money as a pool shark.

Pablo: *Actually he made most of his money going to the bars because he was a pool shark and he would come with money, you know, but at the same time he would be drunk so we would have to see Mom and Dad argue all the time...loud enough for 4 kids to get scared.*

Narrator: At school, in rural Texas, Pablo learned early that there are two choices: be a bully or get bullied.

Pablo: *... if you aren't one of the bullies, then you are one of the ones getting bullied.*

Narrator: He seemed to love the thrill of a fight, in the school yard, or in the neighborhood where he lived. He even pursued fighting as a sport.

Pablo: *I love boxing on punching bags and stuff like that, just for the exercise of it.*

Narrator: As a teen, he played a lot of volleyball, softball and basketball—an athletic body and a certain attitude.

Pablo: *... attitude, I guess, as a fighter.*

Narrator: Pablo appeared very enthusiastic about gaining insight into his own behavior, his past, and his relationship with his wife. But he remained focused on his primary goal: the return of his little girl to their home. He spoke of change and of God.

Pablo: *I don't think anybody can really change without Him. That's my belief ... you know do whatever works for you but definitely look at yourself for a minute 'cause if you don't, then you will never really know what you are. ...*

Narrator: For many people, crisis brings them closer to their spiritual side.

Pablo: *I have always believed in God but I never believed in it wholeheartedly and now I believe a little bit more stronger. I have never been a crier and when this happened with my daughter, I prayed to God and I just busted out in tears, so I definitely feel there is somebody listening to me.*

Pastor: I wonder what is really happening in Pablo's mind. Although he tries to intimidate people with his image as a fighter, I suspect that the fighter image covers over some deep pain that no one has ever helped him to deal with. Pablo's life as a child sounds like a nightmare to me; maybe the reality that his daughter is suffering because of the abuse at home will make Pablo more open about how he suffered as a child, and how he can find healing instead of abusing others. I think his sudden interest in prayer is a start, but so much more is necessary.

Narrator: The story of their involvement with the criminal justice system was complicated. In the aftermath of a particular incident of domestic violence, Nala went to the police. She volunteered that she was the first to attack but that Pablo fought back harder and she wanted their story on file. This prompted law enforcement to contact DHS who did a home visit and at that point took the child from the home on the suspicion of child abuse. No charges were ever laid, but the suspicion concerning the child remained.

Advocate: Nala began to realize that the violence between her and Pablo was affecting her ability to be a good mother to her baby. Then, when the authorities suspected that the baby was being abused, she knew she had to do something or she would lose her. It took a lot of courage for her to go to the police, since she knows firsthand that the cops don't always treat Latinos fairly. Let's face it, the system is racist. But her fear for her child's safety overcame her fear for what they might do to Pablo. She figured Pablo could fend for himself, but the little one needed all the help she could give.

Narrator: Like many men in the batterers group, Pablo drinks to excess.

Pablo: *[Y]ou know alcohol is a downer, it just ruins everybody's life pretty much, so I am not invisible to it and it's got it's hands on me and obviously it came back to bite me in the rear end. . . . I am not untouchable.*

Narrator: Raised Catholic by a father who practiced his faith and a mother who was rather indifferent to hers, Pablo found comfort from his Christian background even though he never embraced it fully.

Pablo: *I don't like to play two-faced but I like the words, I like the words from the Bible and that is what he* [their pastor] *preaches to me, so I love to hear it. . . . And the book we study on the secret to family happiness and everything that's in there, the Bible backs up, so I believe it. If it was coming from somebody's mouth that had a hunch, I would be like ummm, you know, it doesn't sit well in my stomach.*

Pastor: Pablo looks for comfort and support from his faith; it is important to him that he feels loved and forgiven by God. But it seems that Pablo doesn't listen when the Bible addresses the ways in which his life needs to change. Rather than being challenged to love and protect and care for his family, he seems to be content to think that God forgives him for his faults, so the abuse continues. He is focused on how God and others love him, not on how to love others.

Narrator: Learning to love others is very hard word, especially so for someone with the life challenges of Pablo. As he seeks therapeutic support, Pablo is very pleased with the skills of the group's facilitator. And the spiritual tone of the agency, and its staff, is a huge bonus for him.

Pablo: *She will quote a Scripture from the Bible every now and then, but she won't push God onto anybody. . . she has it memorized and that is about it. It think it's just enough so that it won't scare somebody away that doesn't believe or make them mad or upset. . . if you can have backup, it might as well be God.*

Pastor: That is the kind of comfortable Christian message that Pablo wants—God can be his "backup" without him having to believe or get upset (or change his behavior).

Narrator: From Pablo's point of view, the intervention has helped him remain violent-free through this very stressful period of their daughter in foster care. He even jokes about it.

Pablo: *I am telling you, if my brothers, or someone, has a problem I could probably repair it for them right there on the phone. . . . I have learned a lot and with the stress that me and my wife are going through right now, I think without the tools that I have, I would have crumbled a long time ago. . . . I got plenty of tools on me now.*

Advocate: One of the things that Nala found really difficult is that she loved Pablo—she loved his toughness and charm and she thought he would be a good father. Yet below the surface, she said he was a volcano ready to erupt. She never knew when it was going to happen or what the consequences would be. She got tired of living in fear—he wore her down. Even though she's tough, she would get hurt really badly—she was no match for him.

Narrator: Pablo admits that he can get angry pretty easy.

Pablo: . . . one of those short fuses. . . [but]. . . with all the help that I am getting and all the people in my life, all of a sudden, I think I am able to address things easier and keep it calm instead of boiling. I am warm.

Pastor: That comment worries me. Pablo is not recognizing that he has a controlling personality; he is just learning that with extraordinary effort he can keep it bottled up inside without exploding in violence. I am afraid that having a longer fuse will just make for a more violent explosion when it eventually happens.

Narrator: With an army of people attempting to give them support, Nala and Pablo are staying the course. He is in a drug rehab program and a batterer's intervention group, they are in a parenting class, both are having individual psychotherapy, Nala meets regularly with the DHS worker, and they both meet weekly with their pastor.

Pastor: Pablo also seems to be extraordinarily capable of bringing a host of people to his side to keep him from being violent instead of taking responsibility himself. In a sense, he is now controlling a whole army of people who are serving his needs. Are we unwittingly encouraging his controlling behavior instead of challenging it?

Narrator: The supervised visitation takes place at church; one of the elders from the congregation brings their daughter from the foster family to them at church. After the service, the elder returns the child back to the foster home. They see her on two other occasions per week, bringing their total hours of weekly visitation to four. The minister comes to their home each week, has met with the facilitator of the parenting program, and with the social worker at DHS. He is certainly committed to a community response to Pablo and Nala's problems.

Advocate: Supervised visitation is a particularly dangerous time for a mother who has been abused. Nala was so eager to see their child but Pablo would use their time together to make her feel guilty. He said that it was her fault that their baby was not living with them. It was only a few hours a week but sometimes those visits would put her right back to square one—doubting herself and being revictimized.

Narrator: Six months later we interview Pablo again. The child has been returned to Nala on the condition that the couple lives separately. They have complied with this DHS order, but it is causing financial strain. Pablo is allowed to see their daughter in supervised contexts, but not at Nala's place of residence. Pablo is now living with his parents. It simply was not possible for them financially to have two separate living spaces. Yet, they needed to fulfill the DHS no contact order. So his parents let him move back home. It has been a long time since Pablo lived at home with his folks. In prison—a result of four DWIs—he had learned some new skills, taken his GED, became certified as a plumber and a drywaller, and upon his release quickly became financially stable. We learn that a year out of penitentiary Pablo met Nala. His positive attitude toward life, coupled with his good looks, made him hard for Nala to resist. This same attitude has helped him stay in the program and continue in his employment. At the sixth month mark in the batterer intervention program, Pablo is still attending classes, working at the same job and hoping that soon he will be reunited with his family. Using the mantra from AA of one day at a time, Pablo notes that if he stays the course, and fulfils all the obligations, it will happen, he just needs to be patient.

Pablo: *. . . one day at a time is that tool belt that I am adding together. . . .*

Pastor: Pablo still sees himself as in control; his plan is being fulfilled. That is one area where I think Christian faith might help—to trust his future to God, he would have to give up control. But I don't think he is willing to do that—in his own life or in the lives of others.

Narrator: When we return one year later to interview Pablo again, he is not available to see us. He has gone back to drinking and Nala has taken their child and gone back to Texas. The couple is seeking a divorce.

LEARNING FROM THE STORIES OF MEN WHO HAVE ACTED ABUSIVELY

Ned, Chris, and Pablo are all real men—living and worshipping in a church community, probably not unlike the one in which you, the reader, might be attending. They are all dangerous men, having acted violently towards a partner that they promised to love and cherish until death drew them apart. They have all fathered children. They all claim to love God. They have all sought—and received—some form of assistance from the Christian community and its leadership in the aftermath of violence at home.

Unfortunately, there is no reason to believe that Ned, Chris, or Pablo have turned from their violent ways. They do not appear to take full responsibility for the hurt they have caused others. There are elements of remorse, to be sure, disappointments in themselves and others. But interwoven through these personal accounts is a persistent feeling of victimization. Sometimes they claim victimization at the hands of their (past) partner; sometimes it is the system with which they are most agitated. The end result, though, is much the same. They do not believe that they personally need to make fundamental changes in the way they think or the way they behave.

For men found guilty by the criminal justice system of victimizing an intimate partner, this personal account of *victimization* may be a little difficult to understand. Yet, when they first enter any program—and especially a mandated one—most of the men are defensive, unsure what to expect, angered at having been ordered to come, feeling sorry for themselves and a long way from developing empathy for those they have hurt. One of the advantages we have observed in a faith-based program, is that there less talk of forced separation, court orders, restraining orders and other demands of the criminal justice system. Here there is more of an emphasis on learning—to act in caring ways, to alter your behavior, to think before you act, to change your way of thinking. Yet, many men are not ready for this type of intervention until they have been forced by the criminal justice system to understand fully the consequences of what they have done to others, the harm they have caused.

Advocate: It's hard to not get jaded in my line of work, but I see other guys, smart ones, milk the system. It's like they need to be the center of attention and they'll get it any way they can. But the bottom line for me is making sure that the women are safe, no matter how many programs the guy is in.

Batterer intervention groups differ, the personnel differs, the curriculum differs, and so does the tone. Some groups focus more on punishment: on what you did that was wrong. From the point of view of many of the men we have interviewed, the faith-based group focuses on helping you to change who you are and what you do. It offers insight.

Advocate: No matter what type of intervention program the men are in, it has to be tough enough to hold them accountable for their violent actions. Insights are all well and good but actions speak louder than words when lives are at stake.

Some of the men claim that this focus in the faith-based group on *insight* is in stark contrast to the focus in other groups on your choice to abuse. *Choosing to abuse*, they say to us, with an element of sarcasm in their voices and their eyes rolling as they speak. We feel their skepticism. Not surprisingly, most of the guys resist this. They feel that *no, I don't have a choice, I am backed into a corner....*

Advocate: People always have a choice—men can choose to be abusive and women can choose to leave.

The program we have studied is organized with the notion of *consumer choice* as an important element. It *treats* the men as if they make a choice. This impacts the environment in several, important ways. Since the faith-based program believes that the men make a choice, and treats them accordingly, and the men themselves believe that they make a choice, then the mandated group attendance ordered by the court takes on a very different feel given that it is cloaked in the language of *choice*. It is true, of course, that the men do not need to attend the faith-based program, but they do need to attend one of the groups in the local area.

The reputation of the agency within the criminal justice, therapeutic and advocacy community is solid. While some do not personally endorse their faith-added approach, there was no sense that their work was compromised by religious persuasion, nor any evidence that the agency was proselytizing clients, or pushing a faith-based agenda, or reluctant to accept clients from a variety of faiths (or no expressed beliefs). Perhaps surprisingly, the men were more critical of the agency's reluctance to talk about matters spiritual than they were to suggest that matters of faith were pushed. Several very religious men were quite annoyed that the agency did not express more openly a faith-based perspective on their lives or journey. Yet, other men referred to how well group facilitators were able to call religious men to accountability, particularly by refusing to accept their attempts at justifying abuse using the language of the Scriptures or their faith traditions.

Advocate: This is what I mean by actions speaking louder than words. Lots of women get fooled by the words of their partners after they have completed an intervention program. The men say they have changed but once life goes back to normal, once the novelty has worn off and the bills are due, or someone gets sick, or someone loses a job, then the abuse starts up again. They cannot seem to cope with normal, day-to-day life. Many guys work the system, where they use the conflicting messages they are getting from different agencies to justify practically anything they are doing.

Pastor: It is difficult and frustrating for pastors when they are not included in the process. As a pastor, I might have been able to help a man continue to make progress after his time within the program has ended, or at least help him not fall back into old patterns. Seeing the downward spiral begin again makes me keenly aware of my unpreparedness to respond to the needs of both victims and perpetrators of domestic violence. I wish I had been better trained for these situations.

For those men who had been incarcerated, some connected with their faith during their stay in prison. But, in almost all cases, they were *reconnecting* with a faith that had been nurtured much earlier in their life, rather than adopting a totally new frame of reference. In each case, however, there were three essential elements: (1) the reconnection with *faith* brought warmth to a cold reality about their life and circumstances and offered a new language—*the language of the spirit*—to conceptualize the way forward. It offered words for a new start, turning away from the past and embracing a new beginning; (2) the reconnection with one's spiritual life brought *hope*—that tomorrow could be a better day. This fuelled motivation to change, an eventual willingness to become accountable—not just as a mandated criminal justice response to the wrong that had been committed, but a decision to begin to do the work of altering how one thinks and how one acts; and (3) the reawakening of a past connection to faith brought *charity*, a community of people—religious by choice and/or tradition—that embraced the language of change, the hope of a better tomorrow and random acts of kindness to those who had stumbled.

The faith-based batterer intervention program we studied combined these three elements in interesting ways, though it was never named as such. Each of the workers was a person of faith, but it would be inaccurate to conclude that they shared a religious world perspective. They did not. What they shared was a religious language, cultivated from a variety of traditions, for a new start. Staff spoke of that new start in different ways, to each other, and to the men. This language spilled over in conversation to other workers from the criminal justice perspective and within the advocacy community. It was clear to us that throughout the domestic violence community within the local region, professionals understood that the faith-based group spoke and acted the language of faith, that they maintained hope for change, and that they went to great lengths to offer charity (in terms of kindness and assistance) towards men who had acted abusively.

However, the faith-based agency and staff were steeped in reality—they were not unfamiliar with the culture of violence, the abysmally low rates of long-term dramatic change, nor were they unwilling to accept the evidence of clients who gave up hope and stopped *doing the work*. But, like many parole and probation workers, judges and clergy, hope kept them doing their work, despite countless examples where hope had failed, recidivism had occurred, and change needed to be calculated in very small measurement indices.

CONCLUDING WORDS FROM A PASTOR

From my perspective as a pastor, these actual interviews with batterers are a reminder of how complex these situations are and of how important it is that pastors not seek to respond to these individuals on their own. Few pastors are adequately trained to provide the kind of help that these men need. At the same time, it is also obvious to me in such situations that pastors and congregations can offer a great deal in terms of spiritual care, encouragement, and accountability provided that we are part of a coordinated community response to domestic violence. Most pastors are well trained in ways that would provide the kind of spiritual support and social environment that would encourage an abuser to remain in the program and apply the things they are learning. If pastors were aware of the directions and goals that the programs encourage, they might also be able to facilitate important ongoing supports after the program ends. Such coordination requires good working relationships between clergy and agencies in the community, which are often lacking.

These stories also remind me of the complexity of the effect that domestic violence can have on a congregation. Obviously, the church needs to respond to those who are victims, but pastors and congregations often find themselves in the very difficult and sometimes uncomfortable position of providing spiritual care for both a victim and the perpetrator. In addition to that difficult task, the pastor must be concerned about the possibility of potential future victims. Many perpetrators whose past abusive relationships have ended soon begin searching for a new partner ("who won't cause the same problems as the last one") and they may look for vulnerable women within the congregation—women who may be convinced because of their Christian faith to overlook past sins and believe that the abuser has truly changed due to the profession of a conversion or renewal experience. Through sermons and other teaching, the pastor should seek to make the church a safe place. Even when a perpetrator leaves a congregation, the pastor still may have concerns about the next congregation he chooses to attend. Should the congregation be warned? Or would such a warning be futile in the face of the perpetrator casting doubt on the reputation of the previous congregation?

I am also reminded of the importance of maintaining hope. From my own experience as a pastor, I know that conversations with abusive men can be very discouraging and frustrating—especially when one is aware of the terrible hurts they have caused. I have great admiration for those who work in batterers' intervention programs, not only for the important work they do but for the genuine compassion they show. If we are going to end domestic violence, the solution must include the ways that we respond to perpetrators.

CONCLUDING WORDS FROM "ONE OF THE MEN"[4]

As I think about my own life, and the lives of so many guys I know, we haven't been very successful in keeping our family lives safe and peaceful. Most of the guys I've met in this intervention program have had very rough lives and that includes me. Starting in our childhoods we began hanging out on the streets with other kids who were interested in drinking, using drugs, sex, and getting into trouble with the law. Our homes weren't happy, our parents didn't get along, and we were getting "beat" for minor issues. So we sought refuge on the streets with others like ourselves. I saw it all around me. We started out with minor skirmishes with the law and just about everyone ended up in serious legal trouble, often charged with DUI's, assaults and domestic violence. Most of us guys started having kids at a really young age—it was a macho kind of thing—how many kids do you have? But we never thought about caring for those kids, supporting those kids, being there for those kids. Our girlfriends/wives and our kids suffer.

After attending this batterer intervention program, we can see there is a better way—but getting there is so difficult. We love our women, we love our children, yet we can't seem to pull ourselves out of the spiral of negative thinking and action. The hope that we learn to develop—for a loving and peaceful family life—keeps us "doing the work" necessary for change. But when things go wrong, we lose our jobs, our relationships end, or when we are drawn back to drinking and drugs, that hope fades. When I think about my own life, and the lives of so many of the guys I have met in this program, it is at this point—where hope is gone—that we begin to return to what we know and to who we know. We begin thinking and acting in irresponsible and abusive ways again and again. When I completed my 52-week program I believed I had no help, no one to turn to anymore. The cycle we know so well rears its ugly head and once again, we all suffer.

CONCLUDING WORDS FROM AN ADVOCATE

The primary concern with faith-based batterer intervention programs from the perspective of an advocate is first and foremost the safety of abused women and their children. Advocates work hard with survivors

---

4. This section has been written by Barbara Fisher-Townsend based on our fieldwork with men who have acted abusively.

in order to empower them to make changes that will ensure a violence-free future. So many religious women have hope that things in their marriage will change but the hope that their violent spouse will change is often premature and unrealistic. Of course change is always possible but often it is more realistic for women to initially place their hope in themselves and their ability to make wise decisions.

Abusive relationships erode a woman's self-esteem, her ability to make her own decisions, and rob her of the resources necessary to carry them out. Consequences of the abusive cycle include giving up power and control and dependency on the abuser. Survivors need practice in making and carrying out decisions that ensure peace and safety in their families. This is a long and challenging journey which is often disrupted by premature reconciliation. If a marriage is truly salvageable, then a violent spouse will respect the time and space his wife needs to get her life on track. Churches and religious leaders can help in patiently supporting a survivor's healing journey while holding perpetrators accountable for the consequences of their actions.

6

More Than a Simple List

David Horita

THE THEME OF LOVING, reflecting, and pursuing justice together is important and timely. Although our society seems capable of massive self deception and avoidance regarding the issues of domestic violence, it is clear that this is a pressing issue of significance to all of us.

However, while we must transform and bring justice to our society through our joint efforts and strategic alliances, we also remember that helping the people around us to change and be changed must occur one person at a time. True transformational leadership strategizes at a macro level, operates tactically at a programmatic level, but will always need to express love at a micro level. We can create structures, programs, seminars, and organizations that will alter the face of society over time, but the people we encounter in these gatherings will need to be cared for one by one.

One passage of Scripture that is frequently overlooked by both the casual and committed reader of the Bible is Romans 16[1]. The first twenty-three verses of this chapter contain a series of greetings that the Apostle Paul wanted passed on to some of his friends in the Roman church. It is as exciting to most of us as watching a seemingly endless slide show of our parent's old friends. It is as exhilarating as reading a shopping list or memorizing a list of vocabulary words for a language we will never speak. We are as pumped up by Romans 16 as we are

---

1. All Scripture references are from the New International Version, 1978.

when we read the Old Testament genealogies of "who begat whom." In short, it bores us and we skip the verses.

It is worth noting that Romans 16 is still the Holy Scripture. Theologically speaking, we believe that it is the Word of God divinely inspired by the Holy Spirit as he spoke through individuals in history. Like all Scripture, it has both an historical setting and eternal relevance. Thus it follows that this chapter, like all of the chapters of the Bible, ought to be important to us. At the same time, it is hard to ignore the reality that this chapter is nothing more than a list of names that appear to be totally disconnected from our lives. The truth is that I skipped my graduation ceremony at University because I didn't want to endure the reading of an endless list of names. Another fact is that I barely made it through my youngest son's high school graduation last June and it proved necessary to phone out for a coffee delivery if I was to survive it. Most of us are not overwhelmed by reading or hearing lists of any sort, never mind a list created two thousand years ago as part of some Apostle's private life.

So what is the value of a list of names in Scripture that is apparently unrelated or relevant to us in any way?

Minimally, it is worth noting that the list in Romans 16 includes some fascinating names that are fun to think about simply for their own sake. While doubting that any of us would want to encumber our own children with these monikers, we do need to acknowledge that they are extremely expressive. There are names like Epenetus, Ampliatus, and Asyncritus. Perhaps these were people who felt sorry for something, talked too much, and couldn't keep a beat. It leaves me wondering if the individuals changed their names later in life to match their character, if they were descriptive nicknames, or if somehow their parents had more prophetic insight than my wife and I when it came to naming our children. For example, the name Narcissus also appears in this list. Since the story of the self-loving Narcissus would have been well known in the Roman world, this appears to have been an unfortunate name to stick on your new-born. Philologus receives a greeting from Paul in verse 15, perhaps because they both belonged to the same book club. Phelgon puts in an appearance in verse 14, with his shy and stable personality possibly inspiring early theories of temperament by Galen of Pergamum[2], and later by Alfred Alder and Erich Fromm.[3]

Unfortunately, other than having a little fun with names, this list in Romans 16 remains just that—a list. No doubt the list mattered to the Apostle Paul, but it doesn't particularly matter much to us. For the majority of people, the lists of names that are valuable to us are the ones formed by our own experiences, our own travels, and our own interactions.

OUR OWN MEANINGFUL LISTS

I have a list of names hung on the wall in my bedroom that would be of interest to very few people other than me. It is a list of names signed on a baseball bat by nine year old boys at the end of a baseball season, in which I had the privilege of coaching them. Although it was a number of years ago, the names of the Surrey Mariners written on the bat in permanent marker still matter to me. Some of these names I value deeply. Jody and Jeremy are two of the names. Both of these young men began the season wanting to quit baseball due to some negative experiences on other teams and coaches, in which they had felt undervalued and certainly not appreciated. Their parents felt that it was good for them to play a team sport so the young men were playing that season on my baseball team whether they wanted to be there or not. Mostly, the reality was "not." They were sure they were in for another long season of playing right field or sitting on the bench. Fortunately our team had a good year developmentally, relationally, and competitively so that by the end of the season Jody and Jeremy had decided they liked team sports. They wanted to return for the subsequent year. I continue to encounter Jeremy now and then, as a couple of years later he decided to give his life to Jesus Christ and now is involved in a study group along with my son. There were a lot of good things that year, and it didn't hurt that we won the championship.

However, my favorite name on the Mariners baseball bat is Dylan. Dylan is a boy that I will always remember because he phoned me prior to our first practice to explain why we didn't want him on our team. Phoning from a phone booth so his mother wouldn't hear him, he was

2. Online, "The Four Temperaments."
3. Ibid.

matter-of-fact in describing his flaws in both baseball and life. It took quite a while on the phone to convince young Dylan that his responsibility was to come and have fun, and it was our coaching responsibility to help him become a good player. As we got to know him, it was not surprising to discover that Dylan came to us from a dysfunctional and abusive family with a long history of addictions.

The day that Dylan phoned me I had just completed reading Pat Conroy's autobiographical novel *My Losing Season*, in which he poignantly describes his journey through domestic violence and abusive behavior within the sporting community.[4] It was an emotional reminder of the power of children's sports to help or to hurt young people. As I learned nine-year old Dylan's story, I was struck by the opportunity I had been given to impact his young life in a positive way. With baseball practices and games, I would have a five month window of four to five days a week, two to three hours per day, to help Dylan find support, love, and success. It was the biggest responsibility I would have that baseball season.

Part way through our baseball season, Dylan decided to quit the team because he believed he was letting us all down by striking out too often. He believed we would lose the championship because he wasn't a good-enough hitter and he didn't want the pressure of not "failing" the team. After a number of attempts on the part of all the coaches to convince him that he was a valued part of the Mariners, he continued to say that he needed to quit. At that point, one of our premier nine year old players who had been eavesdropping on the conversation asked if he could talk to Dylan. They went for a walk across the baseball diamond, returning about twenty minutes later with Dylan saying he had decided that he could stay and play. When the opportunity presented itself, I asked my son, Timothy, what he had said to Dylan. Timothy told me "Well Dad, I just told him to watch my legs when I was up to bat. Every time I go up to bat I am so afraid of getting hit by the ball or striking out that my legs shake. I told him to watch me, because all of us feel the same way. Dylan thought he was the only one." As you can probably guess, one of the names written on the baseball bat that I am particularly attached to is "Timothy."

At the end of that Mosquito ball season, Dylan made it on the All-Star team. I love the name of Dylan being written on a bat, on my wall,

---

4. Conroy, *My Losing Season*.

in my room. It is a continual reminder that every person matters, and every name has significance.

The list of names found in Romans 16 was an important list to Paul; it was a continual reminder of his investment in people and their investment in him. The first person mentioned on Paul's list is Phoebe, who likely carried the letter to Rome on behalf of the Apostle. By mentioning her first, Paul was making a strong statement countering his own culture and time, attributing high praise and prestige to a woman in a patriarchal society. He states that Phoebe was a servant of the church, a deacon, and a huge help to many people. It is hard to imagine that Paul was not aware of the centuries of debate that he was stirring up by greeting Phoebe when he does and in the way that he does.

Paul's next greeting was to Priscilla and Aquila, whom he describes as people who had risked their lives on his behalf. Most of us can fondly remember people who went out of their way to be loyal or supportive to us when we were desperate for encouragement. Every time we consider these loyal friends, it generates feelings of warmth and appreciation. This would have been true for Paul as well, deeply moved by friends who went to the most extreme limits to be part of the team.

Neither was Paul ever likely to forget Epenetus, whom he describes as "the first convert to Christ in the province of Asia." Epenetus was the beginning; the first sign of hope; the initial work of grace; the start of an ever increasing ripple of Christ followers throughout Asia. Ultimately, Epenetus would prove to be the forerunner of millions and millions of people whose lives were transformed by the love of God throughout Asia and around the world. The reality is that most of us today are part of the outworking of the gospel of Jesus Christ that began with this one name. Paul never lived to see the full harvest that began with this one person, but he did know that Epenetus was the first. Epenetus would forever be on Paul's list.

Mary is commended by Paul in verse 6. All we know about her is that "she worked very hard" on behalf of the church. A number of years ago I had the joy and challenge of planting a new church. It proved to be exhilarating, stressful, and a lot of work. Among the most humbling experiences in beginning a church was to watch a few of the older members of our team consistently work behind the scenes doing anything that was required. They never stood at a pulpit, never served on the board, and never got any acclaim for any of the success of the church plant and yet the church only grew because of their lives of service. I thought then and continue to think now that they are the people who will have the big houses in heaven. They are the ones who most fully express the heart of Jesus described for us in Philippians 2, where we are told that Jesus "did not consider equality with God something to be grasped, but made himself nothing. . . ." In Romans 16, Paul remembered the hard work of Mary. She was noticeable for her humility and service. She deserved to be on someone's list.

In verse 13, the Apostle isolates Rufus, who "was chosen in the Lord," and whose mother had been like a mother to Paul. While not sure what this meant to Paul, I assume it means she fussed over him and worried about his nutrition and eating habits. Not mentioned in this passage is the probability that the father of Rufus was Simon of Cyrene, who carried the cross of Jesus to Golgotha (Mark 15:21).[5] This rich heritage would have been known by Paul. Both Rufus and his mother belong in this list.

As we wander through the greetings of Paul at the end of his letter to the Roman church, we could look more closely at each of the people mentioned and discover why they matter. These names make a difference because the people were important to Paul and to the gospel Paul was sacrificing his life to spread. While together we must continue to strive to change the society in which we live at a macro level, we can never forget that individual lives are transformed at a micro level. People only come to know that they are loved and matter to God when we choose to actively love them. We make a difference by being loving people. We positively redirect the life of any single person by loving that one person.

The two commandments

It is interesting to look back in the history of the church and to learn from the lives of past saints. One form of devotion to God began in the deserts of Egypt in the 3rd Century through the leadership and

---

5. Murray, *Romans*, 231.

teachings of Anthony the Great (Anthony of Egypt, 251–356 AD)[6] and Pachomius (292–348 AD).[7] Many scholars consider these individuals to be the progenitors of the Monastic movement, which is still prevalent today in a variety of forms. The monastics believed that removing obstacles to a whole-hearted love of God required them to live a disciplined and isolated life in which they took religious vows of renunciation. Whether in religious communities (monasteries) or in isolation (hermitages), these early ascetics committed themselves to such things as poverty, chastity, and service.

Many of the Monastic Orders did extensive good for a lot of people, substantially assisting in the development of agriculture, medicine, and education.[8] But as is often the case with religious practice, there were more extreme forms of monasticism that were developed that were less helpful. One such group were known as the Stylites, or Pillar Saints.[9] They believed that the mortification of their bodies would ultimately lead to their salvation, and went to severe limits to ensure that salvation. The first of these, Simeon Stylites the Elder, climbed a pillar in 423 AD in order to live on top of the pillar and focus on intensifying his relationship to God. One of the followers of Simeon, Saint Alpius stood upright on a pillar for over fifty-three years. When unable to stand any longer, he remained on top of his pillar lying on his side for the final fourteen years of his life.

Obviously, there are a lot of questions to be asked about how a person could remain standing for fifty-three years, what he would eat, and what happened when lightning struck. There are also other questions that are best left unasked and we will not pursue. However, it is very clear that these individuals were willing to take radical steps in order to live out their personal commitment to God. These were people that took seriously the command of Jesus to "love the Lord your God with all your heart and with all your soul and with your entire mind" (Matt 22:37). While we have many unanswered questions about the wisdom of this extreme mode of religious practice, it is hard not to respect the essential nature of their faith.

---

6. Dowley, *Eerdmans' Handbook*, 205.
7. Ibid, 206.
8. Walker. *A History of the Christian Church*, 125–128.
9. *New Catholic Encyclopedia*, 750.

Unfortunately, these same saints of old seem to have skipped the words of Jesus stated in Matt 22:38, where we are told that the second greatest commandment is like the first, in that we are to "love our neighbor as ourselves." It is very difficult to choose to actively love people when we are spending all of our time balancing on the top of a pillar. We might even consider that a life of total isolation, focussing only on our personal relationship to God, has within it the seeds of narcissistic selfishness. Minimally, we know that without a wholesale love of God and a commitment to helping others, we will never be able to fulfill the entire teaching of Jesus. Religion in itself may lead us to the top of a pillar, but an encounter with Jesus will always direct us towards the people that he came to earth to save.[10]

If we choose to live our lives on a pillar, then there will never be a significant list of names that are part of our lives. When we live our lives many feet above the grit and dirt of life, there will be no community surrounding us when we need it. There will be no refuge for those who are fleeing violence in their town or home. There will be no church filled with people seeking together to live out both commands of Jesus. There will be no support, no love, and no pursuit of justice.

If we choose to live our lives on a pillar, there are no Rufuses that become part of the fabric of our existence. Life in isolation means there are no families we have been privileged to share in rebuilding, no children saved from abuse, no men we see transformed, and no women who begin to learn that they were always important to God. Selfishly, when we withdraw from the people around us we impoverish our own lives. Without engagement with the hurting people that we walk beside every day, there are no Phoebes on our list who begin to create new paradigms of thinking. Without the sharing of our lives, there are no Epenetuses who become our children in the faith. Without a list of boring names that is uniquely our own, there are no Priscillas and Aquilas who have stood by us in the best and the worst of times. If we take only the first great command of Jesus to love God without adding the second to love people, there is nobody who comes to mind when we pause to ask ourselves how our lives have made a difference.

---

10. The original concept of pillar saints being used in juxtaposition to Romans 16 comes from a sermon by John Ortberg heard years ago at Willow Creek Church, Barrington, Illinois.

If we have chosen to be a follower of Jesus Christ, then we would strongly affirm that we value every life and every person regardless of age, stage of life, gender, or ethnic origin. We would vehemently argue that every person we have ever laid eyes on deserves dignity, respect, justice, and love. At least, I deeply hope that we would say these things. But if we have chosen to live our lives on our pillar of choice in isolation from the world, then we likely have very few people who are a part of our list of important names. The unfortunate reality is that far too many people in the church of Jesus Christ today still choose a life totally separated from the painful realities that most are encountering on a daily basis. In any given week in any given church, we will encounter people who believe that their purity, their theology, or their righteousness is so profound that they cannot lower themselves to engage in the ugliness of the society in which we live. Instead, they hold firmly to the belief that if they pray enough, fast enough, study enough, and attend enough meetings then the world will certainly improve. We might never refer to them as extreme monastics or Stylites but the actuality is that they might as well be living on a pillar. An examination of their lives would reveal a complete commitment to the first great commandment and a total absence of the second. They may well know the words, but the way they steward the resources of their lives prove that the words have little meaning. It may be that nobody has ever told them that it is impossible to live out the first great command if we are not willing to fully engage the second. We cannot actively love God without caring about the people God loves.

A biblical picture of true spirituality

It is this same concept of caring for people as a demonstration of devotion that the prophet Isaiah was addressing when he wrote the words of Isaiah 58. The chosen people of Israel were angry that God seemed to ignore their impressive spiritual pedigree and religious actions. In verses 2–3, we see the leaders and priests of Israel asking for answers and intervention from God on their behalf, but expressing frustration at His lack of response:

> For day after day they seek me out; they seem eager to know my ways, as if they were a nation that does what is right and has not forsaken the commands of its God. They ask me for just decisions and seem eager for God to come near them. 'Why

have we fasted,' they say, 'and you have not seen it? Why have we humbled ourselves and you have not noticed?'

The response of God, through Isaiah, was that they had retreated into a heavily spiritualized world of compartmentalized faith where their words were proven untrue by their actions. Isaiah points out that even while fasting they continued to exploit their workers, to fight among themselves, and to act wickedly. He ends with the query "is this what you call a fast, a day acceptable to the Lord?" (Is 58:5). It is as if God were saying to Israel, "Are you joking? Do you think I can't see the emptiness of your words when your actions towards people prove the opposite?"

Isaiah then describes the kind of spiritual focus that God desires to see in His people, saying, "Is not this the kind of fasting I have chosen: to loose the chains of injustice and untie the cords of the yoke, to set the oppressed free and break every yoke? Is it not to share your food with the hungry and to provide the poor wanderer with shelter—when you see the naked, to clothe him, and not to turn away from your own flesh and blood?" (Is 58:6–7). These words are a huge challenge to each of us who have grown our spiritual muscles in a wealthy and entitled Christian milieu. We have learned to say the right things in the right way and at the right time. We have been schooled in the correct way to pray, to practice spiritual disciplines, and to tithe. Too often, we have been taught that writing a cheque (needed as it may be!) is the same as involving ourselves in the intricacies and complexities of downtrodden people. Fortunately for each of us, Isaiah 58 is an "if, then" kind of passage. If we begin to act with concern in the lives of people, then God does intervene in miraculous ways. The rest of Isaiah 58 delineates the many beautiful outcomes that could be expected if Israel were to begin living with a vibrant inner love for God that is continually expressed through an active love for people. The prophet tells them that when they call, God will answer; that healing will take place; that the Lord will guide them and satisfy their needs; that they will be like a well-watered garden; that they will rebuild the ruins of their land; and that they will be called Repairers and Restorers.

The wonderful certainty is that when we choose to spend our lives building a list of names of people with whom we have meaningfully entwined our lives, God promises to work. God does answer and healing does take place. It is still possible to repair lives and restore people. When we refuse to live our lives on a pillar but instead determine to become involved loving our neighbors, the Lord does satisfy their needs as well as our own. Once we move from high level strategy to mid-level tactics to an active micro-level loving, then these words of the prophet Isaiah become the promise of God to us and to people who are on our list.

Building our own list

If we were to write our own list today, much as Paul did in his greetings of Romans 16, that list would tell us a lot about ourselves and our lives to this point. That list might be long or short and could include family, friends, co-workers, or people we have just met. Each of our lists would also include names of people who have shared the grace of God with us, allowing us to more fully be enveloped by the love of God at a time when we were desperate to experience it. For those of us fortunate enough to have a loving and supportive family, the names of our father and mother would be at the top of our list. Some of our lists include names of people that we have been given opportunity to help reclaim out of terrible violence and fear. It could be individuals who are hesitant to trust but are just beginning the journey of experiencing justice and love. It is worthwhile to regularly pause and let these names, these life credits, scroll through our minds. They tell us all we need to know about ourselves and perhaps sometimes more than we want to know.

Savor these names. For the many people who have served faithfully in the realms of social justice, domestic violence, and family restoration, some of these names on your list are people you have been able to help save. Of course the full truth is that if you have been involved in this arena of society for very long, then there will also be names on your list that you read with deep sorrow. Actually, if you have been involved with caring for people in any substantial way, then there are individuals who are written on your list who release joy in the memory, and others who will always carry a shade of grief.

Brittany was one such individual. It is a name that means absolutely nothing to any of you reading this, but is a person that will forever be etched on my heart.

I met Brittany playing softball. We were placed on a team together in a mixed recreational league and got to know each other fairly quickly. She was originally from Guyana but had just moved to the west coast with her young daughter in an attempt to simplify her life. She had recently left a difficult relationship in Montreal and was also looking to escape a tumultuous and highly dysfunctional extended family saga. You have heard the same sort of story a hundred times and it won't really help to tell it again.

Over a period of time, my wife, Jo-Anna, and I got to know Brittany very well. She joined us for a few barbeques at our home, and ultimately began to ask us more about our relationship with Christ. Brittany recognized that she wanted a deeper and important connection with God, began to attend some of our small group gatherings, and ultimately made a profound decision to give her life to Jesus. You should know that there are times when introducing someone to Jesus is a little too much like reading a textbook on the subject, such that I leave the conversation not really knowing whether or not there is any heart-transformation that has occurred. The person may have prayed a suggested prayer but not much else actually happened. Not so for Brittany. Her commitment to Jesus was heartfelt, emotional, volitional, and life changing. It was one of the times when you know that the angels of heaven are having a party over the life that was just changed.

About the same time, the father of Brittany's daughter, Joe, decided to move to the west in order to restore their relationship. He was a pleasant and honest guy who was willing to put in the time and energy to try and make things work with Brittany. Over a period of about a year they came to church together and sought assistance from counsellors in order to build a sustainable relationship. Throughout the year they lived in separate rooms at a boarding house and spent so much time in discussion that they referred to it as the "group home." During the same year Joe also made a decision to become a follower of Christ although it was an uncertain and shaky level of faith, at best. At the end of the year, Brittany and Joe chose to get married and to have another child within the boundaries of matrimony.

Tragically, when the reality of marriage and an increased family began to become concrete to Joe, he decided that he couldn't be tied down to that level of commitment and left to "find himself with some other woman." The result was that Brittany was alone when baby Mattias was born. She found herself alone, other than the fact that she had a great church family, small group friends, and close connection with my wife and myself. Even with a high level of church community support, it was a painful time for Brittany and her young faith. It was terribly difficult, until a few months later when Mattias died of crib death. Then it became almost impossible.

Brittany hung on to her church, her friends, her surrogate family, and to her faith. She struggled, talked, prayed, read, and sought God. She began to volunteer time in our church office in order to be around other Christ followers a little more. She and her daughter hung around our home and the homes of other friends. Most of all she fought for her belief in God to deepen.

Through all of this time, God was working in the heart of Joe. Like the prodigal of Luke 15, he was in a far country when he "came to his senses" and decided to come home. It is an understatement to say that Brittany had mixed feelings about the idea of Joe returning to her and her daughter's life. But in fact, God had been transforming Joe and he had recognized that he had been running from God as much as he had been running away from family responsibilities. Joe was changing and ultimately after months of difficult conversations so did his relationship with Brittany. It was a miraculous and rare renewal of both love and grief as they came back together.

After another year had passed they decided to adopt a child and wanted the entire experience to be one of praise to God. Before they got very far down the adoption line, however, they discovered that Brittany was pregnant again. For them, it was a nine month period of celebration. Brittany and Joe deeply believed that God had given them another chance, together, to do it all over and to do it right.

The day that Brittany and Joe brought home their new son, Andrew, from the hospital, our small group had a party at their home. It was a bitter-sweet kind of gathering, as we talked about both Mattias and Andrew, and about the journey of Brittany and Joe. Brittany pulled out her Bible and directed us to Psalm 139, where she read that "when we were woven together in the depths of the earth, your eyes saw my unformed body. All the days ordained for me were written in your book." Brittany talked of how God knew what He was doing, even in taking Mattias to be with Him. But she also talked of her continuing desire to be with her son. She turned to me and said, "I could never give up my faith now, because it has cost me too much to keep it." The evening was wonderful and painful all at once.

A couple of hours after we went home from our small group meeting, Brittany's aorta split while feeding Andrew, and she went home to be with her Lord and with her son Mattias. It was a horrible period of time for the family, for our small group, and for our church. But it was a time in which we also learned for ourselves how to apply the words of Brittany that she could never give up her faith because it had cost her too much to keep it.

The name of Brittany means very little to you, other than it is another of the sad stories that life seems to bring our way. While Brittany is never going to make it on your list, she will always be on mine. I had the joy of helping her to meet Jesus, and she helped me to know him in a different and deeper way.

I don't want to see your list of names. I have no history with those people, no meaningful experiences, no joy in life, or shared stories of pain. I have ascribed no meaning into their lives and there is no relationship of value. Your list has cost me nothing and given me nothing. However, if you have chosen to not live your life on a pillar, then you do have a list that means something to you. It is a list of names of people with whom you have history, a list of individuals and families to whom you have ascribed meaning and built relationships. The odds are high that having these people on your list has cost you a lot.

Paul's list of names in Romans 16 is part of his life story. It is the best of who Paul was, and what Paul did with the people of Rome. In a similar way, Paul wrote to the church in Thessalonica and reflected upon another list of names. He wrote that these people were his glory, his hope, and his crown. They were his living resume in heaven.

Justice will only be found, society will only be transformed, and love will only be experienced when we realize that our list of names is anything but boring. True transformational leadership strategizes at a macro level, operationally implements plans at a tactical level, but will always need to express love to one person at a time. Sometimes the best use of our time is to stop and remind ourselves of whose list we have been on and of those who are now on our unique list of names. It is a tangible expression of the grace we have received and the grace we are privileged to share.

BIBLIOGRAPHY

Bruce, F. F. *The Letter of Paul to the Romans*, TNTC. Grand Rapids: InterVarsity Press, 1999.

Conroy, P. *My Losing Season*. New York: Knopf Doubleday Publishing, 2002.

Dowley, T., et al. *Eerdman's Handbook to the History of Christianity*. Grand Rapids: Eerdmans Publishing Company, 1977.

Motyer, A. *Isaiah, An Introduction and Commentary*, TOTC. Downers Grove: InterVarsity Press, 1999.

Murray, J. *The Epistle to the Romans, NICNT*. Grand Rapids: Eerdmans Publishing Company, 1965.

"*Stylites.*" In New Catholic Encyclopedia, Vol. XIII. Washington: Catholic University of America, 1967.

"The Four Temperaments," citing Kagan, J. *Galen's Prophecy: Temperament In Human Nature*. New York: Basic Books, 1998. [online Wikipedia].

The Holy Bible, New International Version. Grand Rapids: Zondervan Corporation, 1978.

Walker, W. *A History of the Christian Church*. New York: Charles Scribner's Sons, 1970.

7

A Framework for Understanding Risk and Protective Factors of Intimate Partner Violence within a Larger Social Context

Victoria Fahlberg

DOMESTIC VIOLENCE, ALSO REFERRED to as intimate partner violence (IPV), occurs between partners who have an on-going intimate relationship and usually live in the same household. The violence primarily occurs in the home and an initial intervention can take place when the victim or others break the silence. Treatment strategies emphasize helping the victim to find physical and psychological safety, which often means moving from the home into a shelter, where advocates can help the victim with the economic, legal, and mental health services she may need to live safely. The legal approach towards batterers can vary by region, but most commonly batterers are mandated into anger management programs or programs specifically for men who batter. Depending on the severity of the offense and the willingness of the victim to testify, a batterer may be incarcerated. Domestic violence does not just impact the victim. It has been found that approximately 3 to 10 million children are exposed to intimate partner violence (IPV) annually.[1]

Interventions to help victims and bring perpetrators to justice usually occur after the violence has happened and up to now those interventions have been primarily focused on the individuals involved in

---

1. Carlson, "Children's observations," 147–167.

the violence. The purpose of this chapter is to look at an "ecological" model for understanding the confluence of factors that can increase the risk of IPV as well as those factors that act to protect against IPV. An ecological model includes individual variables that can impact IPV, such as developmental history or personality. However, the model recognizes that individuals live within a social context that exerts complex interactions within their family, community, and the larger society. In addition, individuals often belong to various communities that can influence their attitudes, values, and behavior, such as their neighborhood, church community, extended family, and friends. Finally, the risk of domestic violence is also impacted by the attitudes and values found in the larger society that can work to both increase or decrease the risk of domestic violence. The significance of utilizing a model that takes into account the many outside influences that impact individuals in their daily lives allows for more entry points into intervention and, more importantly, into prevention. After laying out the known risk and protective factors at each level, a short discussion will follow regarding the implications of how the model can be used to reduce the incidence of intimate partner violence. Development of the model

This ecological model was first proposed by Bronfenbrenner[2] and focused on human development. Several theorists,[3] whose work focused on child maltreatment, continued to develop the model, looking at the etiology of maltreatment as the actions and interactions of protective and harmful factors, within the many layers of the human ecosystem. Although some theorists[4] applied the model to batterers, theories of violence against women remained primarily focused on the individuals involved, or proposed a socio-cultural explanation based on patriarchy. However, while not denying the developmental history or personality of individuals, nor male dominance as the foundation for gender violence, Heise[5] proposed an ecological framework for understanding violence against women. She reviewed studies from interna-

2. Bronfenbrenner, "Toward an experimental ecology of human development."

3. Belsky, "Child maltreatment"; Cicchetti, et al. "Developmental perspectives"; Star, R., Ed. "Child abuse prediction"; Kaufman & Zigler, "The intergenerational transmission of child abuse."

4. Carlson, "Causes and maintenance of domestic violence"; Dutton, *The Domestic Assault of Women*; Corsi "Violencia familiar: Una Mirada Interdisciplinaria."

5. Heise, "Violence against women."

tional and cross cultural research as well as data from North American social sciences to determine specific risk and protective factors that can impact domestic violence. Her study initiated the use of the ecological model for understanding the risk and protective factors of domestic violence and currently both the World Health Organization (WHO) and the Centers for Disease Control and Prevention (CDC) utilize the ecological model for creating prevention strategies for intimate partner violence.

So what does an ecological model look like? Various models have been proposed although currently the CDC uses the model below to demonstrate the multi-layers of influences on individuals.[6]

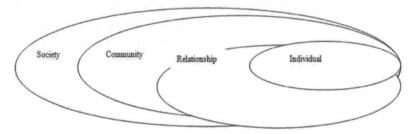

Contained within each of these layers are both risk and protective factors. Another, slightly more detailed way, to view this model that incorporates multiple layers of risk factors looks like this:

THE INDIVIDUAL

Risk and protective factors for men

In a standardized population-based household survey that took place in ten countries from 2000 to 2003, the World Health Organization found a number of factors that increased the risk of domestic violence among men.[7] Many of these risk factors have also been noted in previous studies. These risk factors include: witnessing domestic violence as a child, having a partner who witnessed her mother's abuse as a child, being physically maltreated as a child, having an absent or rejecting father, having a partner with a history of child sexual abuse, controlling

---

6. Valle et al. *Sexual and Intimate Partner Violence.*
7. Abramsky et al. "What factors," 109.

their partner's behavior, having problems with alcohol, and having a partner who has problems with alcohol. Other studies have also found these factors to put men at risk of perpetrating domestic violence.[8]

Additional risk factors have been found, including: childhood poverty, aggressive behavior by age 15, low academic achievement,[9] hypermasculinity,[10] being emotionally abusive, forcing sex with a partner, using illegal drugs, having an attitude that condones marital violence, being depressed, being stressed,[11] being emotionally dependent, insecure, and having low in self esteem, low impulse control[12], and race—where African American men are found to be more than two times as likely than their non-Hispanic white counterparts to commit domestic violence.[13] Protective factors are less studied, as it seems apparent that men who do not have identified risk factors will be more protected from battering their partners than those with the risk factors.

The World Health Organization study did note that men who had at least a secondary education and/or had a partner with at least a secondary education were better protected than men with lower academic achievement. Regularly attending church was also found to be a protective factor that decreases the risk of domestic violence[14] with this protective effect stronger for African American and Latino men than their non-Hispanic white counterparts.[15]

---

8. Heise, "Violence against women," 10; Silverman & Williamson, "Social ecology," 147–164; Hindin et al. "Intimate partner violence," 127–164; Foran et al. "Alcohol and intimate partner violence," 1222–1234; Gil-Gonzalez et al. "Alcohol and intimate partner violence" 278–284; Leonard, "Alcohol and intimate partner violence," 422–425; Ellsberg et al. "Wife abuse," 241–244; Kyriacou et al. "Emergency department-based study," 502–506; Rodgers, "Wife assault" 1–22.

9. Moffitt et al. "Findings about partner violence."

10. Parrott et al. "Effects of hypermasculinity," 70–78.

11. Stith et al., 22

12. Kantor et al. "Dynamics and risk factors."

13. Ellison et al. "Race/ethnicity, religious involvement, and domestic violence," 1094–1112.

14. Ellison et al. "Are there religious variations" 87–113; Ellison & Anderson, "Religious involvement" 269–286.

15. Ellison et al.

Risk and protective factors for women

The World Health Organization study[16] found a number of factors that increased the risk for a woman to be battered by her partner. These risk factors include: witnessing domestic violence as a child, having a partner who witnessed domestic violence as a child, having been sexually abused as child, having a partner who was physically abused as a child, being younger in age, having low socio-economic status, having an attitude that is supportive of wife beating, having problems with alcohol, having a partner who has problems with alcohol, experiencing non partner physical or sexual violence when over the age of 15, and having a partner who fights with other men. Other studies have also found these factors put women at risk of domestic violence.[17] Additional risk factors that have been found include: transgressing gender norms,[18] co-habitating rather than being married,[19] using physical violence on her partner, being depressed, and fearing future abuse.[20] In the United States, race is also a factor, as African American women with similar demographics are 2.5 times more likely than non-Hispanic white women to be victims of abuse.[21]

Protective factors are often thought of as absence of known risk factors. For example, the World Health Organization study identified protective factors, including: having at least a secondary education, having a partner with at least a secondary education, being older in age, having higher socio-economic status, being formally married and having a faithful partner.[22] Additional protective factors include: being older at age of first intercourse, having a greater sense of mastery, and being unemployed.[23] Finally, like men, regular church attendance also has been found to decrease the risk of domestic violence, and is stron-

---

16. Abramsky et al. 12.

17. Hindin et al. 15; Gazmararian et al. "Prevalence of violence" 1915–1920; Jasinski, "Pregnancy and domestic violence" 47–64; Caesar, "Exposure to violence" 49–63; Byrne et al. "The socioeconomic impact" 362–366.

18. Jewkes, "Intimate partner violence" 1423–1429.

19. Li et al. "A multilevel analysis" 532–539; Ellsberg et al. "Wife abuse" 241–244.

20. Stith et al. 22

21. Ellison et al. 27.

22. Abramsky et al. 12.

23. Li et al. 32.

ger for African American women than both their non-Hispanic white and Hispanic counterparts.[24]

Risk and protective factors of the couple

In utilizing an ecological framework, there is an understanding that individual characteristics alone may not account for the occurrence of domestic violence. This framework adds the issue of interactions between partners as an additional risk factor possibly accounting for the occurrence of violence between couples. These potentially risky interactions occur when there are disagreements about parenting, when stressors enter the family, when the couple lacks strong communication skills, and when there are negative influences in the general family environment.[25] Some of these factors overlap with those that can also be classified as individual factors, an issue that demonstrates the complexity of narrowing down exactly which variables can produce intimate partner violence, and therefore makes it difficult to predict which couples are most at risk. However, some factors are unique to the couple relationship, and therefore it is important to examine these factors as well.

The World Health Organization study[26] found that woman with children from previous relationships, men who were intimate with other woman during their relationship, men who have many partners, couples co-habitating rather than living in a formal marriage, and women working when her partner is unemployed, all contributed to greater risk of violence occurring in the relationship. In addition, this study found that when both partners had less than a high school education, when both had experienced abuse as a child, when both had witnessed abuse of their mother during childhood, and when both had a problem with alcohol, the risk of violence increased as well. Relatedly, others[27] also found that problems with alcohol increased risk for violence in the relationship. Yet other studies showed that marital conflict/discord, male dominance in the family, male control of wealth in family, first time parenting, an unplanned or unwanted pregnancy, lack of social

24. Ellison et al. 27; Ellison & Anderson, 29.
25. Little & Kantor, "Using ecological theory" 133–145.
26. Abramsky et al. 12.
27. Heise, 10.

support, poor conflict management, stress, and lack of resources also increased risk of violence in the relationship.[28]

Strong social bonds and strong marriages work to protect families against partner violence.[29] Some speculate that these factors are associated with an internalization of norms that conform to society[30] that help the couple pull together to manage their households and protect against negative influences in the neighborhood.[31]

A qualitative study by Suzuki et. al[32] looked at adults who had witnessed violence between their parents as children yet had grown up to demonstrate health and resiliency. They found that as children, these adults had a closeness to someone in their family of origin (usually a parent or sibling), and as adults they physically distanced themselves from their family of origin, accepted the imperfections of their family of origin, had retained some values from their family of origin, and eventually reconnected with a parent.

Risk and protective factors at the community level

People belong to a variety of communities that include their neighborhood, extended family, religious institution, ethnic group, and even virtual communities such as Facebook. While it is recognized that belonging to communities outside of one's nuclear family could provide both risk factors as well as protective factors, the evidence of impact on domestic violence is indirect and therefore more difficult to demonstrate. However, some studies have begun to help in understanding what community factors may have the most influence on increasing or preventing domestic violence. Most current research focuses on the neighborhood, although some studies are beginning to look at the role of religious communities in relationship to domestic violence.

Neighborhoods with greater unemployment, poverty, low per capita income, resource deprivation, and concentrated disadvantage seem

---

28. Heise, 10; Li et al. 3; O'Campo et al. "Violence by male partners," 1092–1097; Janiski, 28; Fox et al. "Economic distress," 793–807.

29. Lackey &Williams, "Social bonding," 295–305; Lackey, "Violent family heritage," 74–98; Sampson et al. "Does marriage reduce crime?" 465–508.

30. Ibid.

31. Bandura, "Self-Efficacy" cited in Li et al. 32.

32. Suzuki et al. "The experiences of adults," 103–121.

to be at increased risk for domestic violence.[33] Some authors suggest that poverty can lead to stress, frustration, and a sense of inadequacy in some men for not fulfilling their culturally defined role as provider.[34] Social isolation from any community is also found to be a risk factor for increased potential of interpersonal violence.[35] In societies with a low level of violence, extended family and community members feel that they have a right to intervene.[36] Delinquent peer associations, which have been specifically linked to sexual coercion and rape[37] as well as physical and psychological abuse,[38] appear to be strong predictors of male gender violence in addition to men's increased beliefs of entitlement to abuse female partners, and the belief that battering is justified.[39] Higher levels of neighborhood crime[40] and cynicism regarding the legal system were also shown to be risk factors.[41] Neighborhood residential mobility is an inconsistent factor.[42] It is possible that in low income neighborhoods where people feel trapped and hopeless, intimate partner violence could increase, whereas in low-income neighborhoods where residents have access to social services and/or believe in the possibility of upward mobility, at least for their children, one might find lower rates of domestic violence.

If risk factors—including poverty, especially concentrated poverty; social isolation; delinquent peer associations; including men's increased beliefs of entitlement to abuse female partners; the belief that battering is justified; and higher levels of neighborhood crime and cynicism regarding the legal system—then it would seem that the lack of these risk factors would protect against domestic violence. For example, higher

33. Andrews, "Developing community systems," 1–9; Stark et al. "Wife abuse," ; O'Campo et al. 52; Strauss et al. "Behind closed doors," ; Miles-Doan, "Violence between spouses," 77; Benson et al. "Neighborhood disadvantage," 207–235; Van Wyk et al. "Detangling," 412–438.

34. Heise, 274; Dobash & Dobash, "Violence against wives."

35. Dobash & Dobash, "Violence against wives."

36. Heise, 275.

37. Alder, "An exploration," 306–331; Malmouth et al. "Using the confluence model," 353–369.

38. DeKeseredy and Kelly, "Woman abuse," 25–52.

39. Silverman & Williamson, 14.

40. Andrews, 62.

41. Frye. "The informal social control" 1001–1018.

42. Ibid, Miles-Doan, 66; Benson et al. 67; Van Wyk, 68; Li et al. 38. .

income, social connection to others, healthy peer relationships, less neighborhood crime, and trust in the legal system could help to reduce incidences of domestic violence. In fact, studies have found social cohesion and social control to play a role in reducing violent victimization at both the neighborhood and individual level.[43] Sanctions against domestic violence in a community also function as protective factors. These sanctions can be formal, such as laws against domestic violence or policies like providing housing vouchers for low income residents, or they can be informal, such as neighbors feeling a moral pressure to intervene. Having a place of safety, such as a shelter or home of a family member was also found to be a protective factor.[44] Informal "helpers" were found to function as protective factors only when they had an attitude that did not blame the victim.[45]

While most studies have focused on neighborhoods as communities, church communities also can function as a protective factor. Church communities are viewed as supportive to abused women, especially among African Americans.[46] Nancy Nason-Clark (1996) found that 55.1% of 250 evangelical women had been involved in supporting an abused woman by offering emotional, physical, or spiritual support, in addition to making a referral to a secular agency or minister, or providing advice, or counseling as either a friend or professional.[47]

In the qualitative study by Suzuki et al[48] who interviewed adults who, as children, had witnessed violence between their parents yet had grown up to demonstrate health and resiliency, some additional protective factors were found that resided outside the home environment. First, as children, they had a social support system, including peers, outside the home. Second, they had important adults in their lives, such as extended family members, teachers, coaches, and friends' parents who also provided them with support. Finally, many had been involved in extracurricular activities such as after-school activities, sports, and

---

43. Sampson & Morenoff, "Ecological perspectives" 1–22; Sampson et al. "Assessing 'neighborhood effects,'" Frye, 78.

44. Counts et al. "Sanctions and sanctuary," 99.

45. West & Wandrei, "Intimate partner violence," 972–986.

46. Krause, "Exploring race differences," 126–149.

47. Nason-Clark, "The Battered Wife," 109–137.

48. Suzuki et al. 61.

art, all of which acted to increase their self-esteem, were positive reinforcements, and were ways to escape from their families of origin.

Risk and protective factors in society

Few studies have been done to date that attempt to link the act of violence between partners to variables in the larger society. It is also important to note that local differences on the prevalence of intimate partner violence within countries often have greater differences than across national boundaries,[49] which emphasizes the importance of interventions occurring at the community level. It has also been found that even where cultural norms allow men substantial control over female behavior, perpetrators of domestic violence usually exceed the norms.[50]

However, research has produced some cultural and societal factors that might give rise to higher levels of domestic violence, but currently these factors, while reasonable, do not have empirical evidence to back them up.

A cross cultural study by Yodanis did find that the higher women's occupational and educational status the lower the prevalence of sexual violence, but this concordant relationship was not related to physical violence.[51] Another ethnographic study of 90 societies explored cultural patterns of wife beating.[52] An analysis of the data from this study suggests that the frequency of domestic violence is greater when men have economic and decision-making power in the household, women lack easy access to divorce, and adults routinely use violence to resolve conflicts. This study also found that domestic violence is lower for women whose work groups are all female. Heise postulates that societies with a cultural definition of manhood related to dominance, toughness, male honor, and rigid gender roles are risk factors for domestic violence, while a lack of strongly defined gender roles is a protective factor.[53] Other researchers have reasoned that higher rates of domestic violence will likely be found during times of war or social upheavals and where

49. Valle et al. 57.

50. Rosales et al. "Encuesta Nicaraguense," 11; Johnson, "Dangerous domains"; Romero, "Violencia sexual y domestica," 11.

51. Yodanis, "Gender inequality," 655–675.

52. Levinson, "Family violence in cross-cultural perspective."

53. Heise, 10

violence is commonplace and people have easy access to weapons.[54] It is also reasonable to believe that laws at the national level aimed to reduce domestic violence, like those at the community level, will have a protective impact on women. For a large list of possible risk factors at the societal level, see who has broken down these factors into four areas: Cultural, Economic, Legal, and Political.[55]

DISCUSSION

Understanding risk and protective factors that interact within an individual's entire social context allows for many points of intervention. While most spending necessarily goes to help victims find physical and psychological safety, it is important to begin to think about preventing, or at least reducing, intimate partner violence from ever occurring. At an individual level education is generally viewed as the best way to help people, particularly young people, understand the terrible consequences of domestic violence for the victim, perpetrator, and their children. Education can also help build new skills for resolving conflicts without the use of violence, as well as effective communication skills. Since we know that witnessing domestic violence as a child for both boys and girls, physical abuse of boys, and sexual abuse of girls are strong risk factors for future domestic violence, it is important to reach out to children who have suffered from violence or witnessing violence before it's too late. In the United States many of these children are identified through child protective services. Perhaps mentoring programs could be developed since we also know that having a significant adult in the life of the child helps to protect against future abuse. Adult role models such as teachers, coaches, leaders of boy scouts and girl scouts can also provide support to children who are witnessing domestic violence.

Regarding the relationship of the couple, parenting programs, offered at community centers or places of worship, could be provided for couples whose profiles indicate risk factors that lead to child abuse and/ or domestic violence. Informational brochures could be created that help parents gain information about child development and how to build healthy relationships with their children. These initiatives could

---

54. Valle et al. 11.
55. Heise, 46.

be designed to help decrease risk factors of the couple as well as teach them how to be good parents.

At the community level, schools could partner in providing the time and place for programs focused on teaching students about healthy, non-violent relationships. Collaborations with religious organizations, or perhaps non-profits that work with youth, sports clubs, or within the scouting field, could also help. Having speakers address neighborhood groups about the issue of domestic violence and the importance of intervening would surely generate discussion of the issue and give neighbors the chance to think as a group about how family privacy is viewed among them. Certainly churches have many opportunities to reach out to youth in their congregations through Sunday School and youth group meetings, while adult congregants can be reached through adult Sunday school, Bible Studies, and even sermons on the importance of healthy, non-violent relationships in the home.

In the larger society, it is important to advocate continually for laws that will impact sexual and domestic violence as well as violence towards children—such as mandatory arrest laws. It is also important to advocate for government funding for prevention programs and campaigns that focus on prevention.

The better that risk and protective factors are understood at all levels of society, the better equipped everyone will be to work together towards a society that abhors violence, especially violence in the home, the place where one is supposed to find love, safety, and security. How a community—whether a neighborhood, extended family, religious congregation, or other group—responds to domestic violence will have a significant impact on reducing the occurrence of violence in the home.

BIBLIOGRAPHY

Alder, C. "An exploration of self-reported sexually aggressive behavior," *Crime and Delinquency*, 31 (1985) 306–331.

Abramsky, T., et al. "What factors are associated with recent intimate partner violence?" Findings from the WHO multi-country study on women's health and domestic violence. *BMC Public Health* 11 (2011) 109.

Andrews, A. B. "Developing community systems for the primary prevention of family violence: family and community health," *The Journal of Health Promotion and Maintenance*, 16(4) (1996) 1–9.

Bandura, A. "Self-Efficacy: The exercise of control," (1997), New York, NY: WH Freeman & Company,. Cited in Qing Li, et al. "A Multilevel analysis of individual, household, and neighborhood correlates of intimate partner violence among low-income pregnant women in Jefferson County, Alabama," *American Journal Public Health* 100(3) (2010) 532–539.

Belsky, J. "Child maltreatment: An ecological integration," *American Psychologist*, 35 (1980) 320–335.

Benson, M. L., et al. "Neighborhood disadvantage, individual economic distress and violence against women in intimate relationships," *Journal of Quantitative Criminology* 19 (2003) 207–235.

Bronfenbrenner, U. "Toward an experimental ecology of human development," *American Psychologist* 32 (1977) 513–531.

Byrne, C. A., et al. "The socioeconomic impact of interpersonal violence on women," *Journal of Consulting and Clinical Psychology*, 67 (1999) 362–366.

Caeser, P. L. "Exposure to violence in the families of origin among wife abusers and maritally nonviolent men," *Violence and Victims*, 3 (1998) 49–63.

Carlson, B. E. "Children's observations of interparental violence. In A.R. Roberts (Ed.), *Battered Women and their Families*, New York: Springer (1984) 147–167.

Carlson, B. E. "Causes and maintenance of domestic violence: An ecological analysis," *Social Service Review* 58(4) (1984) 569–587.

Cicchetti, D. and R. Rizley. "Developmental perspectives on the etiology, intergenerational transmission and sequelae of child maltreatment," *New Directions for Child Development*, 11 (1981) 31–56.

Corsi J. "Violencia familiar: una mirada interdisciplinaria sobre un grave problema social," Buenos Aires, Argentina: Paidos (1994). Cited in L. Heise, *Violence against Women: An Integrated, Ecological Framework* 4(3) (1998) 262–290.

Counts, D. A., J. Brown, and J.Campbell, (Eds.), *Sanctions and Sanctuary: Cultural Perspectives on the Beating of Wives*. Boulder, CO: Westview, 1992.

DeKeseredy, W. S. and K. Kelly. "Woman abuse in university and college dating relationships: The contribution of the ideology of familial patriarchy," *Journal of Human Justice* 4(2) (1993) 25–52.

Dobash, R. R. and E. Dobash. *Violence Against Wives*, New York: Free Press, 1979.

Dutton, D. G. *The Domestic Assault of Women: Psychological and Criminal Justice Perspectives*. Newton, MA: Allyn and Bacon, 1988.

Ellison, C. G., et al. "Race/ethnicity, religious involvement, and domestic violence," *Violence Against Women*, 13 (2007) 1094–1112.

Ellison, C. G. and K. L. Anderson. "Religious involvement and domestic violence among U.S. couples," *Journal for the Scientific Study of Religion* 40 (2001) 269–286.

Ellison, C. G., J. P. Bartkowski, and K. L. Anderson. "Are there religious variations in domestic violence?" *Journal of Family Issues* 20 (1999) 87–113.

Ellsberg, M.C., et al. "Wife abuse among women of childbearing age in Nicaragua," *American Journal of Public Health*, 89 (1999) 241–244.

Foran, H. M. K. and D. O'Leary. "Alcohol and intimate partner violence: A meta analytic review," *Clinical Psychology Review* 28(7) (2008) 1222–1234.

Fox, G. L., et al. "Economic distress and intimate violence: Testing family stress and resource theories," *Journal of Marriage and Family* 64 (2002) 793–807.

Frye, V. "The informal social control of intimate partner violence against women: Exploring personal attitudes and perceived neighborhood social cohesion," *Journal of Community Psychology* 35(8) (2007) 1001–1018.

Gazmararian, J. A., et al. "Prevalence of violence against pregnant women," *Journal of American Medical Association* 275 (1996) 1915–1920.

Gil-Gonzalez, D., et al. "Alcohol and intimate partner violence: Do we have enough information to act?" *European Journal of Public Health* 16(3) (2006) 278–284.

Heise, L. "Violence against women: An integrated, ecological framework," *Violence Against Women* 4(3) (1998) 262–290.

———. "Violence against Women: The Hidden Health Burden," Discussion papers No. 225, Washington DC: The World Bank. Cited in UNICEF Violence Against Women, *Innocenti Digest* 6, 1993.

Hindin, M.J., S. Kishor, and D.L. Ansara. "Intimate partner violence among couples in 10 DHS countries: Predictors and health outcomes," DHS Analytical Studies. No 18, Calverton, MD: Macro International, 2008.

Jasinski, J. L. "Pregnancy and domestic violence: A review of the literature," *Trauma, Violence and Abuse* 5 (2004) 47–64.

Jewkes, R. "Intimate partner violence: Causes and prevention," *Lancet* 359 (2002) 1423–1429.

Johnson, H. *Dangerous Domains: Violence Against Women in Canada*, (The Nelson Crime in Canada Series) Ontario: International Thomson Publishing, 1996.

Kaufman J. and E. Zigler. "The intergenerational transmission of child abuse," Cited in D. Cicchetti and V. Carlson (Eds.) *Child Maltreatment: Theory and Research on the Causes and Consequences of Child Abuse and Neglect*. New York: Cambridge University Press, 1989.

Kaufman Kantor, G., and J. L. Jsiniski. "Dynamics and risk factors in partner violence," Cited in: J. L. Jasinski and L. Meyers Williams(Eds) *Partner Violence: A Comprehensive Review of 20 Years of Research*, Thousand Oaks, CA: Sage, 1998.

Krause, N."Exploring race differences in a comprehensive battery of church-based social support measures," *Review of Religious Research* 44:2 (2002) 126–149.

Kyriacou, D. N., et al. "Emergency department-based study of risk factors for acute injury from domestic violence against women," *Annals of Emergency Medicine* 21 (1998) 502–506.

Lackey, C., and K. R. Williams. "Social bonding and the cessation of partner violence across generations," *Journal of Marriage and Family* 57 (1995) 295–305.

Lackey, C. Violent Family Heritage: The transition to adulthood and later partner violence," *Journal of Family Issues* 24 (2003) 74–98.

Leonard, K. E: "Alcohol and intimate partner violence: When can we say that heavy drinking is a contributing cause of violence?" *Addiction* 100 (2005) 422–425.

Levinson, D. *Family Violence in Cross-cultural Perspective*, Thousand Oaks, CA: Sage, 1989.

Li, Q., et al. "A multilevel analysis of individual, household, and neighborhood correlates of intimate partner violence among low-income pregnant women in Jefferson County, Alabama." *American Journal of Public Health* 100(3) (2010) 532–539.

Little, L. and G. Kauffman Kantor. "Using ecological theory to understand intimate partner violence and child maltreatment," *Journal of Community Health Nursing* 19(3) (2002) 133–145.

Malmouth, N. M., et al. "Using the confluence model of sexual aggression to predict men's conflict with women: A ten year follow-up study," *Journal of Personality and Social Psychology* 69 (1995) 353–369.

Miles-Doan, R. "Violence between spouses and intimates: Does neighborhood context matter?" *Social Forces* 77 (1998) 623–646.

Moffitt, T. E, and A.Caspi. *Findings about Partner Violence from the Dunedin Multidisciplinary Health and Development Study, New Zealand*, Washington, D.C.: National Institutes of Justice, 1999.

Nason-Clark, N. *The Battered Wife: How Christians Confront Family Violence*, Louisville, KY: Westminster John Knox Press, 1997.

O'Campo, P., et al. "Violence by male partners against women during the childbearing years: A contextual analysis," *American Journal of Public Health* 85 (1995) 1092–1097.

Parrott, D. J., and A. Zeichner. "Effects of hyper masculinity of physical aggression against women," *Psychology of Men & Masculinity*, 4(1) (2003) 70–78.

Ramirez, I. L. "The relationship of acculturation and social integration to assaults on intimate partners among Mexican American and non-Mexican white students," *Journal of Family Violence* 22 (2007) 533–542.

Rodgers, K." Wife assault: The findings of a national survey," *Juristat* Service Bulletin 14 (1994) 1–22.

Romero, M. "Violencia sexual y domestica: Informe de la fase cuantitativa realizada en el centro de atencion a adolescentes de San Miguel de Allende," [Sexual and Domestic Violence: Report from the Qualitative Phase from an Adolescent Center in San Miguel de Allende.] Mexico City, Population Council, 1994. Cited in L. A. Valle, *Sexual and Intimate Partner Violence Prevention Programs Evaluation Guide*. Centers for Disease Control and Prevention, National Center for Injury Prevention and Control, 2007.

Rosales, J., E. Loaiza, D. Primante, and A. Barberena. "Encuesta Nicaraguense de demografia y salud, 1998," [1998 Nicaraguan demographic and health survey] Managua, Instituto Nacional de Estadisticas y Censos, 1999. Cited in L. A. Valle, *Sexual and Intimate Partner Violence Prevention Programs Evaluation Guide*. Centers for Disease Control and Prevention, National Center for Injury Prevention and Control, 2007.

Sampson, R. J. and J. D. Morenoff. "Ecological perspectives on the neighborhood context of urban poverty: Past and present," Cited in J. Brooks-Gunn, et al. (Eds). *Neighborhood Poverty: Vol. 2. Policy Implications in Studying Neighborhoods* New York: Russell Sage (1997) 1–22. Cited in V. Frye. "The informal social control of intimate partner violence against women: Exploring personal attitudes and perceived neighborhood social cohesion," *Journal of Community Psychology* 35(8) (2007) 1001–1018.

Sampson, R. J., J. D. Morenoff, and T. Gannon-Riley. "Assessing 'neighborhood effects': Social processes and new directions in research." *Annual Review of Sociology*, 28 (2002) 443–478. Cited in V. Frye, "The informal social control of intimate partner violence against women: Exploring personal attitudes and perceived neighborhood social cohesion." *Journal of Community Psychology* 35(8) (2007) 1001–1018.

Sampson, R. J., J. H. Laub, and C. Wimer. "Does marriage reduce crime? A counterfactual approach to within-individual causal effects," *Criminology* 44 (2006) 465–508.

Silverman, J. G. and G. M. Williamson. "Social ecology and entitlements involved in battering in heterosexual college males: Contributions of family and peers," *Violence and Victims* 12(2) (1997) 147–164.

Starr, R. "Child abuse prediction: Policy implications," 1982. Cited in D. C. Bross, et al. (Eds.) *The New Child Protection Team Handbook*. New York: Garland, 1988.

Stark, E., et al. *Wife Abuse in the Medical Setting: An Introduction for Health Personnel*, Monograph 7, Washington, D.C: Office of Domestic Violence, 1981.

Stith, S. M., et al."Intimate partner physical abuse perpetration and victimization factors: A meta-analytic review," *Aggression and Violent Behavior* 10 (2004) 65–98.

Strauss, M. A., R. J. Gelles, and S. K. Steinmetz. *Behind Closed Doors: Violence in the American Family*, New York: Doubleday, 1980.

Suzuki, S., R. Geffner, and S. F. Buckey. "The experiences of adults exposed to intimate partner violence as children: An exploratory qualitative study of resilience and protective factors," *Journal of Emotional Abuse* 12 (2008) 103–121.

Valle, L. A. *Sexual and Intimate Partner Violence Prevention Programs Evaluation Guide*, Centers for Disease Control and Prevention, National Center for Injury Prevention and Control, 2007.

Van Wyk, J.A., et al. "Detangling, individual partner, and community-level correlates of partner violence," *Crime and Delinquency* 49 (2003) 412–438.

West, A. and M. L. Wandrei. "Intimate partner violence: A model for predicting interventions by informal helpers," *Journal of Interpersonal Violence* 17 (2002) 972–986.

Yodanis, C. L. "Gender inequality, violence against women, and fear: A cross-national test of the feminist theory of violence against women," *Journal of Interpersonal Violence* 19 (2004) 655–675.

PART II

Working to Strengthen Individuals within Family Life

8

Realizing the Potential of Second Stage Programming

Lorrie Wasyliw

INTRODUCTION

For women and their children who make the difficult choice to leave an abusive relationship, the road ahead can look daunting. Whether the leave-taking comes abruptly as a result of a traumatic incident involving police or emergency responders, a desperate decision when believing they are "at the end of their rope," or the outcome of an implemented and carefully thought out plan, there are common markers that highlight their situations. At this critical time, women often feel isolated and are unsure of their personal capacity to make good decisions and move forward. It is easy to become overwhelmed with the enormity of beginning again. This challenge, coupled with the impact the abuse has had on the woman, often makes it very difficult for the woman to navigate this journey alone. The special needs for safety, security, and support are often integral for a future healthy life. An additional factor that plays a significant role is limited access to stable, safe, and affordable housing.

In this chapter, we will focus on the potential ministry that a second stage housing program provides for those who find themselves at this crossroads. The opportunities to provide key services of housing, supportive relationships, and advocacy are significant. Having someone who understands the dynamics and impact of abuse walking alongside them in their quest to conquer the barriers, re-establish their lives, and become independent can mean the difference between freedom or returning to an abusive relationship. Both women and their children, if any, need a safe place to belong.

Second stage experience

W.I.N.G.S. (Women in Need Gaining Strength) began in New Westminster, British Columbia in 1997, as a result of a common vision to demonstrate responsibility toward the issues of social justice in our society today. The realization of the extent of domestic violence in our society propelled us to focus our efforts specifically in the area of violence against women and children. A second stage housing program was one of the opportunities that emerged as we grappled with how to practically support women. In May 2001, we opened *Chrysalis Place*, providing supportive subsidized housing for 7 women and 4 children for up to one year. Our shared experiences of graduating over 75 women are discussed in this chapter. The names and some details of the women's lives have been changed out of respect for their privacy.

Challenges faced by women who have chosen to leave abusive relationships

Sadie was married to a very successful school principal. They lived in a beautiful home in a lovely neighborhood. To all outward appearances, he was well respected and regarded as a skilled, capable, and kind supervisor. Life at home was the opposite. Sadie was treated like a slave. She was often kept locked in a room while he was away. Often she was not given enough food to eat. Sadie had lost hope of being able to get away from this situation because she knew that no one would believe her story. She had no family or friends she could turn to. When the physical abuse began, she contemplated suicide. Then one day her husband treated her very aggressively in public and someone else called the police. When the police arrived and evaluated the situation they made a decision that Sadie needed to be removed from her home and taken to a safe place.

Petra married her childhood sweetheart. It wasn't until she was expecting their first child that her husband began to direct a barrage of verbal and emotional abuse towards her. The level of abuse escalated as time went by and she became accustomed to living with it. She spent every day doing what she could to keep incidents from happening. It wasn't until she recognized that her three children were being very negatively impacted by the abuse and that her husband had begun to treat them the same way that she knew she needed to safely plan how to leave.

For women like Sadie and Petra who face the difficult dilemma of leaving an abusive relationship, the journey that has brought them to this place is unique to them as individuals yet marked by common characteristics. The cost of staying is devastating; the cost of leaving is overwhelming.

Debilitating impact of abuse

Initially, the most important thing that we needed to grasp was an understanding of the multitude of losses women experience when they leave. First and foremost is the loss of a woman's relationship with her intimate partner, the father of her children, the one who is often her provider. For many women, it is not the relationship they want to end, it is the abuse. We first met Hillary five years ago when she left for the first time and took refuge in our emergency shelter. She found that the relational bonds with her abusive husband were stronger than she could manage and even though her mind was telling her that it was a futile endeavour to return, his continuing emotional demands of her were a lever to draw her back into the relationship. It took over five years and several leavings before Hillary faced the sad reality that no matter how much she loved her partner and tried to make the relationship work, the abuse continued. She came to our second stage program feeling very hopeless and confused about her internal turmoil.

Another loss involves the loss of a woman's "dream," that of a happy family life. A woman's identity is often based on her role in relationships and when a relationship fails, it is easy for her to feel it must be because of some inadequacy in her. She is usually a woman who has tried to "fix" the relationship and invested much time and effort into changing herself—changing anything and everything she can to try to end the abuse. Sylvie was another woman who was drawn back to her marriage several times, mostly because she desperately wanted the security of a happy family life. In addition, her desire to have a child outweighed almost everything else. Her efforts to attain the ideal she envisioned did give her a child, but her futile efforts to stop the abuse robbed her of her dignity and self-worth, leaving her with a significant sense of failure and shame.

For other women, particularly if they are a woman of faith or a woman of a non-mainstream ethnic culture, the decision to leave involves the loss of her community and possibly the support from her own family if they don't agree with her decision. When a woman's family or community does not support her, this actually places her in an unsafe, potentially dangerous situation. Keisha, a woman from an ethnic culture, found that she couldn't have any contact with her family as they would trace the phone number she was calling from and immediately tell her husband any details she disclosed to them. From their perspective she needed to come home and make the best of the situation in order to save face for the family. Stacey experienced significant pressure from her pastor and the elders in her church to quickly "forgive" and return to the marriage or she would be disciplined by the church and removed from membership. She received this directive in the immediate aftermath of her husband making threats to her safety and that of her son. The that Stacey experienced, while virtually held as a prisoner in her own home, gave her a sense of disconnection from others and left her without a community. Women need a safe place to belong.

An important lesson we have learned is to never underestimate the debilitating impact of abuse. Whether it be physical, mental, emotional, psychological, or spiritual, abused women are vulnerable in many ways. Marilee had been told so many times she was incapable and useless, she had begun to believe it, leaving her mired in a deep depression. Some women turn to alcohol and illicit drugs to numb the pain inside; others experience depression and anxiety that a medical doctor might simply prescribe a prescription drug to solve, rather than seeking a long term solution for the underlying cause.

Statistics from various sources indicate that, on average, a woman will leave an abusive relationship up to nine times before she leaves permanently. Internally overwhelmed and vulnerable, women like these need a safe place to belong.

External impacts

Leaving a relationship can also mean the loss of a woman's home. There are numerous women who know that when they walk out the door they will never be able to return, even to retrieve basic essentials. Others know that they will never be able to retain all their possessions. Imagine for a moment going home today and finding your home had burned to the ground, leaving nothing behind. You would likely regard this as being a very devastating event and feel quite overwhelmed by all the immediate decisions to make, paperwork to complete, and practical arrangements to secure. Now think about facing this loss without the benefit of house insurance, access to a credit card, or cash in your bank account, and already feeling debilitated, hopeless, and uncertain about your capacity as a person. For many of us, it is simply unimaginable. When we first met Brenda, she only had a backpack with simple essentials within. Everything else had been left behind and would never be retrieved. Her sadness about sentimental items left behind was heartfelt. Finding a new place to belong was the beginning of her journey to peace and safety.

It is disturbing to realize the connection between abuse and homelessness. One regional homelessness plan says, "Violence against women is a cause of homelessness. Women fleeing abusive situations may find themselves with nowhere to live. . . . North American and other studies have shown that a high proportion of homeless women disclose domestic violence as a chronic feature of their family life or as a precipitating factor in their current homeless episode."[1] Several other studies have noted that the multiple and overlapping barriers to housing that many women face after leaving violent relationships compromise women's safety and well-being, put them at risk of housing instability and homelessness, and, at times, force them back to abusive partners.[2] "Addressing women's housing and housing instability is understood to be one of the key service areas in supporting women who leave violent relationships, alongside other services such as counselling, income and legal support, and employment programs."[3] "Moving between various types of accommodation that lacked security of tenure and/or failed to provide a sense of safety. . . directly impacted on the women's ability to obtain a life free from violence and to heal."[4]

---

1. *3 Ways to Home*, 32.

2. Champion et al. "*The impact of housing*"; Davies et al. "*Safety planning with battered women*"; Shinn et al. "Predictors of homelessness," 1651–1657.

3. Hague and Mullender, "Who listens?" 568–587; Jones, "The distinctive characteristics," 113; Paterson, "(Re)constructing women's resistance," 121–145.

4. Champion et al., 3.

Another important aspect we needed to understand was the barriers these women face in moving forward. Leaving can often thrust a woman into poverty. The loss of financial security is very real to those women who have spent the majority of their time within the home and without a job. Women who have been in a relationship since they were quite young and don't have any work experience face a potentially lengthy employment search. Women who have never had the opportunity to be in control of their own finances need to quickly learn how to budget and manage daily expenses. Tameika had never been allowed to shop or to have money. She didn't know how to open a bank account, use a debit card, or pay for bills. She had no idea of how much it cost to pay rent or utilities. She needed time to acquire some basic skills before she could look for a job. Women who need to get back on their feet before they can work might not be eligible for supplemental income and an exemption from work.

Abused women usually do not have the belief that they will be able to support themselves financially. YWCA Canada notes that "just over half of single parent families headed by women are poor, and more than half of single mothers rely on welfare at some point."[5] Often there aren't any supportive social networks, family, or friends who can respond to the crisis and provide practical assistance.

Women who are working often find it impossible to juggle both the demands of their job and the complexities of leaving an abusive relationship at the same time. Many are forced to take a leave of absence. For others, their inability to perform well in their employment responsibilities leaves their employment status in jeopardy. Lilly was laid off from her position about four months after she left her husband. While seemingly sympathetic to her situation, the reason given by her employer was a poor performance review. The truth was that Lilly was so ravaged by the impact of abuse and dealing with the challenges of leaving she hadn't been able to meet the standard of "business as usual" at work. Tahlia, who had worked side by side with her husband in the family business for many years, had to give up her job in order to be safe.

Unfortunately, many of the government ministries that these women need to access are not set up with their challenges in mind,

---

5. *International Women's Day Bulletin*, YWCA Canada, www.ywcacanada.ca/data/publications/00000058.pdf

making navigating through different systems an intimidating process. There is a plethora of government forms, requirements, documents; the list goes on and on. For women who do not speak English as their first language and are not fluent, there are additional obstacles of translating information into a framework they can understand and respond to effectively.

Parenting is another area where the dynamics dramatically change when a woman leaves. It is common that a man's abusive behaviour has fostered disrespect for the woman and undermined her parenting authority, creating a toxic influence on daily family life. Her decision to leave might be met with anger and anxiety by the children. She might need some solid support to build her confidence to parent alone. It is hard work to rebuild each child's life individually and as a family. The list is long when it includes items like establishing custody, securing child maintenance payments, and negotiating access arrangements.

If the police have been involved in her situation, a woman might face a long journey through the legal system. It might include filing police statements and affidavits, applying for a restraining order, and submitting impact statements, etc., with limited legal assistance.

Whether it is financial instability, navigating through systems such as welfare, legal aid, child services, police and court processes, re-establishing of parenting abilities, or searching for a new home, there are many obstacles to overcome on the journey to peace and safety. Coupled with these challenges is the realization of the debilitating effects of domestic abuse on a woman—leaving her often in a state of depression, anxiety, and without any self-esteem. Women need a safe place to belong.

Opportunities to meet challenges through second stage programming

Defining second stage programming

A second stage program is ideally designed to support women moving forward with their lives and facing
many of the challenges outlined above. The ultimate goal of the program is to walk alongside a woman on her journey to healing and recovery from the impact of abuse and eventually living an independent and healthy life.

The key services of housing, supportive relationships, and advocacy are significant aspects to accomplish the goal and can be provided through a variety of program structures. Not every second stage program looks the same. Some are staffed by volunteers; others have been able to secure a funding source for paid staff. Some are large, others are small. Facilities may range from complete community living (everyone has their own sleeping areas but all other areas are common space) to self-contained housing units. The average duration of a program is between one to three years. Program elements and guidelines vary from minimal to extensive.

For a church or faith community, a second stage ministry is a wonderful opportunity to

respond compassionately and express the unconditional love of God in a practical way to vulnerable women and children. I believe the impact of this ministry in both the faith and broader community demonstrates the heart of God in the broken world around us.

Support for healing

Each woman within our one year program is assigned a one-to-one support worker who comes alongside them for the duration of their involvement in the program. An initial meeting focuses on identifying needs and setting individual goals to be accomplished. The woman meets with their support worker at least every other week to review their progress and encourage re-evaluation and new goal setting. These meetings also serve to allow the support worker the opportunity to monitor the mental, emotional, and physical health of the woman, thereby helping her to recognize areas that may need extra attention.

Giving women time and space to rest and heal, to work through their feelings, and to understand and make sense of the abuse they have endured is central to the support offered. Louise came to us with many losses to mourn. Along with the demise of her marriage, she was despairing a recent miscarriage as well as losing her mother six months earlier. She needed time to go through a grieving process in an understanding environment. Monica had been married for thirty-five years when she made her decision that she couldn't continue to exist in her marriage. She was not aware of how impactful the abuse had been over such a long period of time. She needed long periods of peace and rest to begin to rebuild from the debilitation she had experienced.

Mallory had completely believed the words of her husband when he told her repeatedly that there was no possible way she could manage without him, she was not a fit parent to their two year old twins, and she would never be able to find a job because no one would be willing to hire someone who was so useless. Her self-worth was non-existent. She needed to gain a new understanding and appreciation of her worth and capacity to succeed.

Tahlia was riddled with guilt and shame over the consequences faced by her husband in their community because of her decision to leave. Because she had been an unpaid employee in the family business, her departure forced her husband to restructure the workplace and incur higher operating costs. As well, he was shunned by his family and cultural community for not being able to "keep her in line." Tahlia needed to realize that she was not responsible for the consequences of his abusive behaviour.

One of the key features of supporting healing and recovery is to provide information about abuse to those who have been caught up in it. Information brings understanding and clarity to confusion. Our program takes women through a specific ten-week group experience giving the women the opportunity to learn about themselves, reflect on their experiences to gain new understanding, and focus on healing. A considerable number of women believe that they are the only ones who feel the way they do and that no one can understand. There have been many "Aha!" moments for women as for the first time they have understood why their partners might have reacted or behaved the way they have. Lindsay, a mother of three children, had been puzzled by her husband's reaction to her suggestion for a special family outing. His angry response was highly disproportionate to the situation and his verbal assaults left her feeling that she had done something terribly wrong. To add to her confusion, her husband came back to her within a few hours and magnanimously agreed to participate in the event. When the day came, however, he was withdrawn and unresponsive throughout the outing, which served to ruin the time for the entire family. She came to an understanding that family priorities would always be secondary to her husband's plans and his need to control her.

Support through life skill development and advocacy

Giving opportunities for women to set individual goals and experience success in reaching them is an integral element of a second stage program. Broad categories range from getting settled, restructuring financial affairs, navigating through legal matters, pursuing education or employment goals, life skills development, home management, multicultural issues, strengthening parenting skills, recreation, building connections with a faith community, and referrals to counseling or medical professionals. These needs are met in a variety of ways, both within the program and through referral and advocacy.

Our program provides a regular topic-themed group. Topics are often chosen by the women themselves and may include everything from grief and loss, issues of faith, self-worth, and boundaries, to practical things like budgeting, parenting skills, and healthy nutrition. Information is provided on child development and behavior, dealing with medical, legal, financial, and social services, and opportunities for education, training, and employment. One of Rose's daughters was swayed by her father's attempts to win her affection. With his indulgences of her every desire that her mother could not afford, he successfully turned her against her mother and she became very angry with her mother's decision to leave. It was important for Rose to understand her daughter's perspective. By gaining insights into her behavior, she needed to learn how to effectively respond.

For many abused women, they might have enough inner strength to survive but not to speak up for themselves. For these women, advocacy is an important aspect of support. Dorothy's husband was determined that he would punish her for leaving him by keeping her young son from her. He had the financial ability to hire a lawyer and put every possible obstacle in her way. Multiple court appearances, disclosure statements, and mental health assessments had led her down a long and arduous path to reclaim a relationship with her son. She needed someone to be by her side as she faced this relentless battle.

Amber was placed on a wait list for a medical procedure that would help provide a long term solution to a major health issue. Her lengthy wait had far exceeded the normal time limit and she was both exhausted and becoming more physically unstable every day. She needed letters of support to gain the professional attention she required. Jessica had a handicapped child and found that her situation "fell through the cracks" because the government system would not fund her to be her child's primary caregiver. She needed someone to research how to challenge that system and advocate for an exemption for her situation. Tameika needed to learn how the banking system worked and how to make and live within a realistic budget. In each of these situations, advocacy was a key ingredient to help them move forward.

The final challenge of a second stage program is to support women to investigate and secure safe and affordable long-term housing in a community of their choice.

Support through building community

Our program also encourages community living and sharing with other women. We find that often women who have lived in an abusive relationship find it difficult to socialize and interact with others in healthy ways. Many women recognize that one of the effects of abuse is a sense of isolation and loneliness. It is important to build relationships within a safe community. Women can share experiences, feelings, and resources with other women who are or have been in similar situations, and deep trusting relationships develop. Living in community creates the ability to role model responsible decision making, co-operative problem solving, respect for individual differences, and healthy coping strategies—exploring what healthy relationships should look like.

Fun is a key ingredient in healing, the ability to reclaim life and joy. Our program offers regular social events such as monthly resident meetings, "Popcorn and a Movie" nights, a monthly Souper Supper, Thanksgiving and Christmas dinners, birthday parties, etc.

Through building community, we become their family and they become ours. They have a safe place to belong.

LESSONS LEARNED

The faith response to women and children within and without the faith community has unfortunately been, for the most part, minimal. Others have taken the lead in confronting this issue and responding to those impacted. We believe the church should be in the forefront of this work, emerging from the shadows to boldly claim peace and safety for our communities. We understand that providing this ministry calls for an intentional focus, a determination to overcome obstacles, and a coordinated effort to accomplish. The role of the church community should be an integral part of any community-based service to support families in crisis. We have learned some important lessons along the way and share them here.

Determine program foundation and values

Every human being represents the Imago Dei or "the Image of God."[6] Accordingly, each woman and child we have the privilege of serving is a worthy image bearer. In response, we chose to state as our mission *"to provide women and children in need the opportunity to gain strength and to live according to their true worth."* It is clear from Scripture that God hates violence and does not condone abuse in relationships; rather He calls for loving, responsible relationships within the family unit.[7] It is also clear that the heart of God is to protect the innocent, to be tender towards those who have been wounded, mistreated, neglected, and abandoned,[8] and to call his people to respond on His behalf and take action on the things that matter to Him.[9]

We found that having a mission statement, governing principles, and values have created the ability to establish a strong foundation for our program, foster personal growth, and provide a healthy and safe community environment. Corresponding values provide a solid framework for the relationships. Our program values grew out of a staff discussion on the things we felt would be of the highest 'universal' value to our program residents. We chose eight values to surround all of our interactions: respect, individual worth, healthy community, personal responsibility, honesty, safety and security, confidentiality, and celebration.

Develop clear program guidelines and support elements

It is important to have guidelines that provide specific ways to demonstrate the values. We want the women to know that we realize this is a very difficult time for them and we are here to help them through this next phase of their journey. Guidelines are designed to facilitate a safe and productive stay for everyone. Important considerations in-

---

6. Gen 1:27.
7. John 13:34, 35; Gal 5:22, 23; Eph 5.
8. Ps 10:14–18; 146:7–9.
9. Mic 6:8; Isa. 61:1

clude protecting information about the location of the program and the residents as well as aspects of living communally and sharing common space.

Have a solid case management system

There are times when a woman's situation can be so complex it is difficult to track. Between a variety of tasks and appointments, it can be very busy. We have found that a case management approach can help streamline all the supports needed by the woman, as well as integrating her individual plan into an overall program plan. We do this through regular check-ins. We also use a "Five Month" and a "Nine Month" review where both the woman and her one-to-one worker fill out a form and then meet together for discussion. The purpose is to help adjust and/or refocus the woman and ensure that she is meeting the goals that she wants to meet, as well as to see if those goals have changed or been achieved. Some women may choose to leave after six months while others feel they need to continue on for the full twelve months. The nine month review assists the woman in planning her next steps and preparing to move on to the next phase of her journey.

Celebrate and evaluate

The importance of celebrating milestones, whether big or small, cannot be underestimated. Any time there is the opportunity to reinforce belief in personal worth and ability, or experience of success, is a sacred moment. We look for these moments and use them to build women up and help them to see their potential and capacity to achieve.

It is really valuable to give women the opportunity to share their experiences with you. It could be through an evaluation form that inquires about different facets of the program you have designed. We like to hear how a woman feels differently about herself, the goals she has accomplished, and what she has learned. We have also received many helpful recommendations that have helped us to improve our program.

Rewards

Each woman we serve comes with a story of unimaginable mistreatment at the hands of the one they love. Some stories are much more violent than others, but all with the same devastating and debilitating impact—a life that is now broken, a soul that is shattered, a woman who feels no safety, a hopelessness that can't imagine an optimistic future. As we serve, we remind ourselves of the role that we believe God has asked us to fill: reflecting His character, being His "face," serving as a sacred and practical expression of our faith in God and our relationship with Jesus Christ, communicating the hope of the gospel. And then we have the profound privilege of watching God at work in the lives of these broken individuals. It is a great privilege to meet needs with the resources of Jesus Christ.

> Then the King will say to those on his right, "Come, you who are blessed by my Father; take your inheritance, the kingdom prepared for you since the creation of the world. For I was hungry and you gave me something to eat, I was thirsty and you gave me something to drink, I was a stranger and you invited me in, I needed clothes and you clothed me, I was sick and you looked after me, I was in prison and you came to visit me." Then the righteous will answer him, "Lord, when did we see you hungry and feed you, or thirsty and give you something to drink? When did we see you a stranger and invite you in, or needing clothes and clothe you? When did we see you sick or in prison and go to visit you?" The King will reply, "I tell you the truth, whatever you did for one of least of these, you did for me." Matt 25:34–40.

Graduation hour

Our most rewarding time is the 'Graduation Hour.' Every woman who successfully completes the second stage program is 'graduated' in a private ceremony with staff. During this hour we take time to discuss her plans and dreams, and then each staff who is present gives a verbal affirmation to the woman. This is always a very emotional time as we focus on how far she has come in her journey toward healing. We honor her with a journal that has been started by affirmations written to her by the various staff members. We let her know that the rest of the journal is for her to write her own story as she moves on from us, noting that *she will always be a part of our family.*

During her 'Graduation Hour,' Petra told us that the relationships she had developed with us during the program had renewed her hope and trust that people truly cared about her. She affirmed that she felt safe, loved, and special for the first time in her life. During her 'Graduation

Hour,' Sadie told us that this was 'the best day in her life so far.' What made it the best day for her was the knowledge that she would always be part of our family, that we believed in her and affirmed her capability to pursue a good life for herself, and that she indeed was a person who was of great worth and value to her Creator.

Hearing comments regularly such as, "This was the first time I have been loved—no one has ever loved me before," "This was the first time I felt like I belonged somewhere," "You have been a lifeline to me, I feel like you saved my life," "You took me in when I had no one and nowhere to go," "I have seen God in you," "Being here will stay with me for the rest of my life," tell us that we are doing sacred work.

Jolene wrote a note back to us several months after she completed the program, a note that reinforces our call to respond to broken women and children: *"It has been a while since my kids and I have left this wonderful place. Life, pain and violence were the reason that brought me to your door, to give the opportunity to meet wonderful human beings like you. You were my strength and support during many dark days. My only support. I thank God everyday for bringing good hearts like yours to my life. Every time I think about you, a feeling of love, care, and peace comes to my mind. Thank you so much for being part of my journey in life. Thank you for your time, support and love, giving us the support we badly needed during this difficult and scary time in our lives. You were the light along the dark and empty road I was on."*

CLOSING CHALLENGE

A passage that many women strongly identify with is in Psalm 55:

> Listen to my prayer, O God, do not ignore my plea; hear me and answer me. My thoughts trouble me and I am distraught at the voice of the enemy, at the stares of the wicked; for they bring down suffering upon me and revile me in their anger. My heart is in anguish within me; the terrors of death assail me. Fear and trembling have beset me; horror has overwhelmed me. I said, Oh, that I had the wings of a dove! I would fly away and be at rest—I would flee far away and stay in the desert. I would hurry to my place of shelter, far from the tempest and storm. Confuse the wicked, O Lord, confound their speech, for I see violence and strife in the city. Day and night they prowl about on its walls; malice and abuse are within it. Destructive forces are at work in the city; threats and lies never leave its streets. If

an enemy were insulting me, I would endure it; if a foe were raising himself against me, I could hide from him. But it is you, my companion, my close friend, with whom I once enjoyed sweet fellowship as we walked with the throng at the house of God.

What is our responsibility before God to women who, through no fault of their own, become the 'homeless,' the 'widows,' and the 'orphans' because of the scourge of domestic violence; women who are forced to flee their homes because of domestic violence; women who are left alone, homeless, friendless, and abandoned. Who will help? Where can these women go? Can we rise to the challenge? Has God called us to this ministry? Can we seize the opportunity of coming alongside these women to support them? These are the questions that faced our organization several years ago and our answer was YES! "let them come to us" (Mk 10:15), for we serve a God of grace and compassion. We have seen firsthand the devastating impact of abuse that permeates abusive relationships, bruises both visible on faces and reflected in eyes. We have also seen the awesome restorative work of God. We have definitely found second stage programming a treasure beyond compare—giving women a safe place to belong, next to the heart of God. "In righteousness you will be established. You will be far from tyranny and oppression; you will have nothing to fear and terror will be far removed; it will not come near you." Isa 54:1

9

Best Practices for Supporting Victims of Domestic Violence in Rural Communities

Julie A. Owens & Rhonda Encinas

DESPITE THE POPULAR NOTION of easy, peaceful country living, rural women are as much at risk for domestic violence as are their city-dwelling sisters. The common notion of abuse victims as poor, non-white women living in high-crime urban areas has long been dispelled as myth by numerous scholarly studies published over the past few decades. It is clear that women living rural lives—in small towns, on family farms or isolated back roads, in mountain hollows or desert areas, on small islands or on native lands, for example—suffer from the same abuses as those living in metropolitan areas. Many circumstances of rural living, in fact, may exacerbate the danger for these victims. Further, since isolated areas typically lack robust social service programs, those living in these areas may more frequently reach out for help to the church and its leaders. Pastors, staff, and lay ministers in rural churches therefore must understand the challenges these victims face and know how to respond effectively.

In this chapter we will discuss issues of specific concern regarding domestic abuse in rural families. We will not outline the basic "do's" and "don'ts" of supporting abuse victims, since that information is readily available elsewhere, including the two PASCH books previously published by Wipf & Stock.[1] We believe that the most essential needs of

---

1. *Beyond Abuse in the Christina Home: Raising Voices for Change*, C. Kroeger, N. Nason-Clark, B. Fisher-Townsend, House of Prisca & Aquila Series; *Responding to*

both rural and urban victims alike are the same—to be believed, treated with respect and complete confidentiality, assisted with safety planning and personal needs, and offered on-going empowerment-based support. Additionally, domestic violence offenders, regardless of locale, need to be held solely accountable for their abusive behavior (including non-physical forms of abuse), which may increase their opportunities for making positive changes.

About the authors

We are survivors of domestic violence who discovered we had experienced similar challenges while being abused by our husbands in the rural settings where we each resided. Julie married at thirty-two and lived with her new husband on an isolated Texas country road, eight miles from the nearest town. She had not lived in the area long and her family was many thousand miles away in Hawaii. With no other houses in sight, and no one to hear the constant barrage of verbal assaults and threats, her abuse was completely hidden. Although Julie worked full time in a local public school and had many friends, her husband acted quickly to isolate her after their marriage. He commandeered the family car for his use alone and insisted on driving her to and from work. His obsessive jealously, all night rages, and constant harassing accusations and threats left no physical marks but took a terrible toll on Julie, who had become pregnant just weeks after the wedding. After only three months of marriage, she slipped out of town one day after her husband went to work. Following a three month separation, the couple attempted carefully planned trial reconciliation in Julie's family home in a very small coastal town in Hawaii. After a brief period of calm, she was again subjected to escalating psychological abuse. She was threatened with violence but was not physically assaulted until after she filed for divorce almost a year later. To punish her for leaving him, her estranged husband broke into the house and attacked Julie and her father, a prominent pastor, with a knife. Years later, her ex-husband is still in prison. Over the years, Julie has developed numerous secular and faith-based programs for victims and now oversees domestic violence and sexual assault efforts in a very large, mostly rural area of the southern state where she now resides.

Abuse in Christian Homes: A Challenge to Churches and Their Leaders, N. Nason-Clark, C. Kroeger, B. Fisher-Townsend, House of Prisca & Aquila Series.

Rhonda married young and lived with her abusive husband in the same small Southern California desert community where she grew up. Her family was well known and she knew and was known by many of the community members. Her boyfriend was unfaithful and controlling before their marriage, but with no experience of abuse, she did not anticipate the escalation to physical violence. By the age of twenty-two, Rhonda was already a battered wife and the mother of two children, living at the edge of the desert in an isolated cluster of about twenty homes.

Despite her family's high profile in town and the fact that her parents were both active community leaders, no-one except her in-laws knew about the extreme physical and psychological abuse that Rhonda experienced on a regular basis. When at last she left her husband after twelve years of marriage, she moved nearby within the same small town. With her abuser in the area, numerous challenges and obstacles confronted her. Because of unrelenting harassment, Rhonda was eventually forced to flee into hiding with her young children. Years later her ex-husband was murdered. She remarried and now lives in a very remote mountain community in the Northwest where she operates the Christian domestic violence ministry she founded. Her all-volunteer ministry offers Christian-focused victim support groups, Bible studies, a women's jail ministry, individual and court advocacy and two free abuse shelters.

Why focus on rural victims?

Looking back on our own experiences and those of the hundreds of victims we have since supported, the impact of rural living is undeniable. Despite the differences in our circumstances, we faced many of the same barriers while being abused. Among the insights and issues we will address are rural mores, geographical isolation, limited transportation, anonymity/confidentiality, availability of weapons, use of alcohol/drugs, justice system/legal challenges, safety challenges, scarce community resources, limited employment and housing options, a lack of trained domestic violence helpers, stalking, and suggestions for addressing challenges. Each of these issues made our paths out of the violence more difficult and treacherous. We will also offer suggestions for addressing these challenges.

How big is the problem?

It is estimated that twenty percent of Americans and Canadians live in non-metro areas, scattered across vast land areas.[2] Existing research suggests that while in general, individuals living in remote areas are much less likely to witness violent crime; women in rural areas are just as likely as those in cities and suburban locals to report being a victim of intimate violence.[3] Unfortunately, data-based studies focusing on rural populations are limited, and studies of rural domestic violence are particularly scarce.

Generally, official statistics do not count any crime as having occurred unless someone reports it to law enforcement and a report is filed by an officer. While violence against women is notoriously underreported, it is estimated that in the United States approximately one out of every three women is physically or sexually abused at some point in their lives.[4] We therefore operate from the assumption that approximately one third of rural women have been or will be abused, and this is a very large number of women indeed. In a recent survey of rural Ohio women, however, a shocking 81 percent of respondents stated that they personally knew local women who had been sexually assaulted.[5] No doubt most of these crimes were never reported, as is typically the case with sex crimes. To think that one of every three women sitting in the pews of any given church is abused can be overwhelming. These numbers are staggering and can seem exaggerated and inflated to the uninitiated. It is safe to say that society at large is woefully uninformed about the ubiquity of domestic violence, and that therefore victims are rarely identified, even when they are right in the room with us, or we see them on a regular basis, especially if they do not fit any stereotypes we may hold.

Some rural victim populations are even more invisible and isolated and less likely to report an assault to authorities. We have observed in our work that the already significant problems of battering victims are almost certainly exacerbated if they are members of a chronically underserved rural minority group.

2. United Nations Secretariat, *World Urbanization Prospects: The 2003 Revision.*
3. Websdale, N. *Rural Woman Battering.*
4. *Commonwealth Fund Survey*, 1998
5. DeKeseredy and Schwartz. *Dangerous Exits.*

There has been little racial or religious diversity in most rural areas of North American; the majority population has been primarily white and Christian. The exception would be areas where native peoples live in community, historically Indian reservations, and Alaskan and Hawaiian native lands. However, this has begun to change in the past few decades. Racial minorities such as Hispanics and Asians are now moving to rural communities where they have heretofore been absent or underrepresented. Some minority victims in remote communities may be immigrants who do not even speak English or understand their legal rights. In recent years, too, gay and lesbian individuals have become more comfortable leaving cities in favor of small towns and slower-paced rural living. They may find themselves more socially isolated than heterosexual peers and less apt to be fully embraced in small traditional rural towns and faith congregations that tend towards conservatism. Victims in any of these minority groups, and others not mentioned specifically, such as the hearing impaired and frail elderly, may thus be further isolated from sources of support for a variety of reasons.[6] Therefore, it is incumbent on the faith community to make special efforts to provide outreach and support, offering culturally relevant services in order to identify the abused adults and children in their midst. The best way of doing this in our experience is to identify and partner with the official and unofficial leaders in each community and provide them with training about violence against women and the resources available to them. Numerous web-based free resources exist that provide multi-lingual printed literature and the previously mentioned National Domestic Violence Hotline provides free translation in over 150 languages for callers.[7]

Rural mores

Individuals living in most rural and remote communities pride themselves on being self-sufficient, although family ties and bonds of loyalty tend to be strong. Traditional values and gender roles are the norm, with women frequently attached to the home in unique ways. Men

---

6. Pennsylvania Coalition against Domestic Violence. *Helping Rural Battered Women*.

7. Hot Peach Pages is a global list of abuse hotlines, shelters, refuges, crisis centers and women's organizations, as well as domestic violence information in over 80 languages. http://www.hotpeachpages.net.

are expected to be tough and resourceful. When young males misbehave, the old explanation still typically offered is: "Boys will be boys." A variety of studies in recent years have demonstrated a pronounced rural tendency towards male dominance. In the 2009 book *Dangerous Exits: Escaping Abusive Relationships in Rural America*, the researchers reported that, "Male dominance and supremacy are displayed through symbolic leisure activities as well as more severe manifestations of controls (sometimes violent). Interpersonal violence for these men may be a form of proving to themselves and others their essential masculinity and heterosexuality, as they define it."[8] Recognizing the relationship of such mores to violence against women, organizations like A Call to Men, founded by Tony Porter and Ted Bunch, concerned Christians, challenge men through seminars and other means to reconsider their long-held beliefs about women and to "break out of the Man Box"[9] in an effort to create a more just society. They achieve this by encouraging change in the behaviors of men through a re-education and training process that promotes healthy manhood.[10]

Rural families are often large, and in many cases, live together in extended family units on shared land. Survival of the individual may be dependent on survival of the larger family unit, particularly in the case of family farms and small family-run businesses. A strong connection to the land is often integral to rural individuals' sense of self. Poverty is a factor for many and it is common for families to work together to grow their own food or hunt for game. In such areas, non-traditional families are rare and single mother-led households are an exception to the norm. When families break apart (even when violence is not the cause) it is often necessary for single women to leave their home communities and the land to which they are so connected in order to find work and a community where they will fit in socially.

Perhaps even more so than in urban areas, where education about domestic violence is more readily available, intimate partner abuse in remote areas is often considered the result of bad choices made by victims rather than bad choices made by abusers. Information about

---

8. DeKeseredy and Schwartz. *Dangerous Exits*.

9. See fn 10.

10. Porter, A. *Breaking Out of the Man Box*. http://www.acalltomen.com/page.php?id=54 ; A Call to Men TED talk, http://www.ted.com/talks/tony_porter_a_call_to_men.html.

the causes of domestic violence is scarce, and old myths and misconceptions die hard. Common stressors such as unemployment may be blamed for family violence, alcohol is frequently cited as the cause as well. Victim-blaming attitudes abound and it is not unusual to hear statements that focus on victims' behavior:

> She should not talk back to him—she knows what pushes his buttons. She just doesn't know her place." "She's not a very good wife. She needs to do better job of taking care of her responsibilities so he doesn't have to discipline her so much." "He's a really good man. She must have pushed him over the edge. His people have short fuses and she should have known better.

Families in rural areas are expected to keep their personal business to themselves and to not "air their dirty laundry" or discuss family matters with others. Author Deborah Fink has noted that historically, "A woman would not ask anyone for help, because the prevailing attitude held that she had made her bed and must lie in it. People didn't talk much about marital problems, because such things were private."[11] Such attitudes remain common today amongst country folks. Even in emergency situations, some may be very hesitant to ask for help because they are used to handling things themselves. Medical and mental health crises may be dealt with at home, for reasons that are practical, traditional, financial, or personal. Involving professionals may only be possible by traveling to urban areas, and those who do so may be considered by some to be "weak."

Geographic isolation

Nearly all individuals who are battered by their partners are isolated in various ways. Isolation is an extremely common method of control used by abusers to systematically sever the victim's ties with family, friends, supportive church members, and anyone else who may believe and support them. The enormous power and control exerted by an abuser is greatly threatened by these potential external resources.

Like other rural victims, our isolation was intensified due to the remote areas where we lived. There were no neighbors to hear Julie's husband when he flew into screaming rages and berated her for hours on end. He routinely ripped the phone from the wall and threw it across

---

11. Fink, D. *Agrarian Women*.

the room or hid it from her. Rhonda's husband at times removed the receiver and took it with him when he left the house. When he traveled, he insisted that she stay in contact with him via CB radio, a common form of communication in rural areas, especially before the advent of wireless phones. When he was traveling and out of CB range, he made sure that his buddies checked up on her regularly with their own CBs. Julie's husband insisted that she carry a pager so he could contact her at all times. Today, wireless phones can be a lifeline for domestic violence victims who can maintain possession of them. Some areas, however, are so remote that cell phone coverage is not reliable or available at all. Victims who do use wireless phones must be warned that abusers often track or stalk victims by secretly activating the optional global positioning system (GPS) feature.[12]

We have both known victims whose abusive partners have relocated their families to remote communities, purposely isolating them from the support of their friends and family and making it easier to control their movements. Battered women may literally be held hostage in their own homes for days and no one will know. We have worked with those who have been handcuffed to beds, locked in closets, chained in tool sheds, or confined in isolated mobile homes. More frequently, however, batterers isolate their victims in unique ways that are not against the law.

Weather and transportation challenges

Poor roads, extreme weather, lack of transportation, and the difficulty helpers face when attempting to locate remote homes (with perhaps no street address) are additional factors that compound the challenges for rural victims. Abusers frequently use the rugged terrain or inclement weather to their advantage. We can recall numerous victims who were deprived of clothing or shoes, especially in winter, to prevent them from leaving home. Others have been punished by being locked out of their homes, especially at night and in the winter. Such an experience is not only terrifying for the adult victims but it is also torture for children who fear their mother will die. In Rhonda's area, winter lasts nearly six months and the danger of hypothermia and frostbite in these instances, not to mention hungry bears and cougars, is very real. Such

---

12. See the Safety Net Project for more information on cyber stalking and other technology-related safety concerns http://nnedv.org/resources/safetynetdocs.html.

abuse, however, does not usually meet the legal criteria necessary for arrest to occur or a protective order to be issued.

Extreme weather conditions can also create transportation difficulties for rural victims. Snow, swollen streams, and deep mud on unpaved roads regularly affect life in rural areas and may also extend victims' periods of isolation with their abusers. In Rhonda's community, a four wheel drive (4WD) vehicle is an absolute necessity. No other vehicle can navigate the deep snow and unplowed roads that must be routinely navigated. Abusers frequently deny their victims access to the 4WD vehicle, effectively isolating them for weeks or even months at a time.

Even in temperate weather conditions, transportation may be a major barrier. Many batterers prevent their partners from obtaining a driver's license. Though we each had licenses, neither of us had independent sources of transportation after we married. No taxis or buses existed in our counties, as is usually the case in remote areas. On many occasions, our husbands hid the car keys from us. On one occasion, Julie's husband took the spark plugs out of their car when she threatened to flee. When either of us was allowed to use a car, the mileage was monitored. Once, Julie was forced her out of the car onto a long lonely country road, although she was pregnant and had worked all day. There was no sidewalk or shoulder, making the long walk home quite dangerous. With no phone or neighbors nearby, she was trapped even more than a woman in an urban or metropolitan area might be.

It should be noted that even when a victim of abuse does have her own vehicle, an abuser will often sabotage it or manipulate circumstances to deprive her of that vital link to the outside world. Numerous victims, including Julie, have had their car windshields smashed, rendering their vehicles illegal to drive and/or uninsurable. Tires are frequently slashed. Sometimes brake lines are even severed. Abusers may refuse to assist with the victim's car payments, purposely causing the vehicle to be repossessed. Insurance payment may be withheld or policies cancelled. Many abusers go to great lengths to ensure that their victims will be housebound, and we are frequently amazed by the clever control tactics they employ.

Some extremely rural communities, such as Alaskan fishing villages or remote islands, are accessible only by small planes and only when weather permits. Victims living in these uniquely isolated areas have sometimes waited days to be evacuated after physical or sexual assaults. As time passes and victims remain weathered-in, bruises can heal and DNA evidence (especially after a sexual assault) can become lost or degraded. Abusers may coerce or threaten victims into changing their minds about reporting the abuse or leaving the premises. Victims may re-think a prior decision to report the abuse or to leave their abuser, especially if they are threatened.

Regardless of the weather, victims in remote locales face the very real likelihood of delayed police and medical response when they call for help. Small law enforcement and emergency service agencies have limited staff that must cover a wide geographic area. In Rhonda's community, two police officers cover an area of nearly eight hundred square miles during the day. At night, only one officer is on duty. Not only is this a concern when an assault is actually taking place, victims with civil protection or no-contact orders may not be able to receive immediate help when abusers violate those orders. Typically, by the time an officer arrives, abusers have fled and no arrest is made. Discouraged victims may determine that taking out a protective order will only ensure their abuser's rage and endanger them further.

Churches and ministries that serve rural communities should be prepared to assist with the transportation needs of victims. Volunteer drivers, free car repairs, needed parts such as a new tire, a gas gift card, a bus ticket out of town, or even a donated used car have all made major differences in the life of domestic violence victims. Many victims have told us that without the practical help ministries and churches have provided, needs that other agencies typically do not provide, they would likely have been forced to return to their abusive partners. Collecting emergency funds for such needs is a wonderful way to support victims and survivors. By partnering with local social service agencies that can screen and refer victims in need, faith organizations can serve as a lifeline to rural abuse victims and their children.

Confidentiality Issues

Confidentiality and anonymity are critical to the safety of domestic violence victims. Abusers who are tipped off that their victims have "let the cat out of the bag" may retaliate and punish them harshly for disclosing the family secret. It is very important for helpers to understand that while a call to law enforcement is certainly appropriate if an assault is in process, confronting an abuser or reporting his prior domestic abuse to authorities may further endanger a victim. Abusers may be questioned by authorities, only to beat the victim later for 'getting him into trouble.' Even when an arrest is made, abusers are typically bailed out or released quickly, returning to punish their victim. Faith leaders in rural areas need to be familiar with the domestic violence laws in their particular state, as they differ widely. In rare cases, mandatory reporting of domestic violence may be required, although this is rare unless a victim is disabled or elderly.[13]

In rural areas, potential responders are likely to be acquainted with (or even related to) the victim, the abuser, or their families. This intrinsic barrier to victim anonymity and confidentiality can make it more difficult for victims to reach out for help. In small towns, it can seem as if everyone knows everyone else. In Rhonda's case, this was nearly true, as we have stated. Her father was a volunteer firefighter and on the local volunteer rescue squad as well. The other members of the squad were all family friends. Rhonda's husband was armed and routinely threatened to shoot anyone who responded if she called for help. Since she was unwilling to put her father and friends in danger, she never reached out.

When law enforcement does become involved, peace officers, magistrates, and judges who know the batterer socially may be less likely to recognize the severity of an assault. Any of these individuals could be his neighbor, fellow church member, former classmate, coworker, a hunting buddy, lodge fellow, or even his relative. Additionally, rural families frequently own and routinely monitor a police scanner and calls to law enforcement are overheard. An abuser's family member or friend may even appear at the scene before the police arrive, warning him to leave to avoid arrest. If the person involved has never seen the abuser become violent outside the home (which is likely) he may not believe the victim is telling the truth. Those who do know about the abuse may purposely minimize it or even cover it up.

Some rural communities are fortunate enough to have a domestic violence shelter. In these places it is almost impossible to keep the shelter location confidential. This adds yet another layer of difficulty for victims. Abusers may appear at the door, making demands or behaving in a threatening manner. In Julie's state, a woman was tragically mur-

---

13. State domestic violence and related statutes may be found at the Women's law website http://www.womenslaw.org/statutes_states.php.

dered by her stalker husband while in a rural abuse shelter. In another rural shelter, the staff was taken hostage. While these situations are extremely rare, they are not unheard of, and they demonstrate the length that some batterers will go to in order to punish their victim for leaving them. They also clearly illustrate the need for rural shelters.

Sometimes other individuals may appear at a shelter on the abuser's behalf. We have heard of cases in which pastors appeared uninvited, attempting to coerce a victim into returning home and "submitting to her husband's authority" or "keeping the peace." Julie recalls a time when a police officer showed up at a shelter in an effort to obtain information about his buddy's wife who was hiding there. Another time a batterer pounded on the door of a Christian safe house Julie managed shouting and insisting that his wife come out and agree to drop the protective order she had been granted that morning.

Seeking treatment for abuse-related injuries will present an additional confidentiality challenge to a victim. Clinics and other free medical services are rarely found in rural communities and the same few doctors tend to treat everyone. Health care providers have a unique opportunity to identify and assist victims, however, if they know the perpetrator well, they could be tempted to question or downplay the seriousness of the abuse.

As a general rule, domestic violence best practices dictate that only the individual(s) working directly with a victim should have access to records about the abuse. Domestic violence offenders are notorious for finding ways to acquire written records and use them against their victims, particularly in court. Advocates are trained to make any notes brief and factual, and keep all documents under lock and key. Computer records are password protected. This is a critical component of protecting victim confidentiality. Unfortunately, it is one which is often not considered by those not formally trained in victim advocacy or bound by a professional code of ethics.

If your church offers services or support to victims of abuse, it is imperative that protocols for enhancing their confidentially be established and maintained. This includes how records are kept and who has access to them, but also other confidentially-enhancing procedures as well. For example, it is helpful to provide a safe place for victims to park if they need to drive to your facility. Abusers often cruise around town looking for their partner or former partner's vehicle. Additionally, well-meaning acquaintances may mention seeing her vehicle to her partner, not knowing that her visit was a private matter and that such a seemingly harmless statement may cause her to be interrogated or abused.

The increased availability of weapons

While batterers can and do inflict immense damage with their hands alone via beatings, strangulation, etc., when abuse results in death a weapon is usually involved. Weapons such as firearms and knives tend to be readily available in rural areas where wild animals may live and hunting is a way of life. Axes and pitchforks are also commonplace and often used as weapons.[14]

Any weapon can be deadly, however, scholarly research indicates that access to firearms alone yields a more than five-fold increase in risk of intimate partner homicide, suggesting that abusers who possess guns tend to inflict the most severe abuse on their partners.[15] In remote areas, firearms are often kept in the home and also carried in vehicles, making them easily and readily accessible to an abuser. A study in a rural Iowa county, for example, found that 85.8 of people living in farm households reported having firearms and that 61.1 percent of people living in rural towns owned them. Twice as many farm households as town households claimed to have a loaded, unlocked gun on the premises.[16] This is significant, since people who have guns in their home are also twice as likely to be killed by guns as are those who do not have guns in their home.[17]

Rhonda estimates that most families in the rural area where she resides own approximately fifteen different firearms, all with different uses or for hunting various types of game. Deer, rabbit, and bird hunting are a way of life and provide sustenance for many rural families who would otherwise not be able to afford to put meat on the table. Individuals frequently hunt along roadsides or from their trucks, which are equipped with gun racks to accommodate rifles and shotguns. Hunting is not only a necessity to many; shooting is also taught for

14. Men's Violence Against Rural Women, Crisis Connection, http://www.crisis-connectioninc.org/domesticviolence/rural_battered_women.htm.

15. Campbell, J.C. et al. "Risk Factors for Femicide." http://www.ajph.org/cgi/content/abstract/93/7/1089).

16. Nordstrom, D. L. et al. "Rural Population Survey," 112–116.

17. Nagourney, E. "Linking Guns and Gun Violence."

defense against dangerous animals and target shooting is a popular hobby. Children are trained at a young age to handle firearms in a safe and respectful manner. Rhonda's children are typical and her sons and daughters alike grew up as experienced hunters. Though she recalls domestic violence victims she has worked with being threatened with firearms on occasion, given the ubiquity of guns in her very rural locale, this has occurred with relative infrequency.

Whether they live in urban or rural areas, firearms—particularly handguns and semi-automatic weapons—are not uncommonly wielded by abusers who attempt to intimidate their victims. Julie has worked with the former partners of both military service members and law enforcement officers who frequently used their service weapons to threaten or terrify them. Other women have reported to her that their batterers played Russian roulette with them, raped them with gun barrels, waved or slowly cleaned their guns in front of them in an intimidating manner, or fired the gun right next to them, simply to instill fear. Many stories of pets harmed by firearms have also been shared in her support groups and Julie's ex-father-in-law, who terribly battered his wife and young children, once forced them to watch him shoot and kill the children's pet dog. Such trauma is likely to leave a lasting impact and may result in symptoms of traumatic stress.

We have also had our own terrifying experiences with weapons. Rhonda recalls that her husband always kept a loaded .44 sitting on a counter in their home. He wanted to be sure she saw it and knew he always had access to it. The message it conveyed was clear: "Don't even think about crossing me or leaving me." The night before Julie left her husband and fled to her parents' home, she told him that she was considering a trial separation. He later awoke her during the night, threatening to kill himself, a loaded handgun to his heart.

As mentioned previously, later assaults on Julie and her father also involved knives. Cutting instruments and knives in particular, are very often involved in domestic violence situations. They are found in every household and are easily used to threaten, cut, tear, or stab objects and victims alike. The clothing or belongings of victims are frequently destroyed with knives or scissors. Julie's husband shredded the beautiful lace pillows she collected as he waited to ambush her the night she was attacked.

Survivor Michelle Johnson Major, who lives in the foothills of N.C., is a committed Christian and professional artist. Her abusive husband slashed ninety four of her paintings, destroying twelve years of her work, before strangling and leaving her for dead.[18] In the past several years, Julie has been contacted by two rural survivors whose abusers actually carved words onto their bodies with knives. One was the word "MINE." The other was the name of the abuser. Another nearby rural victim was tortured in an especially heinous way, her feet nailed to the floor with a nail gun, then repeatedly cut with a knife. Such assaults seem like unthinkable scenes from horror films, yet we know the very women who have survived these assaults. In each case, these were premeditated assaults intended to torture, control, or punish.

It is no wonder that knives are often also the tool used when victims defend themselves. They are readily available in most homes and may be the only way a victim can "level the playing field" during an assault. We know many victims who have told us that they sleep with knives under their pillows for protection. Knives are perhaps the weapons most often employed by victims during an assault, and many are arrested every year for cutting an abuser who was attacking them. Julie has worked with several survivors of extreme abuse who accidentally killed their abuser after grabbing a knife during a savage beating or rape in their kitchen. Sadly, some of these survivors were sentenced to life in prison despite evidence of years of escalating abuse.

Alcohol and drug use substance abuse does not cause domestic violence, there is a

Among state offices of rural health, substance abuse has been identified as a major rural health concern.[19] While most domestic violence offenders are not alcoholics or drug addicts and there is no causal link between domestic violence and substance abuse, research does frequently indicate high rates of alcohol or drug use by perpetrators during a violent episode. Regular alcohol abuse, in fact, is one of the leading risk factors for intimate partner violence and battering incidents coupled with alcohol abuse may be more severe and result in greater injury. Moreover, women who have been abused are estimated to be fifteen times more likely to abuse alcohol and nine times more likely to abuse

---

18. Major, M. J. Be A Voice Arts http://www.beavoicearts.com/.
19. National Rural Health Research Center Directors Meeting, 2001.

drugs than women who have not been abused.[20] It is not uncommon for victims to report to us that they have themselves used drugs or alcohol to cope, to induce sleep or forgetting, to "numb out," to medicate physical pain, to please their partner, or even to attempt suicide. We have also heard many stories also from victims who were regularly forced to use mind-altering substances by a batterer who controlled them further by manipulating their access to the substance they came to crave.

Methamphetamine (meth or "ice") is an addictive stimulant drug that strongly activates the central nervous system and has become a common problem in rural areas in recent decades. Data from the U.S. Drug Enforcement Administration indicates that of the 11,239 seizures of methamphetamine labs that occurred in 2010, many were in rural areas. Long-term methamphetamine abuse has many negative health consequences, including extreme weight loss, anxiety, confusion, insomnia, mood disturbances, and violent behavior. Chronic users can display psychotic features, including paranoia and hallucinations.[21] We have both supported victims whose abusers used meth and these survivors were some of the most violently abused women we have served. Julie recalls one victim who came to her church's abuse shelter from a rural area after both her knees had been smashed repeatedly with very a heavy steel vacuum cleaner tube. Sometimes the victims themselves have become addicted and have joined their abusers in illegal activities to support their habits.

Since meth is inexpensive and simple to make, it is especially a problem in chronically poor rural areas and regions with high unemployment. Remote areas contain many abandoned buildings, farm houses and barns, and those located on abandoned or rarely used roads are ideal locations for establishment of a meth lab. The ingredients used to make meth can be purchased at local stores, and one of the key items is a chemical commonly used as fertilizer. Since the drug can be cooked in kitchens, garages, and mobile homes, these rural meth labs are difficult to detect.[22]

Alcohol is popular most everywhere, of course, but the states with the highest rates of youth alcohol abuse tend to be the most rural. It is

20. Domestic Violence and Substance Abuse, http://www.ncadv.org/files/SubstanceAbuse.pdf.
21. U.S. Drug Enforcement Administration
22. http://www.raconline.org/topics/meth/.

difficult to determine consumption rates, but there are studies which have indicated that men and women in metropolitan areas are less likely to report consuming five or more drinks in one day than are their rural counterparts[23]. The co-occurrence of violence and substance use adds another layer of complexity for those wishing to help a family in crisis. Abusers who are drunk when they have been assaultive will frequently minimize their responsibility and blame the alcohol, although they may get just as drunk or high with their friends and not beat them up. Battered wives who believe their partners' violence is not a choice he makes but rather a symptom of a disease he has may feel obligated to stay with him because they married "in sickness and in health." Victims who are addicted or who are intoxicated themselves when abuse occurs may blame themselves and perceive they are equally at fault.

Since the issues of domestic violence and substance abuse can interact with and exacerbate each other, best practices suggest that they should be addressed simultaneously. Unfortunately, helpers frequently assume that the violence is a result of a drug or alcohol problem and so it is not addressed separately. A batterer who sobers up will almost always still be a batterer, since giving up these substances will not eliminate his deep-seated belief that he has the right (or perhaps responsibility) to 'keep his woman in line.' When a skilled rural helper does provide assessments for both issues, it will likely be difficult to locate substance abuse treatment for either one or both partners, domestic violence intervention classes for the abuser, and a domestic violence support group for the victim. If the individuals decide to pursue support, they may be forced to travel great distances and wait months for an opening in any of the programs.[24]

Lack of domestic programs, safe shelters, and trained helpers

Even when the abuse is severe and help is nearby, many who suffer will never identify themselves as "domestic violence victims" and therefore will not seek appropriate support services. Rhonda was so convinced that she was a terrible wife that she never talked to anyone about what was happening at home. She was embarrassed and humiliated. Julie disclosed what was happening at home, although she did

23. Eberhardt et al. *Urban and Rural Health Chartbook*.
24. Methamphetamine, Rural Assistance Center, http://www.raconline.org/topics/meth/.

not name it as domestic violence. The problem was addressed strictly as a substance abuse issue despite the fact that her husband had been sober for some time.

Both urban and rural victims, however, will often see doctors for depression or anxiety and/or pastors for counseling. These may be among the very few persons, in fact, that controlling abusers will allow them to see. Sadly, doctors often fail to assess or identify the problem and pastors frequently give the worst advice. Women tell us often that pastors have advised them to pray harder and submit to their husband's authority. Julie was given this advice by several ministers from whom she sought counsel while married to her abuser.

Rhonda has found that that nearly every woman who comes to her rural ministry has been told by a pastor that "divorce is the unforgivable sin" and that she may not leave her husband unless he is unfaithful. One support group member who has been extremely abused by a meth-addicted husband was recently told that she would "have more jewels in her crown" if she stayed in her marriage and submitted to him. She was advised to maintain a loving demeanor regardless of her husband's actions. Such advice has caused many abuse victims to remain with their batterers and no small numbers of them have been killed as a result. Still others have been forced to choose between their faith community and their personal safety, a tragic dilemma.

Victims who reach out to existing domestic violence programs will likely be forced to seek support from an agency that is far removed, sometimes literally hundreds of miles away. Limited social services in rural parts of the country greatly diminish the likelihood that they will have access to trained domestic violence victim advocates, peer support groups, safe shelter, and free legal advocacy. For rural women, any call they make may necessarily be a long distance one. This may be expensive and dangerous since the number will appear on the phone bill for their batterer to see.

Although victims may stay with an abuser for many reasons, most fear leaving due to routine threats that have been made. If previous threats have come to fruition and the ultimate one is "If you leave me, I will kill you" (or the children, or your parents, etc.), victims can become paralyzed by fear. They may be understandably terrified that if they seek help, especially from someone who might confront the abuser without her knowledge, the danger to her and her children will escalate. In rural areas especially, they will struggle to find affordable, safe housing, jobs that provide a living wage, and pro bono legal services that will allow them to leave abusive relationships. Accessing these services, if they are available at all, will likely mean that rural survivors must leave their community. Many have never lived anywhere else and leaving the security of their family and all they have ever known can cause tremendous grief and anxiety.

Stalking

Domestic violence-related stalking is a problem in all geographic areas. Most people believe that a victim of domestic violence will be safe once she separates from her abuser. Unfortunately, leaving does not usually put an end to the violence. Often, in fact, this is the most dangerous time in a relationship. An abuser may escalate his violence in an attempt to force the victim to reconcile with him. He may be furious that she has dared to defy him or may react violently to perceived rejection or abandonment. Post-separation violence can take many forms, including physically or sexually assaulting the victim, harassing her, retaliating by taking legal actions, refusing child support, making threats of homicide or suicide, or hurting or taking away the children. Stalking is a common thread that runs through many cases of post-separation violence and most stalkers are batterers.

Obsessive behavior and stalking heightens the level of dangerousness. Research has established that it is highly correlated with domestic violence homicide (also known as femicide when the victim is female). In a study done between 1994 and 1998, researchers found that in ten U.S. cities, 89 percent of femicide victims who had been physically abused had also been stalked in the 12 months before the murder.[25]

Since victims are so often tracked and hunted down, it is incumbent upon helpers to take this into consideration and assist with careful individualized safety planning. In rural and remote areas, victims typically have a much harder time hiding. There may be only one grocery store, one elementary school, one pediatrician, etc. The likelihood of a victim running into her abuser is very high even if she is not being stalked, and he is not actively looking for her.

25. "Stalking Fact Sheet."

It will be quite difficult for rural victims who are being stalked to keep their location a secret. Even shelter locations will be known to most citizens. In a small community it is virtually impossible to hide a victim and her children indefinitely. This is why victim support programs work closely with others across the state and even across the country to move victims when necessary. Abusers who stalk will likely stake out her work place, the children's school, her parent's house, even her church, and any other place he thinks she may be likely to go. Once a victim is located, it is a simple matter to follow her home. Domestic violence stalkers have even been known to make phone calls to the offices of their victims' doctors, pastors, etc. and tell an unknowing receptionist they are supposed to meet their partner at an upcoming appointment, thereby learning the date and time she will be there. There is no end to the lengths some abusers will go to locate their estranged partner.

Of course most victims will continue to live with their abuser, at least for a time, and even then they may be stalked. Victims often seek support in secret. Those who wish to attend support groups or counseling sessions will have a difficult time keeping their attendance confidential. They may try to convince their partner that they are attending a Bible study, a women's circle, a crafting or life skills class, or mother's support group so he does not prevent them from going. (Often, battered women's support groups are purposely advertised this way for safety reasons.)

Individuals who provide the support groups or counseling sessions may have a difficult time remaining anonymous and therefore should plan accordingly. Advocates that accompany victims to court or assist them with transportation may also be identified by the abuser. Although helpers not often themselves attacked by abusers, for this reason, it is a good idea to have their own workplace safety plans. Some may wish to install an alarm or panic button in their office, especially if they work alone.[26] A crisis response protocol for responding appropriately if an abuser breeches the premises, with a pre-determined alterative exit, is wise.

---

26. See http://peaceatwork.org/ for more information.

Suggestions for addressing challenges

Faith communities that can assist with locating, providing, or funding any advocacy services will be providing a tremendous service. Julie's church for example, opened a transitional safe house and ministry for domestic violence victims. Hospitality House served many families in need and was the only free transitional domestic violence shelter in the state of Hawaii. It was featured in the award winning documentary "Broken Vows: Religious Perspectives on Domestic Violence" as an example of churches can be a part of the solution.[27]

For faith-based rural organizations that want to become a resource for domestic victims, it is recommended that a committee be formed that includes survivors as well as key leadership, and potential helpers. Comprehensive training for the members of this committee, and especially for any individuals who will provide direct support services to victims or abusers, is imperative. Fortunately, numerous resources now exist for excellent free on-line training.[28] Connecting with any local secular domestic violence service providers and your statewide domestic violence and sexual assault coalitions are also strongly recommended. Alliances and partnerships with these resources will prove invaluable when professional assistance, safety planning, legal advocacy, and referrals are needed. For a list of the victim service agencies and coalitions in your area, as well as Christian domestic violence ministries and other important resources, the RAVE (Religion And Violence E-learning) project website is invaluable.[29]

Since violence against women is a community problem, it requires a community response. We have discovered that churches or ministries seeking to get involved should, after educating themselves, seek to educate and enlist local service agencies and organizations as ministry partners. Rotary or Lions Clubs, VFW Auxiliaries, women's church circles, etc. may be good collaborators in these efforts. Rhonda

---

27. *Broken Vows*, www.faithtrustinstitute.org/store.

28. National Resource Center on Violence Against Women http://new.vawnet.org/category/index_pages.php?category_id=867 ; Office for Victims of Crime, Victim Assistance Training Online, https://www.ovcttac.gov/views/TrainingMaterials/dspOnline_VATOnline.cfm; The Rape, Abuse & Incest National Network http://www.rainntrain.org/course/category.php?id=8; The RAVE Project (Religion And Violence E-Learning) www.theraveproject.com.

29. The RAVE Project (Religion And Violence E-Learning) www.theraveproject.com.

has found success enlisting the help of volunteers for her own women's ministry by giving talks at monthly meetings of civic groups. She has found that when she shares real stories of (anonymous) local victims, community member make a 'heart connection' and may be moved to volunteer their assistance. For example, she has found it very helpful to let community groups know if her outreach ministry needs a specific item, such as a van to use for transporting families to shelter or to the county seat for court appearances.

Many churches now offer free space for victim support groups to meet and others have even begun providing the groups themselves as a form of local missions. This can be an immensely valuable and low-cost community service, especially in an area that has no shelter or domestic violence advocacy agency. With the support of her tiny faith community and many dedicated volunteers, Rhonda has offered such groups and Bible studies for years. As a result, hundreds of victims and their children have been given a new lease on life. Rhonda's support group curriculum is one of several specifically developed for domestic violence victims by a Christian survivor.[30]

Offering free childcare for domestic violence victims who are looking for jobs, going to school, or appearing in court is a wonderful to reach out and assist them. Rhonda has had success by recruiting locally homeschooled teen girls to watch victims' children, including during the mothers' support group sessions. When this is done as a girl's school service project, the student learns about domestic and dating violence, which is an added bonus. Local Girl Scouts are another service organization that may be a resource in rural communities.

Many churches already provide food pantries, which can be an important source of food for victims and their children. It is not unusual for an abuser to use food deprivation as a form of control or punishment. We have known victims who developed eating disorders as a result of such abuse. Also, when victims leave their abusers and have limited income, food pantries may be a lifeline. Victims who qualify for food assistance from government social service programs are fortunate. But often victims do not qualify and such assistance rarely provides all of the foods needed to feed a family in a given month. Non-food household supplies, which are unallowable for purchase with govern-

---

30. Bonds, L. and R. Encinas. *Healing Hearts*; K. McAndless-Davis and J. Cory. *When Love Hurts*.

ment-issued food assistance cards can be collected and distributed to victims as well. Items that are necessary but often unaffordable may include toilet paper, disposable diapers, female hygiene items, household cleaning supplies, toiletries, over-the-counter medications, school supplies, and clothing. Including a list of needed items in the church bulletin or local newspaper on a regular basis is a great way to generate donations. It also serves as a reminder both to community members and victims that help is available. Addressing these practical day-to-day needs of victims and survivors means acknowledging that in addition to the violence, they also suffer from secondary effects such as poverty, homelessness, lack of transportation, inadequate nutrition, healthcare (including mental health issues), and support.

CONCLUSION

While we have attempted to be as thorough as possible in this chapter, we have no doubt failed to cover some of the challenges facing rural victims of domestic violence. Given the complexity of the problem, it is simply impossible to enumerate the potential issues in an exhaustive manner. Every victim and every abuser is unique. Likewise, the ways in which a particular church or ministry may choose to respond to the advocacy needs of victims will vary according to the culture and resources in a community. Nevertheless, we believe that with thoughtful prayer and a true desire to "Do justice, love mercy and walk humbly with your God" (Micah 6:8), readers will be guided to respond with the compassionate servant spirit of Jesus, our model Advocate.

BIBLIOGRAPHY

Bonds, L. and R. Encinas. *Healing Hearts, A Bible Study for Women.* Student book and leaders book, 2008. http://leeannbonds.com/hopehealingbooks/index.html.

Campbell, J. C., et al. "Risk Factors for Femicide in Abusive Relationships: Results from a Multi-Site Case Control Study," 93 (2003) *Am. J. of Public Health* 1089, 1092, abstract available at http://www.ajph.org/cgi/content/abstract/93/7/1089).

Cory, J., McAndless-Davis, K. *When Love Hurts: A Woman's Guide to Understanding Abuse in Relationships,* Sandhill Books. http://whenlovehurts.ca/getthe ok/.

Crisis Connection.Inc. *Commonwealth Fund Survey,* 1998.

———. *Men's Violence against Rural Women,* http://www.crisisconnectioninc.org/domesticviolence/rural_battered_women.htm.

DeKeseredy, W. and J. Schwartz. *Dangerous Exits: Escaping Abusive Relationships in Rural America,* Rutgers University Press, 2009.

Eberhardt, M, et al. *Urban and Rural Health Chartbook*. Hyattsville, MD: National Center for Health Statistics, 2001.

Faithtrust Institute. *Broken Vows: Religious Perspectives on Domestic Violence*, a two part training DVD with study guide. www.faithtrustinstitute.org.

Fink, D. *Agrarian Women: Wives and Mothers in Rural Nebraska 1880–1940: Studies in Rural Culture*. The University of North Carolina Press, 1992.

Health and Human Services. "Information for Rural Americans. Methamphetamine," Rural Assistance Center. http://www.raconline.org/topics/meth/.

Hot Peach Pages. http://www.hotpeachpages.net/.

Major, M. J. *Be a Voice Arts*. http://www.beavoicearts.com/.

Nagourney, E. "Linking Guns and Gun Violence Cause and Effect," *The New York Times*, May 27, 2003.

Nason-Clark, N., C. Clark Kroeger and B. Fisher-Townsend. *Responding to Abuse in Christian Homes: A Challenge to Churches and Their Leaders*, Eugene: Wipf & Stock, 2011.

National Coalition Against Domestic Violence (NCADV), The Public Policy Office. *Domestic Violence and Substance Abuse*, http://www.ncadv.org/files/SubstanceAbuse.pdf.

National Resource Center on Violence against Women. http://new.vawnet.org/category/index_pages.php?category_id=867.

National Rural Health Research Center Directors Meeting. "Research Opportunities for Rural Health Research Centers and State Offices of Rural Health." Washington, DC, March 5, 2001.

Nordstrom, D. L., et al. "Rural Population Survey of Behavioral and Demographic Risk Factors for Loaded Firearms." In Prev 7.2, 112–116 (2001).

Office for Victims of Crime. "Victim Assistance Training Online." https:// www.ovcttac.gov/views/TrainingMaterials/dspOnline_VATOnline.cfm.

Pennsylvania Coalition against Domestic Violence. "Helping Rural Battered Women and Their Children: A Guide for Faith Leaders and Religious Communities."

Porter, A. *A Call to Men. Breaking Out of the Man Box*, 2010. http://www.acalltomen.com/page.php?id=54.

———. *A Call to Men, TED talk*. http://www.ted.com/talks/tony_porter_a_call_to_men.html.

The National Center for Victims of Crime; Stalking Resource Center. "Stalking Fact Sheet," (citing J. McFarlane et al., 3 (1999) *Homicide Studies* 300–316.

The Rape, Abuse & Incest National Network. http://www.rainntrain.org/course/category.php?id=8.

The RAVE Project (Religion and Violence E-Learning). www.theraveproject.com.

Safety Net Project. Cyber stalking and other technology-related safety concerns. http://nnedv.org/resources/safetynetdocs.html.

United Nations Secretariat, Population Division, Percentage living in rural areas by country. U.S. Drug Enforcement Administration.

Websdale, N. *Rural Woman Battering and the Justice System: An Ethnography*. Thousand Oaks, CA:Sage, 1998.

Women's Law. "State domestic violence and related statutes." http://www.womenslaw.org/statutes_states.php.

World Urbanization Prospects. *The 2003 Revision, Data Tables and Highlights*.

10

From the Top

What Does It Mean When Catholic Bishops Speak Out on Issues of Family Violence?

Catherine Holtmann

JULIA IMMIGRATED TO A large Canadian city from South America with her family.[1] In her teens she became pregnant and married Carl, a Canadian-born man who was very controlling. *I couldn't have friends; I couldn't leave home; I couldn't dress the way I wanted when I was in my country. He was never home. . . . I basically didn't have a husband and it became really hard on me to just be at home with a kid and not be able to do anything.* She wanted to return to school to continue her education but Carl did not want to spend the money. Julia went anyway *and that's when jealousy started and mental abuse started.* One day he came close to striking her and her young child. Julia said, *I decided to get help and leave—I couldn't take it anymore.* On the advice of a friend, she sought out a Spanish-speaking woman at the city's Catholic immigration center. Maria, a settlement counselor with years of experience working with battered Latin American women in her local Catholic parish, listened to Julia's story. *She gave me exactly the two options—that I had to be in the relationship and try to work it out or just to leave and to go to a shelter. So I took the hard one.* Julia took her child who was a year and a half at the time and went to a shelter run by nuns. *It was kind*

---

1. Julia is a pseudonym, as are all of the other names used in this chapter.

of like a very strict shelter, but it helped me a lot, she said. Julia is raising her son and training to become a settlement counselor for immigrants. At the time that we spoke, she was working with the center's youth programming providing emotional support to immigrant youth who were finding it very difficult to integrate into Canadian society (Agency worker #2, Diocese #2).

This story of Julia and Maria is an example of the ways that the issue of domestic abuse and Catholicism intersect in the Canadian context. In this chapter, their story will serve as a touchstone for exploring both the strengths and weaknesses of the Canadian Catholic approach to domestic violence. Julia is among the significant number of young, non-European Catholics who have recently immigrated to Canada. Maria, having immigrated herself almost thirty years ago, is a member of a Spanish Catholic parish. Both the immigration center where Maria works and the shelter that offered Julia refuge were established by Catholic women's religious communities. Maria and Julia have a strong desire to help newcomers to Canada deal with their problems, some of which included domestic violence. But their story also involves structural challenges that relate to them as Catholics. This chapter is based on the analysis of interview data from qualitative research that sought to review the resources available to contemporary Catholics who deal with the issue of family violence. A little over twenty years ago, the Canadian Catholic bishops, leaders of the largest religious group in the country, publically acknowledged the problem of domestic violence.

CANADIAN CATHOLIC SOCIAL TEACHINGS AND THE STATISTICS ON DOMESTIC VIOLENCE

Social action on the basis of faith has a place at the heart of the modern Catholic Church. Since the late 19th century Catholic leaders have written public statements outlining the church's teachings on critical social issues. Catholic laity have been encouraged by the clergy to read the "signs of the times," emphasizing the profound spiritual relationship between the church and the world.[2] In their day to day lives of work and leisure, Catholics are called to engage in the task of a global transformation of a more just social order that respects the dignity of the individual as well as the common good. Catholic social teachings

---

2. Flannery, *Vatican Council II*.

are structural in their approach to the analysis of problems, critiquing the ways in which political, economic, and social systems serve to deepen inequalities and contribute to human and planetary suffering. Included in the signs of the times that global Catholic leaders have identified were the dignity and rights of women in domestic and public life[3]. Canadian Catholic bishops have focused the general principles of Catholic social teachings on issues of concern to Canadian women since the 1970s.[4] Two statements have explicitly named and denounced domestic violence. The Assembly of Quebec bishops established a special task force and a team of resource persons with direct experience in dealing with domestic violence in the province of Quebec and released the document "A Heritage of Violence: A Pastoral Reflection on Conjugal Violence" (1989). This reflection acknowledged the history and pervasiveness of conjugal violence and named aspects of the church's history and practice that may have contributed to the abuse of women by their husbands. The document was meant to raise consciousness about the issue and was accompanied by a workbook (published in French only) which was to function as a pedagogical tool for clergy and pastoral workers.[5] This was followed in 1991 by a statement from the Canadian Conference of Catholic Bishops (CCCB) called "To Live Without Fear" (2000). Building on the work of the Quebec bishops, the CCCB statement sought "to identify some of the ways that the Catholic community, in collaboration with others, can work for short term and long term solutions."[6] They identified helpful and effective pastoral approaches to domestic violence as:

- taking the woman seriously when she discloses abuse.
- avoiding sentimental clichés.
- following up after the initial contact.
- acquiring an ability to detect abuse.
- becoming informed of the available community resources (medical, legal, shelter, counseling) and working with them.

---

3. Beattie, "Dialogue, difference."
4. Canadian Conference of Catholic Bishops, *With Respect to Women*.
5. SACAQB, *A Heritage of Violence*, 11–13.
6. CCCB, "To live without fear," 74.

- being ready to deal with the profound spiritual questions that arise concerning the woman's relationship with God and her worth and dignity as a person; and
- creating a parish atmosphere where clergy and laity can discuss questions of violence against women openly and sensitively in homilies and other forums and offer concrete support.[7]

Harmful pastoral approaches identified by the bishops included:

- being uninformed.
- counseling premature reconciliation.
- silence about violence against women in parishes; and
- the misuse of Scripture to justify the domination of women.
- The CCCB also encouraged local diocesan structures to deal with this important issue.

The bishops' statements were made during a time when the feminist movement had succeeded in bringing the issue of violence against women to the forefront of Canadian political consciousness. In the early 1990s, after decades of smaller scale research to determine the prevalence of domestic violence in Canada, the United States and Great Britain, Statistics Canada undertook the design and implementation of a national random sample population survey "to assess the nature and dimensions of violence against women."[8] The Violence against Women Survey (VAWS) found that since the age of sixteen, fifty-one per cent of Canadian women had experienced some form of physical or sexual assault in their lifetime. Thirty-seven per cent of women who had ever been married or in a common-law relationship had experienced violence by their partners and fifteen per cent of women in marriages at the time of the survey reported being victims of violence.[9] These statistics are generally understood to be conservative measures of the prevalence rates of violence against women yet hint at the pervasiveness of a climate of abuse and violence in Canada. They provided the evidence needed for shifts in Canadian social policy, legal reform, funding, and services for victims of domestic violence in the years that

---

7. CCCB, "To live without fear," 75–76.
8. Johnson, "Rethinking survey research," 29.
9. Johnson, 37–39.

have followed the VAWS including increased numbers of shelters, pro-charging and pro-prosecution policies in the criminal justice system, and specialized domestic violence courts.[10]

Recent surveys show that the rate of violence in Canadian couples remains steady. The 2009 General Social Survey (GSS) found that six per cent of Canadians with a current or former spouse reported being physically or sexually victimized by their spouse in the past five years.[11] In 2008, sixty-four Canadian women were murdered by their intimate partners.[12] And while younger Canadians are more likely to report being a victim of spousal violence than older Canadians as part of a survey, they are less likely to report the incident to police.

Although the Canadian bishops publically acknowledged and condemned domestic violence over twenty years ago, the persistent rates of violence among Canadian couples illustrate the need for ongoing awareness and action concerning this social problem.

RESEARCH IN THE CANADIAN CATHOLIC CONTEXT

In 2010 I conducted semi-structured interviews with thirty-one people in three dioceses in Canada—one in the Atlantic region, one in central Canada and one in the West.[13] Each of the dioceses reflected the Francophone and English character of Canadian Catholic church. Seventeen of the research participants were women and fourteen were men. Ten of those interviewed were clergy—one bishop, eight priests, and one deacon. Of the remaining twenty-one lay persons, four of these were women from religious orders. I spoke with people working in parishes, shelters, secular and faith-based community agencies, and a variety of diocesan ministries. While I did not set out to speak to survivors, two women, Julia being one of them, asked to speak to me about their experiences of abuse. All of the interviews were conducted face-to-face and digitally recorded except for one, which took place on the phone.

10. Johnson and Dawson, *Violence Against Women in Canada*.

11. Statistics Canada. What the VAWS illustrated is that the rates of violence reported in General Social Surveys are considerably lower due to survey methods. For example, the 1993 GSS showed spousal assault rates of almost two percent. The 1999 GSS rates of spousal assault rose due to improvements in the survey methodology.

12. Johnson and Dawson.

13. I am grateful to the Association for the Sociology of Religion for the Fichter Grant that helped to fund this research.

The interviews were transcribed and analyzed. The analysis involved both inter-diocesan comparisons as well as intra-diocesan comparisons looking for common and divergent themes.

While the reality is that religious families experience domestic violence at similar rates to non-religious families,[14] the response to this issue has been different depending on the particular religious group and its geographical context.[15] What follows is a description of four distinctive modes of the response to domestic violence that characterize the contemporary Canadian Catholic church. These modes include mandatory marriage preparation courses; the bridges in place between Catholic parishes and community services; marriage tribunals and the process of annulment; and significant numbers of new immigrant Catholics. Each of these modes of response will be described as they relate to the Canadian bishops' statements in terms of helpful and harmful pastoral approaches to domestic violence. The review of the findings of the analysis will conclude with some of the gaps or challenges that remain to be addressed.

1. *Marriage preparation courses*

In all three dioceses couples planning to get married in the church were required to complete a marriage preparation course. Julia and her Canadian husband likely took one of these courses. They are based on materials developed by Catholic theologians, some of which are published in Canada, and training in facilitating the programs was provided. The courses were facilitated by married couples and all of the people involved had been doing this for many years and supplemented the course materials with guest speakers, power point presentations and handouts. Courses would be offered a few times per year. Because many of the couples taking the courses were not regular participants in local parishes, the courses included information about the Catholic theological understanding of marriage. This section was frequently facilitated by a priest. The majority of couples taking these courses were in their late twenties or thirties and had been living together, which meant that they had practical experience of the issues being covered

---

14. Nason-Clark, *The Battered Wife*.
15. Nason-Clark and Holtmann, "Thinking about cooperation," in press.

such as communication, finances, sexual intimacy, children, spirituality and conflict.

The French-language marriage preparation courses explicitly address abuse and violence in intimate relationships, providing printed materials on the topic, while the English-language courses only mention them in passing. French marriage preparation facilitators identify the many forms of abuse; point out the signs of abuse; and the cycle of abuse is reviewed in detail with the participants. In one diocese, a regular guest speaker during the session on intimate partner violence in the course was a Catholic RCMP (Royal Canadian Mounted Police) officer who provided a criminal justice perspective on the issue. The English program did address conflict in the session on finances and a facilitator said that she and her husband would mention abuse in the courses they offered. However, there were no printed materials on violence given to English participants. Both the English and French facilitators provided all couples with a list of available community services with phone numbers for marriage counseling, the domestic violence crisis line, and the local shelter.

The inclusion of explicit information about the cycle of violence and abuse in relationships coupled with activities that encourage engaged couples to talk to each other about the issue is a strength of French Catholic marriage preparation programs in Canada. The approach of the English-language programs in this research only indirectly mentioned spousal conflict in the context of finances. This is harmful in that it is unlikely that couples preparing for marriage will raise the topic themselves, particularly in a religious setting. Marriage preparation leaders' ability to break the silence about spousal abuse is critical and sends a message to the many couples unfamiliar with Catholic church teachings on marriage that violence is never acceptable. The fact that leaders in both the French and English marriage preparation programs provided information on local services for victims of abuse and for couples in crisis was a helpful pastoral approach.

2. Bridges between Catholics and community services

Many of the research participants, whether they were priests, agency or diocesan staff, or shelter workers, emphasized the importance of working together with the larger community. Making referrals and collaborating with community agencies was commonplace. In the case of Julia and Maria, several of these partnerships were in evidence. As an active member of her Spanish Catholic parish, Maria had offered a listening ear to women who were experiencing marital problems. Her priest had encouraged her in this work and the parish had helped her to get professional training. It was this training, her immigrant background and reputation within the community that enabled Maria to obtain full-time paid work at a Catholic immigration center. This center had first been established in the diocese by a women's religious order to respond to the needs of Canadian immigrants of all backgrounds and was now publically funded. Upon getting help from Maria, Julia was able to leave her abusive marriage and find safety at a shelter run by another Catholic women's community—again responding to the needs of the broader society.

In part, the bridges between Catholic ministries and the broader community are the result of the historical development of Catholicism within Canada. Members of men's and women's religious orders established many of the public institutions and social services that are now taken for granted in Canadian society—schools, universities, hospitals, orphanages, and senior's homes. In some provinces these services were sold to the provincial government and are Catholic in name only, while in other provinces Catholic institutions continue to complement secular services and in some cases receive public funding.

These services were founded in response to perceived needs and a lack of services in the local context. They continue to operate through the mobilization of religious and secular resources which requires strong networks of community interaction and support.[16] In my research I visited long-established community services, such as the immigration center where Maria worked and Julia volunteered, as well as newer ones that have arisen in response to the signs of the times. In one diocese, two nuns were running a shelter for trafficked women. Their religious order had an international scope and had made a commitment to work on the issue of the global trade of women and girls. One of the nuns had a long history of working with abused inner-city residents and homeless aboriginal youth, and was intimately familiar with a variety of social services. Through her work she realized that there

16. Wittberg, *The Rise and Fall of Catholic Religious Orders*.

was a need for a different kind of facility than the city's women's shelter. Located in the downtown core and established through the efforts of Catholic and Mennonite businessmen, in five years the new shelter had provided refuge for forty-one women from fifteen different countries with ten different religious backgrounds. This shelter was able to operate through the joint support of the local bishop, Christian churches throughout the city (Orthodox Catholic churches in particular), and government agencies offering a variety of services for immigrant and refugee women.

Bridge building between clergy, Catholic ministries, and secular agencies relied on professional networks. Like Maria, the immigrant settlement counselor, there are many Catholic women and men offering assistance to victims of domestic violence who have the wisdom gained from a lifetime of front-line community work. They are constantly utilizing their networks (both religious and secular) in order to ensure funding for their own agencies or to find necessary resources for the people they serve. Even in large cities, these people are known to one another and most importantly, trusted. Trust is established through years of dedicated work by individuals in secular and faith-based agencies. They support one another as each organization plays their particular part in a societal response to social problems. This is an effective Canadian pastoral approach to the problem of domestic violence.

People who are relatively new to the issue of domestic violence, such as several priests that I interviewed, did not have the knowledge and trust of these networks. In Maria's Spanish parish, for example, a new priest replaced the one that had supported her ministry to abused women. The new priest felt that Maria's work was not appropriate at the church—it was not directly religious. He did not value the work that she was doing and it soon came to an end. Maria was able to provide support to abused immigrant women as a settlement counselor however, she was sorry that the atmosphere at the parish level had grown insensitive to the problem of domestic violence. While bridge building between Catholics and community agencies is necessary in providing resources for domestic violence, as Maria's example shows, these bridges are fragile and depend on the support of institutional leaders.

The fragility of the bridges between Catholic churches and social services is even more apparent when the demographics of contemporary Catholic religious leaders are taken into account. Bishops, priests, and the men and women in religious orders, are aging. As their numbers continue to decline, the networks of faith-based and community services that many Catholics have come to take for granted are threatened. In the case of women's religious communities in particular, their demise has consequences for Catholic resources for domestic violence. Nuns were among the pioneers of the feminist movement in Canada, dedicating their lives to overcoming the public-private divide that kept women under the thumb of patriarchy.[17] They have been at the forefront of movements for theological and structural change within Catholicism that has highlighted issues of concern for women—the majority of engaged participants in Catholic churches. As pro-change, justice-seeking Catholic women become increasingly alienated by the institution,[18] what will become of their legacy of bridge-building at the community level? Only time will tell. The lack of awareness of local resources for family violence among newly ordained clergy and the fragility of networks between Catholic and secular services can have harmful effects on the response of Catholics to the suffering in their midst. Another area of ministry of women religious and clergy in regards to domestic violence has been within diocesan marriage tribunal offices.

3. Marriage tribunals

The majority of Catholics who approach a marriage tribunal office do so because they want the annulment of a failed marriage in order to remarry in the church. According to canon law the sacrament of marriage is invalid if either of the partners was not able to enter freely into the covenant. In cases like Julia's, the tribunal process would try to uncover evidence of a history of violence or abuse in both Julie's and her husband's family of origin. Having either witnessed abuse as a child or having been a victim of abuse is highly correlated with a continuing cycle of abuse.[19]

Before an annulment procedure can begin the couple must first be legally divorced. Tribunal staff as well as clergy in this study emphasized that the Catholic church does not want couples who experience violence and abuse to stay together. The tribunal process involves

---

17. Holtmann, "My sister my self."
18. Holtmann, "Workers in the vineyard."
19. Gelles, *Intimate Violence*.

several interviews during which the person requesting the annulment (and the other party if s/he chooses to become involved) has the opportunity to tell the story of her/his courtship and marriage. The tribunal staff question the petitioner about her or himself and her or his family background. With years of listening to stories of domestic abuse and violence, tribunal staff have the ability to ask questions that will help them uncover specific evidence. They are trained in the detection of the signs of abuse. The stories of witnesses, such as family members and friends, are also included in the process, which is in some ways similar to a civil court case. After all of the interviews, stories, and evidence are documented the case is decided by a judicial vicar at the diocesan level and then forwarded for review to the national tribunal offices. In cases of domestic violence where an annulment is granted but there is insufficient evidence to suggest that either the perpetrator or the victim has adequately dealt with the problems that resulted in the marriage breakdown, a note is added to the diocesan records. This warning is meant to alert clergy in case the person wants to remarry within the church. Some form of follow-up needs to have taken place before another marriage can proceed. In fact, clergy throughout the country are prohibited from permitting someone to remarry if the warning from the tribunal has not been lifted from her/his file. While the annulment process may seem very formal and for many, is too time consuming and bureaucratic, tribunal staff spoke movingly of the kind of caring ministry that they perform. Having the opportunity to tell the painful story of marriage breakdown to a representative of the church who is a compassionate and understanding listener is a powerful journey of healing for many abused Catholics. Tribunal staff would refer people to counseling services in the community if they felt it was necessary.

The women interviewed who worked with diocesan marriage tribunals were members of religious orders. One sister was encouraging her order to bring sisters from developing countries to study canon law in Canada. She emphasized that Canadian canon lawyers have been sensitized to the issues of domestic violence. They could interpret canon law and adjudicate marriage cases in ways that acknowledged reality of violence and abuse in Catholic families and recognize violations of the sacramental covenant. This was not the approach in other countries and she hoped that by educating canon lawyers in Canadian universities, her community could help Catholic women in other countries better deal with domestic violence in the context of their faith tradition.

While the fact that at least one religious community in Canada is using the training about domestic violence gained through the annulment process to help Catholic women around the world is encouraging, it is discouraging that more knowledge transfer is not happening closer to home. There is a wealth of knowledge gleaned in ministry to the survivors and perpetrators of abuse literally hidden behind the closed doors of the tribunal offices that could be utilized at a variety of levels within the church. This knowledge could be used in the training of seminarians and in lay formation programs to help Catholic leaders recognize the signs of abuse among couples or families in parishes and to help them find ways of addressing domestic violence, perhaps in homilies or in adult education programs. Parish nurses would also benefit from such training.

Enabling Catholics at the parish level to recognize the signs and name domestic violence is a critical step in working for change, as was identified by the Canadian bishops years ago. This is because not all petitions for an annulment in cases of domestic violence are successful—abuse and violence that begin after a couple is married but is not a part of an intergenerational cycle of abuse is not deemed sufficient grounds for an annulment, regardless of its severity. There are many factors identified in the literature that can increase the risk of violence taking place after couples wed including the young age of partners, pregnancy, low socio-economic status, unemployment, alcohol and drug abuse, the presence of children from previous relationships, living in public housing, the degree of acceptance of traditional patriarchal attitudes, and the threat of separation.[20] Marriage tribunal personnel emphasize to Catholics that in such cases, separation and divorce are the best choice. However, the knowledge gleaned from these stories can be used in ways to identify points of intervention at the parish level and strategies for doing so. This could help Catholics assist couples in preventing violence from erupting and providing pastoral support for vulnerable families. One sister with twenty-two years of experience working at a tribunal dreamed of a ministry of confidential listening

20. Brownridge, *Violence against Women*; DeKeseredy, *Violence against Women: Myths, Facts, Controversies;* Johnson and Dawson, *Violence against Women in Canada.*

at the parish level. She believed that more Catholics need to talk about their relationship struggles in a safe context with individuals trained in asking the right questions—a ministry that did not sentimentalize family life but took seriously the reality of abuse and violence. *It's to be pastoral*, she insisted. *It's to be what Jesus was—he walked on the road and he met everybody and I'm sure they were changed* (Diocesan staff #1, Diocese #1).

4. New immigrant Catholics

The ministry to new immigrants is another distinctive aspect of the Canadian Catholic response to domestic violence arising from this research. Canada has one of the highest per capita immigration rates in the world and, according to Statistics Canada,[21] new immigrants account for the majority of growth in both the population and labor force. Religion is a significant aspect of the identities of many new immigrants.[22] Research has shown that in addition to maintaining ritual practices, immigrant religious groups in North America often become centers of social support and civic engagement.[23] The majority of contemporary Canadian immigrants are from Asia and forty per cent of Asian Christians are Catholic.[24] It is the presence of new immigrants that has helped the Catholic church to stave off the decline that is facing main-line Protestant denominations in Canada.[25] These young, educated and skilled new Canadian Catholics are breathing renewed energy into parishes and Catholic organizations across the country.

Maria was proud of the fact that her Spanish Catholic parish had been the place where she had developed her counseling skills. She described the church as *a settlement place for the people when they arrive here. In any place it's like that—in any country, in any city of any country. . . . [The church] is a place where you know you're going to find people that share a common cultural background and stuff like that. You find people that you share something that started with religion and then the*

21. Statistics Canada, "Immigration in Canada."
22. Bramadat and Seljak, *Christianity and Ethnicity*.
23. Ebaugh and Chafetz, *Religion and the New Immigrants*; Foley and Hoge, *Religion and the New Immigrants: How Faith Communities Form our Newest Citizens*; Warner and Wittner, *Gatherings in the Diaspora*.
24. Fay, *New Faces*.
25. Clark and Schellenberg, "Who's religious?"

rest comes along (Agency worker #1, Diocese #2). She had been among the original members of the Spanish Catholic community and had helped it to respond to the needs of new Canadians. In turn, the church had supported her professional development. She gave a lot of credit to her parish priest who was very open culturally—an immigrant who spoke Spanish, French, and English. As a global religion, Catholicism has been adapted in a variety of cultural contexts. Catholic immigrants can rely on the familiarity of their religious background in relating to Catholics in other parts of the world since the church structures, the core beliefs, and the form and content of the mass are universal.

In this study there were major differences between two diocesan contexts that had a long history of immigration and one with a population of primarily French and English descent. Two of the dioceses had multicultural immigrant Catholic populations while the third had a recent influx of African students to a French-language university. The two multicultural Catholic dioceses had employed immigrant priests in ethnic parishes for many years. In these parishes some masses were celebrated in languages other than French and English and ethnic priests were able to provide pastoral care in the parishioner's native tongue. In the bi-cultural diocese the majority of priests were Canadian-born and spoke either French or English. In recent years throughout Canada, many dioceses have begun to procure African priests on a temporary basis in order to deal with the shortage of clergy. These priests are a strategic response to a labor shortage rather than a response to cultural diversity, however, their presence adds another element to the immigrant character of the Canadian Catholic church.

All research participants were aware of government services for immigrants and refugees. Religious leaders had more limited experiences of working directly with immigrant families and violence than did those working in shelters, agencies or community organizations. For example, the chaplain at the French-language university spoke highly of services for international students on campus and was comfortable making referrals. However, he had never directly spoken to students about violence and abuse in relationships and he was unsure if the topic was covered in marriage preparation courses. Priests from parishes with immigrants spoke about how new Canadians generally came with a more traditional view of family life in which gender roles were rigidly defined. While marriage tribunal personnel, shelter, and agency workers told stories of dealing with immigrant victims of abuse, most of whom had been married prior to arriving in Canada, none of the priests with new immigrants in their parishes had preached a message about the unacceptability of intimate partner violence nor did they have printed information about the issue available in their churches.

Domestic violence in immigrant Catholic families is an issue that requires knowledge and sensitivity about the intersection of the multiple oppressions of race, gender, and class.[26] Research participants serving immigrants beyond the church doors all emphasized the importance of cultural competence. Increasingly, situations involving family violence required a family-centered approach to solutions. Shelter and agency workers were actively increasing their knowledge and skill-base for working with families from a broad spectrum of cultural backgrounds. According to a director of second stage housing who had immigrated to Canada from Africa, best practices include a strength-based approach to immigrant family life. She suggested that religious leaders needed to emphasize love, respect, and mutuality between husbands and wives in marriages as new immigrants struggle with the existing social divisions of Canadian society. Churches need to be explicit about the unacceptability of violence against women and children in Canada as well as providing very practical supports for immigrant families as they settle in their new home. While Catholic leaders are optimistic about the future of the Canadian church due to the vitality of the faith of immigrants, there is a danger of sentimentalizing their situations and thus denying the reality of domestic violence. According to the CCCB statement "To Live without Fear," this is a harmful pastoral approach.

GAPS IN CANADIAN CATHOLIC RESOURCES FOR DOMESTIC VIOLENCE

While the evidence reveals numerous strengths of the Canadian Catholic response to the problem of family violence, there remain gaps. These include the lack of specific training in dealing with domestic violence in the training of clergy; the lack of information on domestic violence from a faith perspective available in churches; and a silence about domestic violence from contemporary Canadian bishops.

26. Crenshaw, "Mapping at the margins."

Of the priests participating in the research who were ordained in the past twenty years since the Canadian bishops publically condemned violence against women, none had received any training on domestic violence in a Canadian seminary. In fact, none of them were aware of the documents from either the Quebec bishops or the CCCB. None of the clergy interviewed had preached a homily that dealt with the topic, although most could recall pastoral situations when they had at least suspected that abuse or violence was a factor. However, few had explicitly addressed the topic with a parishioner. Those that did were elderly priests with many, many years of experience in pastoral ministry and trusted connections to individuals and organizations in the community. For example, one priest was a board member for the local domestic violence advisory council. These priests mentioned that times had changed and that today's Catholics were more likely to directly access secular services than approach a parish priest for help. Several priests did mention ministering to homeless men and ex-prisoners who had violent pasts. The bishop who participated in the research said that the homily is not a time for teaching and issues like domestic violence are not suitable for the liturgy. He felt that social problems needed to be addressed through other ministries in the church and that the church must not duplicate services properly belonging in the secular realm. This situation indicates a gap between the clergy's perception of their ministry and the reality of violence among families of faith at the parish level, despite the CCCB's call for change over twenty years ago. Religious leaders need to be aware of the extent and prevalence of the problem of family violence and speak out about the need for change. Despite changes, priests have an important role to play. The data reveals the changing character of the ministry of Catholic priests in Canada.

As mentioned, dioceses in Canada have begun to rely on migrant priests to deal with clergy shortages. It has become normative for most priests to serve several churches, moving from one to another to preside at sacraments but with little time to form bonds with communities. Sometimes priests are deliberately placed in parishes where they share the ethnicity of the congregation and sometimes not. As the research has shown, Catholics (whether priests or laity) coming from the developing world have more traditional understandings of gender roles in family life and are less likely to identify abuse in the family, at the very least as problematic and at most, criminal. Like their Canadian-born counterparts, immigrant and migrant priests have not been trained theologically or pastorally to deal with the reality of domestic violence in the Canadian context. They do not understand the power that their words might carry when speaking out about this issue in their churches. Instead of providing priests with professional training to deal with an identified concern, Canadian bishops have left them on their own to learn (or not) from their mistakes regarding pastoral care involving violence and abuse. This leaves the most vulnerable—women and children in Catholic families, at risk. Yet many resources already exist within the Canadian church through bridges built at the community level that religious leaders could draw upon to improve priests' knowledge and skills in this regard, particularly in making referrals.

There was no printed information specifically on domestic violence that is sensitive to the needs of Catholic victims readily available in any of the churches that I visited, outside of the materials provided during marriage preparation courses. However, each diocese did have a website that listed diocesan and community services available to Catholics. This could be utilized for disseminating more focused information on the prevalence of and risk factors for domestic violence or linking to web-based resources like the Religion and Violence e-Learning or RAVE Project (www.theraveproject.org). Some priests thought that providing information on domestic violence in the parish should be the role of the social justice committee. Yet, as I have written elsewhere, Catholic women find it difficult to translate their concerns about the problems of Catholic family life into social action at the parish level.[27] Maria's story confirms this challenge. Contemporary Canadian churches seem to be focusing more on providing liturgical and sacramental ministries than helping Catholic laity utilize the principles of Catholic social teachings in moral decision-making and social action. This confirms Baggett's claim[28] that inattention to the complexity of Catholic social thought is leading to civic silencing and civic underachieving among Catholics.

Changes in the laity's ability to grapple with social problems have been accompanied by (or are a result of) a shift in the approach

27. Holtmann, *Heart, Mind and Soul* and "Workers in the vineyard."
28. Baggett, *Sense of the Faithful*.

to Catholic social teachings in Canada on the part of the CCCB. In the early 1990s the bishops established the Catholic Organization for Life and Family (COLF) in order to build a pro-life public education and government lobbying program. Prior to this, issues of women and family life were contextualized within the Canadian bishops' critical approach to broader social and economic issues.[29] Increasingly, however, family life is defined by Catholic leaders as the place where individual life is protected in the face of a culture of death. Catholic women and men who insist on the exercise of personal conscience in the face of moral dilemmas concerning sexuality and procreation have become an easy target for all that is wrong with church and society. Yet a search of the COLF website reveals no mention of domestic violence—certainly a life and death issue for too many women in Canada. Questions must be asked about this silence. Polarization around social justice issues of concern to Catholic women, along with differing approaches to solutions, particularly feminist approaches, have resulted in either conservative rhetoric that blames the victims or uncomfortable silence regarding complex moral problems. It was the feminist movement that brought violence against women to the forefront of public attention, yet feminists did not create this problem. While the Catholic Church disagrees with feminist positions on some issues, the Canadian bishops are on record as having agreed with the feminist critique of domestic violence.

The authority of religious leaders has shifted dramatically in the past fifty years. Increasingly individual believers look to their own conscience rather than to their leaders when making moral decisions. This is as true for Catholics as for other religious traditions and particularly the case for Catholic women.[30] Moreover, the authority of bishops and priests has come into question as a result of the global scandal of clergy sexual abuse. The cover-up of numerous cases of sexual abuse of young boys by priests and the protection of offenders at the expense of victims has shocked and angered Catholics. A profound distrust threatens to develop between Catholic laity and their leaders and this has consequences for those working on the issue of domestic violence at the local level. Despite the turmoil at the structural level, Catholicism remains a meaningful religion to thousands of Canadians who faithfully return

29. McKeon, *Canadian Catholic Social Justice Paradigm*.
30. D'Antonio et al., *American Catholics*.

to mass each week. Religious leaders can play a key role in condemning domestic violence, supporting victims, and calling perpetrators to account,[31] principles in line with the long history of Catholic teachings and action for social justice. In doing so they will better support the many Catholic and secular organizations, individuals and coalitions striving together to save lives and bring healing and wholeness to victims of violence and abuse.

CONCLUSION

This qualitative research with Catholics and community workers in three dioceses across Canada reveal that many Catholics continue to respond to the call that Canadian bishops made over twenty years ago to collaborate with others in responding to the societal problem of domestic violence. Distinctive resources have developed within the Canadian Catholic church. These include mandatory marriage preparation courses with explicit references to intimate partner abuse and violence for French speaking Catholics; the many bridges that have been built between Catholic institutions and public community services, particularly through the legacy of men's and women's religious orders; the wisdom about the many facets of domestic violence that has been gleaned through diocesan marriage tribunals and the healing ministry of listening with compassion that has taken place there; and the ability of Catholic churches to adapt to the religious and social needs of new immigrants from a wide variety of cultures as they come to Canada seeking a better future yet struggling with the stress that the migration process places on their families. These distinctively Canadian responses to domestic violence are evidence of effective pastoral approaches while at the same time some areas of concern have been identified. The research also highlighted gaps in the contemporary Catholic responses, namely the lack of training in responding to family violence in Canadian Catholic seminary education for clergy and laity; the need for more faith-specific information on domestic violence in a variety of languages in Catholic parishes; and the complicated silence on issues of violence against women from Canadian bishops. At a time when the issue of abuse is too often associated with inappropriate responses from the leadership of the Catholic church, perhaps this is the best time to

---

31. Nason-Clark, "Making the Sacred Safe."

further strengthen the Canadian church's resources for family violence. Appropriate words and actions in providing pastoral care to Catholic families suffering in the midst of domestic violence will be one more step in the movement from pain to hope[32].

BIBLIOGRAPHY

Baggett, J. *Sense of the Faithful: How American Catholics Live their Faith*. New York, NY: Oxford University Press, 2009.

Beattie, T. *Dialogue, Difference and Human Development: Gendered Perspectives on Catholic Social Teaching*. Unpublished manuscript, Fredericton, NB, 2010.

Bramadat, P. and D. Seljak, (Eds.). *Christianity and Ethnicity in Canada*. Toronto, ON: University of Toronto Press, 2008.

Brownridge, D. A. *Violence Against Women: Vulnerable Populations*. New York, NY: Routledge, 2009.

CCCB. *With Respect To Women: A History Of CCCB Initiatives Concerning Women in the Church and Society 1971–2000*. Ottawa, ON: Concacan Inc, 2000.

CCCB. To Live Without Fear. In CCCB (Ed.), *With Respect To Women: A History of CCCB Initiatives Concerning Women in the Church and Society 1971–2000* (pp. 73–77). Ottawa, ON: Concacan Inc, 2004

Clark, W. and G. Schellenberg. "Who's religious?" *Canadian Social Trends, Catalogue No. 11–008*, 2–9, 2006.

Crenshaw, K. W. "Mapping the margins: Intersectionality, identity politics, and violence against women of color." In M. Fineman and R. Mykitiuk (Eds.), *The Public Nature of Private Violence: The Discovery of Domestic Abuse* (93–118). New York, NY: Routledge, 1994.

D'Antonio, W. V., J.D. Davidson, D.R. Hoge, and K. Meyer. *American Catholics: Gender, Generation, and Commitment*. Walnut Creek, CA: Altamira Press, 2001.

DeKeseredy, W. S. *Violence Against Women: Myths, Facts, Controversies*. Toronto, ON: University of Toronto Press, 2011.

Ebaugh, H. R., and J. Chafetz. (Eds.) *Religion and the New Immigrants: Continuities and Adaptations In Immigrant Congregations*. Walnut Creek, CA: Altamira Press, 2000.

Fay, T. J. *New Faces of Canadian Catholics: The Asians*. Ottawa, ON: Novalis, 2009.

Flannery O.P., (Ed.). *Vatican Council II: The Conciliar And Post-Conciliar Documents* (Revised edition). Northport, NY: Costello Publishing Co, 1988.

Foley, M. W. and D.R. Hoge. *Religion and The New Immigrants: How Faith Communities Form Our Newest Citizens*. New York, NY: Oxford University Press, 2007.

Gelles, R. J. *Intimate Violence in Families* (Third ed.). Thousand Oaks, CA: SAGE Publications, 1997.

Holtmann, C. *My Sister My Self: Women Religious at Work*. Unpublished manuscript, Boston, MA, 2008.

Holtmann, C. *Heart, Mind and Soul: Catholic Women and Social Action*. University of New Brunswick, Fredericton, NB, 2009.

---

32. *From Pain to Hope* is the title of a report on child sexual abuse by clergy published by the CCCB in 1992.

Holtmann, C. "Workers in the vineyard: Catholic women and social action." In G. Giordan and W. Swatos (Eds.), *Religion, Spirituality and Everyday Practice* (141–152). New York, NY: Springer Publishing Co, 2011.

Johnson, H. "Rethinking survey research on violence against women." In R. E. Dobash and R. P. Dobash (Eds.), *Rethinking Violence Against Women* (23–51). Thousand Oaks, CA: SAGE Publications, 1998.

Johnson, H., and M. Dawson. *Violence Against Women In Canada: Research And Policy Perspectives*. New York, NY: Oxford University Press, 2010.

McKeon, R. *The Canadian Catholic Social Justice Paradigm: Birth, Growth, Decline and Crisis*. University of St. Michael's College, Toronto, ON, 2003.

Nason-Clark, N. *The Battered Wife: How Christian Families Confront Family Violence*. Louisville, KY: Westminster John Knox Press, 1997.

———. "Making the sacred safe: Woman abuse and communities of faith." *Sociology of Religion*, 61 (2000) 349–368.

Nason-Clark, N., and C. Holtmann. (in press). "Thinking about cooperation and collaboration between diverse religious and secular community responses to domestic violence." In L. G. Beaman and W. Sullivan (Eds.), *Varieties of Religious Establishments*. Farnham (Surrey), UK: Ashgate Press.

SACAQB. *A Heritage Of Violence: A Pastoral Reflection On Conjugal Violence*. Montreal, PQ: Social Affairs Committee of the Assembly of Quebec Bishops,1989.

Statistics Canada. "*Family violence in Canada: A statistical profile 2009*." Retrieved 8 February 2009. from www.statcan.gc.ca.

———"Immigration in Canada: A portrait of the foreign-born population, 2006 census." Retrieved from http://www.statcan.ca

Warner, S., and J. Wittner. (Eds.) *Gatherings in the Diaspora: Religious Communities and the New Immigrants*. Philadelphia, PA: Temple University Press, 1998.

Wittberg, P. *The Rise and Fall of Catholic Religious Orders: A Social Movement Perspective*. Albany, NY: SUNY Press, 1994.

11

Church Leaders and Family Violence
Understanding the Challenge

Victoria Fahlberg

Every year, thousands of women and children are victims of abuse in the home, whether in the form of domestic violence or child abuse and neglect. Victims who are members of a religious community often seek help and advice from their church leaders, who may or may not respond appropriately. There are reasons why pastors and other church leaders may handle these situations poorly when they arise in the congregation, yet much of what is written explaining this failure has been focused on the leaders' theological beliefs related to headship/submission in the marriage relationship, and the sanctity of marriage and the family.[1] However, we do need to recognize that theological beliefs are not the only reasons that pastors and other church leaders may fail to give good advice and assistance to women and children in their congregations who are living in homes where they are not safe.

The purpose of this chapter is to look at some additional concerns that challenge pastors when working with situations of family violence in their congregation. These concerns include a lack of preparation; personal difficulties in confronting sexual and domestic violence; the possibility that the church leader may himself be abusive at home or at church; and distrust between churches and secular agencies. Although

1. Nason-Clark, *The Battered Wife*.

every situation is unique, both available data and my personal experiences demonstrate that these challenges are significant obstacles for church leaders to overcome. Once these issues are explored, some solutions will be discussed.

In my personal experience, I have found that churches of various denominations are often ill-prepared to handle situations of family violence or child sexual abuse in their congregations. For example, in 2005 I taught a course at an evangelical seminary that was titled "Abuse in the Church." Nearly 20 students were on in the class and all were working towards becoming pastors or lay leaders in their respective churches. The students came from 17 different church backgrounds, including mainline, evangelical, Pentecostal, and Greek Orthodox. In their first assignment, students were asked to critique their current church policy around the issue of protecting children from child abuse in the church. Only five students found that their churches had a policy, while the remaining students found that their churches had no policy at all. As the five students whose churches had policies critiqued them, it became obvious that they were not only inadequate but also the policies were not being sufficiently implemented. Many of the churches with policies were part of larger denominations that presumably had policies available for individual churches to adopt and adapt for their needs. Most churches had simply not bothered to do so. What made this surprising is that many insurance companies now require churches to have policies on certain issues such as child abuse in order for the church to be protected in the event of a lawsuit.

In their second assignment, the same group of students developed a survey to discover more about abuse in the church. The survey questions covered issues of spiritual abuse,[2] sexual abuse of adult congregants by clergy, and child sexual abuse. A total of 247 congregants responded to our anonymous questionnaire, 43 percent male and 57 percent female, representing a fairly equal balance among the church affiliations previously mentioned. Regarding the questions on child sexual abuse, we found that only half of the respondents were aware of the epidemic of child sexual abuse in American society and only one third had ever heard this issue addressed in church. Overwhelmingly, 87 percent of all respondents reported that they would like to learn more about the issue in church.

2. Johnson and VanVonderen, "The Subtle Power of Spiritual Abuse," 20.

To sum up what we learned from those class experiences:

- The majority of churches did not have policies and procedures that adequately addressed how they should deal with issues of child sexual abuse in the church, even though these situations can create significant risk and liability for a church.
- Only a third of respondents had learned anything about child sexual abuse at church and half were unaware that it had reached epidemic proportions.
- People in all of these different denominations wanted to learn more about child sexual abuse from their church leaders.

Related to these points, if people in the pews lack information about a significant social problem, want to understand more about an issue, and plenty of information is available, then why are pastors so reluctant to teach it, preach it, or work with congregants? Next, both child sexual abuse and domestic violence can lead to unimaginable trauma or even death. Children who witness their mother being battered can have their emotions affected as well as their brain development,[3] and if that isn't enough, forty to sixty percent of batterers also directly abuse the children.[4] The harm is so great that it is imperative that church leaders are prepared to help those in their congregations being abused. Finally, lack of policies and procedures around responding appropriately to situations of child sexual abuse can put a church at risk. With so much at stake, how does one make sense of the lack of leadership in the area family violence on the part of church leaders?

LACK OF PREPARATION

In the second book in this series, McMullin and Nason-Clark[5] reported on a study in which 412 seminary students from three evangelical and one mainline seminary completed a detailed questionnaire about their knowledge and preparation to respond to domestic violence. The majority (61.8 percent) felt that they were poorly prepared or unprepared. Of the sixty-six students getting ready to graduate, the level of preparation was only slightly better, with nearly half (48.4 percent) still

---

3. Bronson, P. and A. Merryman. *NurtureShock*.
4. http://www.domesticviolence.org/common-myths.
5. McMullin and Nason-Clark. "Seminary Students and Domestic Violence."

feeling poorly prepared or unprepared to respond to situations of domestic violence. In fact, only 55.5 percent even knew how to contact a shelter. Although this study may not represent church leaders across the country, it is an indication of the challenge seminaries face in properly training their students on how to handle this sensitive issue.

In fact, many seminaries require only a single course in pastoral counseling for their Master of Divinity degree. When I taught pastoral counseling, this one course covered the following topics:

- basic interviewing and counseling skills.
- how to assess situations in which someone's safety could be at stake.
- how to know when they are in over their head and needed to refer the person to others better equipped to deal with the problem.
- the importance of learning about services available in their community; and
- how they could help their congregants access those services.

In addition to the skills required to work with congregants, there were many specific topics that my students needed to become familiar with: (a) mental health issues, such as depression, anxiety disorders, drug or alcohol addictions, etc.; (b) how to help parents deal with problems with their children, such as learning disabilities, bullying, video game addictions, gang issues, rebellious behavior, and more; (c) how to help congregants through bereavement, to understand the stages of grief and when someone's grief requires special intervention; (d) how to help couples with marriage issues, including infidelity, financial problems, in-law problems, and problems of abuse in the marriage, including sexual and physical violence. Relatedly, one study showed that pastors spend 16 percent of their time solely dealing with marriage issues![6]

Just having enough time to provide basic information on all of the types of concerns that can surface in congregations could fill several courses. Instead of students learning much about any one topic, they learned a little about many, and were therefore not fully prepared to effectively handle disclosures of family violence. Social workers spend years learning how to do these things, yet future pastors were required to learn these skills in just one course. This gap in training results in

6. Ibid, 216.

pastors feeling unprepared to help abuse victims, which can have serious ramifications for those seeking help.

Pastors who have not been fully trained to handle issues of family violence may be reluctant to preach or teach on this issue out of fear that more congregants will disclose abuse to them thus requiring that they provide support in an area they do not know well. Unfortunately, this begets a cycle in which the victims of abuse keep quiet, and as a result the pastor is not challenged to learn more about the issue or how to handle it. Although being prepared to help victims of abuse is very important, it is not vital because pastors who suddenly receive a disclosure of abuse without being prepared can reach out to local domestic violence agencies. Personal issues

Learning about and dealing with victims of family violence can be extremely challenging for those who have personal difficulties with this issue. Many people struggle with hearing stories of abuse because they can be almost too repulsive to be true, and they violate our understanding of a humanity that is created in God's image. Others have had personal experiences with being victimized and have not dealt with these traumatic experiences sufficiently to allow them to move on and help others. Finally, some pastors may themselves abuse their power, either at home or at church, and therefore may either be apathetic towards victims or unwilling to recognize the immorality of abuse. All of these reasons make it more challenging for pastors to speak out against abuse from the pulpit and appropriately support victims of abuse in their congregation.

a. The difficulty of facing atrocities

When seminaries do offer courses on sexual and domestic violence, it may not be a popular subject because it forces a confrontation with the greatest evil known to humanity—the violation of a person by someone they trust, often someone they live with, care about, and perhaps with whom they share children. Family violence is a unique type of trauma. It is about evil being purposefully perpetrated upon the vulnerable by those who are supposed to protect them. It is much easier for helpers to approach and care for victims of trauma that have not been purposefully harmed by someone they trust, because these violations desecrate our beliefs about humanity, and may even make some question the benevolence of God.

When I covered this topic in my counseling course, one of the books I used was called *Predators* by Dr. Anna Salter,[7] which provided such graphic details of how sexual predators think and behave that some in the class had difficulty with the text. How can students sit through a class where we talk about a father butchering his wife and children? How can we talk about a father using his daughter as his sexual play toy when she's only three years old? Even reading those sentences makes us cringe. We don't want to hear about it, we don't want to think about it. How can we talk about the sanctity of the family if we truly admit to ourselves that the family is not sacred—or even safe?

b. Personal experiences of abuse

For some seminary students, it can also be difficult to choose to take classes on sexual or domestic violence because they have experienced domestic or sexual violence themselves. If childhood traumas have not adequately been dealt with taking classes on domestic and sexual violence can stir up traumatic memories that victims often work very hard to suppress. When working with victims of abuse, survivors who have not fully healed can project their own stories onto the victim and therefore not respond appropriately to the unique needs of the victim. While many survivors choose to go into the field of domestic violence support services because of their empathy for other victims, those who have not healed completely often end up becoming overwhelmed and easily cross boundaries that are crucial in a pastoral setting.

Religious people appear to be particularly vulnerable to abuse. In Dr. Salter's book she turns to the voice of a child molester, who was also a minister:

> I considered church people easy to fool. . . . They have a trust that comes from being Christians. . . . They tend to be better folks all around. And they seem to want to believe in the good that exists in all people. . . . I think they want to believe in people. And because of that, you can easily convince, with or without convincing words.[8]

7. Salter, *Predators*.
8. Ibid, 29.

c. The issue of pastors and church leaders as perpetrators

Another reason some pastors struggle with helping victims of abuse is that they themselves engage in abusive behaviors, either at home or at church. In the 2005 study by my seminary students in which 247 church members responded (55 percent women, 40 percent men), we learned that over 48 percent of the people surveyed reported that they had been manipulated by a spiritual leader. More than one in four reported that they had been advised or pressured to act against their own conscience by a spiritual leader and nearly one out of five reported that a spiritual leader had taken control over their life at some time in the past. Over 75 percent of those surveyed reported that they knew someone who had been manipulated by a spiritual leader and more than half (51 percent) knew someone in the church who had been advised or pressured to act against their conscience by a spiritual leader.

When asked how the abuse by a spiritual leader was possible, over 45 percent of those surveyed reported that they had been taught to obey spiritual leaders because the leader speaks with the authority of God and 42 percent of respondents reported that a spiritual leader had used Scripture or theology to manipulate or intimidate them. An additional 62 percent of respondents reported that they were aware of others who had been manipulated or intimidated in this manner. Other spiritual leaders use exclusion from church life, or making a person feel spiritually inferior as a means to gain compliance over church members. In this survey, nearly half of the respondents had experienced this and over 62 percent reported that they knew someone who had been excluded or made to feel inferior by a church leader. This "power positioning" occurs when a pastor constantly reminds the congregation to submit to his authority; he eventually "takes the place of Jesus in people's lives,"[9] Congregants find themselves trapped because they cannot leave the church without permission from the pastor, and if they do, will surely lose God's blessing.

Finally, studies[10] show that between 10 and 39 percent of male clergy members have engaged in sexually inappropriate behaviors with women in their congregation. In our study, a full 50 percent of the respondents said they were aware of inappropriate sexual behavior by

---

9. Fehlauer, "Exposing Spiritual Abuse," 34.
10. Grenz and Bell, "Betrayal of Trust," 24–25.

clergy towards women in the congregation but only a third had ever heard this information provided in church.

Abusers are manipulators who know how to manipulate their victims to their advantage. When the pastor is someone you trust and respect, it is more difficult to attribute such behaviours to them. Not only does it create complete cognitive dissonance with the trust most place in their pastor, but it also puts one in an untenable situation because to accept the truth may require the victim to leave the congregation. This can be complicated in churches where abusive pastors use their authority to control people from leaving the church by developing an "us versus them" mentality.[11] Sometimes pastors purposefully defame those leaving the church and prohibit other church members from contacting these rebels. The abusive pastor tries to destroy the victim's reputation so they have no chance of succeeding anywhere else without him.[12]

When people encounter situations like this, they begin to ignore that still, small voice inside of them telling them that it's wrong, because they don't want to believe it is happening. Many churches do not have a policy on sexual harassment because people in the church don't want to think about the possibility of their pastor engaging in abusive relationships. Perhaps part of the denial of abusive relationships in the church is not only a problem of pastors, but because few of us want to think about abuse, we enable the denial among our church leaders.

Pastors who take advantage of their congregants or are abusive in other environments may deny abuse occurring within families in their congregations because it hits close to home. Spiritual leaders can and do use their authority for good, but also for harm. How could they be giving sermons or teaching Sunday School lessons on the sins of power and control, or the misuse of authority, when they are engaging in the misuse of authority themselves?

It is not easy to learn about, talk about, and support victims of family violence. We are each affected by stories of abuse differently, and we must each be willing to overcome our personal struggles in order to support those in our congregation. Church leaders must be willing

---

11. Fehlauer, *Exposing Spiritual Abuse*, 13, 15.

12. Jean Dimock, our editor at the House of Prisca and Aquila, was very helpful in raising some of these points, none of which the present chapter is able to discuss as fully or as completely as they no doubt deserve.

to recognize that abuse happens, and be able to hear the stories of their congregants, no matter how terrible. Pastors who themselves experienced abuse must seek help and deal with it completely so that they may be able to move beyond the role of victim into the role of care giver.

Finally, pastors, like others, are sinners who, only through the grace of God and power of the Holy Spirit, can live a sanctified life. Church leaders must hold one another accountable to always use their spiritual authority to heal and never to harm. A system of accountability should be in place in every church and all church leaders should have the power to confront sin they see in one another. Before anyone can help a victim of abuse, they must first be at peace themselves, living out a Godly life as best they can.

HISTORICAL DISTRUST OF SECULAR AGENCIES

One final reason that pastors may have difficulty dealing adequately with the problem of family violence in their congregations may be related to their distrust of making referrals to secular agencies and shelters. In addition to teaching in seminary, I also served for ten years as the executive director of a small (secular) non-profit, and for four years, during the Romney Administration in Massachusetts, was a Commissioner on the Governor's Commission against Sexual and Domestic Violence. In these professional settings, as well as my personal experiences in church, I have come to see how little overlap there seems to be in these different spheres of life. I have noticed that many religious people, particularly conservatives, have difficulty in utilizing the services provided by the secular community. As a consequence, when a congregant brings forth a personal problem, such as lack of a job, problems with housing, problems with education, or even problems with adequately feeding one's children, some pastors do not have the information they need about programs in the community that could adequately help in addressing these problems. For situations in which a congregant seeks help with domestic violence, one study of southern pastors found that less than a third knew where and how to refer domestic violence victims to community resources. In speaking with my students about their lack of information regarding social services and programs in the community, I discovered that this lack of information is not the result of being too lazy to investigate what is available. Rather, it appears to be related Christian leaders' lack of trust of secular social services in general but even more specifically around services that can impact families.

a. Early gains in the fight to help DV victims

During the 1970s the second-wave feminist movement succeeded in establishing shelters for women victims and getting earmarked funding for police training that specifically instructs officers on how to approach situations of domestic violence and respond appropriately to women victims of violence. Government and private funding also became available for domestic violence hotlines, for advocates, and for mental health services for victims of violence. During the early years family violence was primarily considered a *family* problem, and batterers and victims were diverted to family court rather than criminal court for *crisis intervention*.[13] It wasn't until the mid 1970s that this model for handling domestic violence cases started to change. Feminist groups in various cities across the country helped women victims of partner abuse to bring lawsuits against police departments for not treating their assault cases as crimes as they would if the assault had been perpetrated by a stranger. Only then did the criminal justice system begin its long journey towards treating a battered woman as a legitimate victim of assault.[14]

b. Beginnings of the conservative resistance

As the feminist movement progressed, conservatives began organizing to beat back the cultural changes being advanced by the new movements sweeping the country. The religious right was especially concerned with promoting traditional family values and condemning feminist principles that threatened the nuclear family. The Christian right was fearful of those elements in the feminist movement that threatened what they believed to be biblical standards. This movement gained momentum in the 70s and 80s, and its leaders were incredibly influential among young Christians. Thirty years later, the young followers of this movement are now those leading churches across the country and continue

---

13. Dobash and Dobash, *Women, Violence and Social Change*.
14. Ibid.

to teach the conservative values they learned decades ago. The leaders of this conservative Christianity had, therefore, enormous influence both then as well as now over the Christian perspective on the family.

Throughout the 1970s and 1980s the New Christian Right was formed. In many respects, the rise of the Christian Right was an organized response to the feminist movement and other cultural changes occurring at the time. The Christian Right focused on gaining political power in order to influence issues that were seen to undermine traditional family structures, such as the Equal Rights Amendment (ERA). The ERA passed in both congressional houses in 1972 and for nearly a decade a battle raged to ratify the amendment in two-thirds of the states, which eventually failed. In 1973, abortion rights were extended by the Supreme Court in the Roe vs. Wade decision, a battle that continues to play a strong role in the cultural battles of our times. Past and current leaders of the Christian Right, including Jerry Falwell, Pat Robertson, James Dobson, Tim and Beverly LaHaye, and others, have focused their voices on promoting values that they believe underpin the preservation of the traditional nuclear family.

c. Violence against children

A combination of the women's movement and the child's rights movement opened the door on another social taboo: child sexual abuse. For nearly three years in the mid 1980s, I worked as a clinical therapist at a men's prison. As I worked with the men, I was struck by how many of them came from homes in which sexual and/or physical violence was the norm. Many of the men I treated at the prison had been perpetrators of child sexual abuse, something that was still rarely spoken about at that time. Other prisoners were victims of child sexual abuse and naturally, some were both victims and perpetrators.

I remember working with one young man who had been physically abused as a child, had witnessed his mother abused by his step father, and later, while serving in the army, was raped, stabbed, and dangled by his feet outside of a two story window by two other soldiers. During the years I spent at the prison I came to believe that violence in the home seemed to underpin most other violence and crime in society. After leaving the prison I worked on a team of sexual trauma specialists, where we had a waiting list of more than 100 children who had been sexually abused. At the time I started wondering if child sexual abuse was as prevalent as it appeared, or if it was only my job that made me feel that way. I began my own private survey, asking close friends and family if they had ever been sexually abused. My hope had been to discover that it was not as omnipresent as it appeared to be, but unfortunately, the more I asked, the more I found. In fact, just two days ago as I was awaiting the opening of a play, I started speaking to the woman next to me, who was probably in her mid to late 50s. During the conversation she asked what I was writing about and when I told her she confided to me that she had been sexually abused as a child, but her mother still was in denial. I am no longer surprised to hear such stories.

However, it was a decade from when I initially started to work in the field of child sexual abuse and a world-wide scandal in the Catholic Church before society began to understand and accept that the places that are supposed to be the most safe—the home and the church—are actually the places where so much abuse occurs. "All the perpetrator asks is that the bystander do nothing. He appeals to the universal desire to see, hear, and speak no evil. The victim, on the contrary, asks the bystander to share the burden of pain. The victim demands action, engagement, and remembering."[15] Even today many people believe that child sexual abuse is perpetrated by strangers, when in fact most child molesters are family members and friends.[16]

d. Where we are at today in helping women and children victims of abuse

So, with women's groups constantly pushing domestic violence and child abuse to the forefront of legislative agendas across the country, by 1989 the United States had 1200 shelters for battered women and their children, sheltering 300,000 victims per year. Funds to help victims of sexual and domestic violence also came from private foundations and individual donors. In 1994 Congress passed the Violence Against Women Act (VAWA) with bipartisan support, which provided funds

---

15. Herman, *Trauma and Recovery*, 7.
16. Finkelhor, *Child Sexual Abuse: New Theory and Research*.

for agencies providing services for victims of rape and domestic violence and specialized training for police, while also providing for new rights for women victims of gender-based violence.[17] This seminal legislation for women was reauthorized by Congress in 2000 and 2005. However, in the past year Republicans in the House have blocked the 2012 reauthorization of VAWA for the following reasons. First, the (liberal) Senate specifically mentions the protection of gay and transgender Americans while the (conservative) House argued that their version was inclusive and gender neutral and included all those who are gay or transgender—mentioning them specifically was no more necessary than mentioning women specifically. Next, the Senate provision would have allowed Native American women to take those who abuse them to court within the tribal legal system. The Republicans argued that this was unconstitutional and replaced it with a proposal that would allow for Native American women to apply for protection orders from US courts. Finally, the House bill didn't give provision for undocumented, abused women to move toward citizenship by cooperating with the police investigation and the Senate didn't want women to fear deportation. Republicans didn't want amnesty for illegal immigrants.

Secular agencies that help abused women and children may have beliefs and values that differ from clergy and congregations. Secular agencies that help abused women often view the empowerment and safety of women as more important than keeping families together, even when the potential danger is low. They believe that nothing about female humanity is inferior to that of male and therefore men, even husbands, have no entitlement of any kind. Nor do they believe that women were created for any specific role in life or in the home; they are free to choose their own destiny. These ideological differences can create difficulties for clergy who may worry that their congregants will get 'brainwashed' by secular organizations or that their faith will be belittled. Secular agencies also pose a threat to still too many clergy who believe that keeping the family together is more important than the safety of women and children.

Additionally, domestic violence organizations are generally led by women while churches are generally led by men who are viewed as having greater spiritual authority than women. Pastors may not be accustomed to working with women who feel confident in their authority

---

17. Lemon, *Domestic Violence Law*.

as leaders in the work of family violence, and who do not recognize the spiritual authority of the pastor.

With so many plausible reasons for pastors and church leaders having difficulty helping those in their congregations with problems of family violence, how can women who need help find that help within those congregations where spiritual leadership has experienced incomplete training and/or uses Scripture improperly regarding gender equality.

HOW CAN WE MAKE CHANGES?

The variety of issues and barriers discussed herein can only be addressed when those in leadership, whether at seminaries or in congregations, make a commitment to address the issue of family violence in their churches.

What the religious community needs to do better:

- seminaries need to better prepare students.
- pastors and church leaders need to increase their understanding and skills for dealing with these issues.
- those leaders in the church who have suffered from abuse must get the help they need to confront their past and then to use their experience as a means to help others and to heal.
- pastors and other church leaders must do a better job of holding one another accountable for using their authority in a way that harms people in their congregations, whether that be through spiritual abuse, sexual abuse, or mishandling situations of domestic violence.
- pastors and church leaders must reach out more to the secular services available in the community, which would require them to understand the ideological differences and find a middle ground, primarily by getting to know those leaders in these organizations and allowing those leaders to have a better understand of the importance of faith in the life of a victim who is also a Christian.
- these leaders must address the importance of sound theology in respect to gender equality and practice this theology in both the church and community.

Pastors must also find a means to hold themselves accountable for their behavior—something beyond the 'investigations' that occur through the denomination hierarchy, which tend to support both the pastor and the *status quo*. All professional 'helpers,' be they doctors, nurses, teachers, psychologists, social workers, and other professionals, are licensed by state boards that provide individual consumers the right to bring complaints. However, because of the separation of church and state, the state cannot monitor abuses by clergy and congregant complaints are left to the politics of the denominational hierarchy where that exists. In cases of independent churches, congregants are often left with no official route to make a complaint to an objective source. The power in churches always resides with the leaders, not with the people in the pews. Churches are not democracies.

What secular society needs to do better:

Society's way of dealing with the problem has been to emphasize services to victims after the violence has occurred. During my four years on the Governor's Commission for Sexual and Domestic Violence, we were charged with making recommendations to the Governor's budget for programs on these issues. Once a year, the women on the steering committee would spend a day creating budget priorities. Every year the vast majority of the money, if not all of it, was allocated to services for victims, rather than to programs for prevention.

It is natural to prioritize the needs of women and children who have been harmed because their pain and need is obvious. But we are all stuck putting band aids on the problem rather than eradicating the problem. We may have more domestic violence shelters than ever before, but we have as many or more victims than we did ten years ago. The problem is complex because it requires an answer to the questions: Why do men physically and sexually abuse women? Why do men sexually abuse children?

Those who work in secular agencies that help women and children need to change their attitude towards working with the clergy. Just as clergy are distrustful of secular workers, so the workers are distrustful of clergy. These workers, mostly women, must find a way to work with clergy in a way that is respectful of the faith of the women in their congregations. They are the experts in sheltering women and children, know how to treat post traumatic stress syndrome and depression resulting from victimization, and work in child protective services to take children out of abusive homes. But they often know nothing of how to help a woman of faith address her spiritual needs and those of her children in situations of violence. In order to fully help women of faith, these secular workers need the clergy as much as the clergy needs them.

BEGINNING STEPS:

There are many different steps that are important in creating a church environment that supports victims of abuse. Some of these steps include:

- creating a definition of abuse that allows both pastors and congregants to identify abusive situations.
- establishing a protocol for dealing with family violence affecting congregants; and
- providing the training and support to pastors to effectively address situations of family violence within the church.

Once these steps are established, the church can begin to consider more active steps to encourage victims to step forward and to take a clear stand against domestic violence and child abuse.

Creating a definition of abuse is not a simple task, and each church may establish a unique definition that fits with their doctrine. Some key components should be consistent, however. First, every church should state that abuse is when one person exerts power and control over another person. Second, abusive relationships always have a clear victim and perpetrator. Third, abuse can take a variety of forms and does need to include physical violence for it to be an abusive relationship. Finally, abuse in the home is not a "family situation," but one that requires the involvement of the community in order to protect the victim from the perpetrator.

Once a definition is established, the church must create guidelines for how its leaders will handle an abusive situation. It is vital for the church to clearly state that in an abusive relationship, the church will stand behind the victim and condemn the actions of the perpetrator, even if the perpetrator is also a congregant. The church should also create a protocol for ensuring safety, which includes protecting confidentiality between the victim and the pastor. Pastors should refrain from attempting marriage counseling in abusive relationships, as this approach is not only ineffective, since victims are not able to speak freely, but this could jeopardize their safety. Finally, the church's protocol should include collaboration with external agencies that specialize in helping victims of abuse. These agencies are much more prepared to provide the wrap-around services that many victims need and can also guide inexperienced pastors in effectively handling the situation.

While establishing a clear protocol for handling abusive situations is essential, it is not sufficient. Pastors must be trained on how to follow the protocol and handle each step appropriately. Churches can ensure pastor preparation in various ways. They can provide in-house trainings by Christian leaders who have expertise in this area and have worked with victims of violence. They can contact local domestic violence specialists at state and private organizations to train pastors. They can then dialogue about the theological issues where they differ so they can find a way to work together. They can encourage or require pastors to become informed on family violence by reading some of the extensive literature available to them. Finally, they can encourage pastors to take a course at a local college or through a domestic violence agency on the foundations of working with victims of abuse. The United States is not lacking in information or resources for people who would like to learn more about domestic violence, and churches should require that their leaders take advantage of these resources in order to best serve their most vulnerable congregants.

The Church could begin by admitting that the family and sometimes the church is not a safe place for some of their members. They could define abuse such that it will be clear what behaviours should be considered abusive. Examples should be provided but abuse should not be limited by concrete examples because unique situations can come up that may not have been considered previously. Once a church defines abuse, procedures need to be put in place that will guide the victim in knowing how to reach out for help in the church that provides her with safety. Procedures should also be put into place on how to deal with the perpetrator and, when children are involved, how to help the children. Similarly, protocols should be in place that enable a child or a parent to express concerns about child abuse without the alleged perpetrator being present. Churches must know the state laws which may mandate that church workers report child abuse to state child protection workers for further investigation. Finally, all churches should have sexual harassment policies and a safe way for victims to report when church leaders have crossed the line with them.

Not only do policies need to be created but the policies need to be enforced. Victims must always feel safe to report abuse. Each congregation must have members who are trained to understand the basics of family violence and how to help victims decide how to proceed. Anyone who is trained to help in these situations must decline from participating when a conflict of interest exists.

While this won't be foolproof, at least it is a start. Remember, there are Christian experts, denominational examples of protocols, and many books and trainings available for those who will help in these situations. If you would like your church to become more involved in understanding how to help victims of family violence, some of the things you can do are:

- Pray without ceasing.
- Give books on family violence to your pastor and church leaders and meet with them to explain how important it is to be able to help victims of violence.
- Ask if your church has protocols for dealing with situations of violence in the home of congregants or inappropriate behavior on the part of pastors, including sexual harassment. If the church has none or the policies are not specific, talk with your pastor about the need for a better policy.
- Let church leaders know that people in the pews need to know what to do in these situations and that they would welcome such information.
- Support victims in your congregation when you know they need help.
- Set up a Walk against Abuse in your church.

As Christians, we must find the strength to confront the sin of family violence whenever or wherever it occurs. We must be willing to learn about it, to listen to the horror of what the victim has to say, and to learn how to act immediately and correctly in order to get the victim out of harm's way as quickly as possible. We must learn how to better discern truth from lies, to understand when to trust but also to recognize the limits of trust as well. This is especially difficult the better we know and respect the alleged perpetrator. Batterers and child abusers have learned how to manipulate and lie with ease. Furthermore, in Dr. Judith Herman's seminal book on trauma, she writes:

> In order to escape accountability for his crimes, the perpetrator does everything in his power to promote forgetting. Secrecy and silence are the perpetrator's first line of defense. If secrecy fails, the perpetrator attacks the credibility of his victim. If he cannot silence her absolutely, he tries to make sure no one listens. To this end, he marshals an impressive array of arguments, from the most blatant denial to the most sophisticated and elegant rationalizations. After every atrocity one can expect to hear the same predictable apologies: it never happened, the victim lies, the victim exaggerates; the victim brought it upon herself; and in any case it is time to forget the past and move on. The more powerful the perpetrator, the greater is his prerogative to name and define reality, and the more completely his arguments prevail.[18]

Only in the last half century has more and more information become available and more and more women and men have started taking a stand against family violence as well as spiritual abuse and/or sexual harassment by a person in church leadership.

No matter what, we can't give up.

> Then Jesus told his disciples a parable to show them that they should always pray and not give up. He said, "In a certain town there was a judge who neither feared God nor cared about men. And there was a widow in that town who kept coming to him with the plea, "Grant me justice against my adversary."
>
> For some time he refused. But finally he said to himself, "Even though I don't fear God or care about men, yet because this widow keeps bothering me, I will see that she gets justice, so that she won't eventually wear me out with her coming!"
>
> And the Lord said, "Listen to what the unjust judge says. And will not God bring about justice for his chosen ones, who cry out to him day and night? Will he keep putting them off? I tell you, he will see that they get justice, and quickly.[19]

---

18. Herman, *Trauma and Recovery*, 8.
19. Luke 18:1–8a. NIV

BIBLIOGRAPHY

Bronson, P. and A. Merryman. *NurtureShock: New Thinking about Children*. New York: Grand Central Publishing, 2011.

Dobash. R. E. and R. P. Dobash , *Women, Violence and Social Change*, New York: Routledge, 1992.

Fehlauer, M. *Exposing Spiritual Abuse*, Charisma House: Lake Mary, FL: Charisma House, 2001.

Finkelhor, D. *Child Sexual Abuse: New Theory and Research*, Free Press: New York, 1984.

Grenz, S. J. and R. D. Bell. *Betrayal of Trust*, Baker Books: Grand Rapids, MI, 1995.

Herman, J. *Trauma and Recovery*, Basic Books: New York, 1992. http://www.domesticviolence.org/common-myths.

Johnson, D. and J. VanVonderen. *The Subtle Power of Spiritual Abuse*, Bethany House Publishers: Minneapolis, MN, 1991.

Lemon, N.K.D. *Domestic Violence Law, 2nd Ed*. West Group: St. Paul, MN, 2001.

McMullin, S. and N. Nason-Clark. "Seminary Students and Domestic Violence—Applying Sociological Research," In Nason-Clark, N., C. Clark Kroeger, and B. Fisher-Townsend (Eds.), *Responding to Abuse in Christian Homes: A Challenge to Churches and their Leaders*, 231–246. Wipf & Stock: Eugene Oregon, 2011.

Nason-Clark, N. *The Battered Wife*, Westminster John Knox Press: Louisville, KY, 1997.

Salter, A. S. *Predators*, Basic Books: New York, 2003.

PART III
Plan for Action

12

Clergy and the Pastoral Response to Domestic Violence

Understanding the Complexities

Steve McMullin

THIS CHAPTER MIGHT BEST be described as a sympathetic critique of the pastoral response to domestic violence. My interaction with pastors as a sociological researcher, my own twenty-seven years of experience as a pastor, and the interaction I have had with survivors and with community responders has led me to believe that the ability or inability of clergy to address domestic violence effectively and to respond to victims appropriately is affected by many factors. Some of those factors may seem obvious, but there are additional important factors that are less apparent and quite complex.

In my interactions with victims of domestic violence, sadly I have learned that far too often pastors have provided advice that is misinformed, unhelpful, hurtful, or even dangerous and that such advice has done damage not only to the victims but also to the reputation and witness of the Christian church in the wider community. The eagerness of clergy to protect the institution of marriage and to keep families together, coupled with a lack of understanding of the dynamics of family violence, can actually keep domestic violence hidden and prevent victims from finding help and safety. Perpetrators of violence can also coax naïve pastors to be their allies in seeking forgiveness and continuing access to victims. Advocates, shelter workers, and therapists in the community who respond to the needs of religious victims of domestic violence may have come to distrust pastors precisely because survivors have told them of the kinds of inappropriate responses from clergy that have become all too well known among those of us who are involved in addressing and responding to domestic violence.[1]

Such distrust does not help. It may confirm in the minds of such pastors that they are waging a spiritual battle and that secular agencies in the community are undermining marriages. It may make religious victims of violence feel forced to choose between the unhelpful advice of the pastor whom they trust in spiritual matters and the strangers who offer help and safety but who seem not to understand the dynamics of faith and the sacredness and spiritual significance of their marriage vows. Even in the face of continuing and perhaps escalating violence, many such victims are likely to choose to continue in their violent situation rather than disregard the misinformed advice of the pastor. For that reason, it is important that those in the wider community who respond to victims of domestic violence understand that a far better reaction to inappropriate advice and actions from particular clergy is to make the effort to include such pastors as part of the community response.

It is important to say that generally I have found that pastors of both mainline and conservative traditions have expressed that they very much want to respond appropriately and helpfully to the needs of those who have suffered because of domestic violence, but that they (especially evangelical Protestant clergy) do not know how to respond or that they (especially mainline Protestant clergy) do not realize the prevalence of domestic violence within the faith community. While working with the *RAVE* project I have met with many individual pastors and groups of clergy from a wide variety of Christian denominations in both the United States and Canada, and in presentations and in discussions of how clergy can be part of the solution it has been my experience that pastors seem quite genuinely to want to be helpful. However, I often encounter what seem to me to be quite extreme examples of misunderstanding, an obvious lack of training and preparedness, and

---

1. Nason-Clark et al., "Building bridges," 222.

a denial that domestic violence is much of a problem in their own congregation. The complexity of the need for clergy to be better informed about domestic violence among Christian congregations is illustrated by the following specific examples.

DENIAL AMONG MAINLINE CLERGY

I met with the senior pastor of a 1,900-member mainline congregation in the United States to discuss how domestic violence impacts members of the faith community. This seasoned pastor with a doctoral degree responded that he had been the pastor of his congregation for nine years, and that during that time there had not been a single case of domestic violence in his congregation. He then surprised me by asking if I was also meeting with pastors of conservative Protestant churches in his community (which I was). He then explained to me that he believed that domestic violence is a big problem in evangelical congregations because of their conservative theology. He also said that spousal abuse would be unlikely to occur in his mainline congregation because of their high level of education and their liberal theology.

When I asked him about his personal knowledge of the local battered women's shelter, the pastor said that he was aware of it and that the congregation had responded from time to time to appeals for diapers or other supplies, but that he had no first-hand knowledge of the shelter and that he had never had the need to refer anyone, nor did he know of anyone in his congregation who had ever made use of the shelter. He seemed quite satisfied that domestic violence is a problem for "other" churches in less educated communities, but not for his church or for congregations like it. What made this conversation particularly disconcerting for me was the reason why I had chosen to meet with that particular mainline pastor: a social worker with connections at the local battered women's shelter had requested that I arrange to meet with him because several members of his mainline congregation were participants in a local support group for battered women. The women had apparently not disclosed to their pastor that they were victims of domestic violence. In that congregation, domestic violence is kept well hidden. Perhaps the victims know that disclosing their abuse to the pastor would destroy the illusion that liberal theology and education prevent domestic violence from occurring.

I had a similar experience when I was invited by a mainline denominational group to talk about domestic violence in the faith community. About two thirds of the people present at the meeting were female. During the discussion following my presentation, there was no mention of the possibility of violence in the homes of their church members, but several male pastors lectured me about the need to confront conservative pastors and congregations about domestic violence in their midst. None of the women present, some of whom were ordained clergy, said anything during the discussion. Immediately after the meeting ended and the pastors left the room, a queue of women lined up to talk with me about friends whom they know in their own congregations who are suffering because of spousal abuse. Clearly these women had not shared those stories with the pastors who had just left the room.

Studies consistently show that domestic violence does not respect educational or economic or religious boundaries.[2] Such stereotyping of domestic violence as something that happens only in other congregations contributes to two problems: first, pastors remain ignorant of the needs within their own faith community, and second, if they think they will be stereotyped, clergy from particular faith groups may be reticent to participate in training opportunities that would provide some of the guidance they need in order to respond appropriately to an incident of domestic violence. For example, it has been our experience that when RAVE has invited a multi-denominational group of clergy to a training event, evangelical pastors rarely attend unless they already know and trust us, and even then their numbers are few. When we invite only evangelical pastors to attend, they are much more likely to respond to the invitation. When I visit with pastors individually, regardless of their faith tradition, it usually takes only a few minutes to gain their trust. Once they are certain that I have come to provide help instead of criticism, I have consistently found pastors to be willing to listen and to be very appreciative of the online RAVE resources.

One other specific example involved a student at a mainline seminary. When I visited her seminary, she told me that although she was unaware of any victims of abuse in her mainline congregation she had

---

2. Sterling et al., *Understanding Abuse*.

attended a weekend training workshop about responding to domestic violence, and then a week later she had briefly mentioned from the pulpit that she had attended the workshop. She was then shocked to receive multiple requests for advice and help from abused women in the congregation who now considered her to be an expert because she had made reference to her brief training experience. Simply informing the congregation that she had attended a workshop about responding to domestic violence provided the permission needed for victims within that mainline congregation to break their silence and seek her out for practical help and spiritual guidance.

Clergy in mainline congregations need to realize that neither liberal theology nor educational background prevent domestic violence from occurring. By idealizing marriage and denying that domestic violence is happening among their congregants,[3] such clergy may unwittingly perpetuate the message that it is better for victims to suffer in silence than to destroy the illusion that all is well among the congregation's families.

BAD PASTORAL ADVICE FROM CONSERVATIVE CLERGY

In my contacts with clergy in evangelical churches, I have not faced the same resistance to the idea that there are victims of domestic violence in their midst. In many cases, the pastors told me that they are very aware of such situations in church families, and that victims have come to them for help. Instead, the problems among evangelical clergy are directly related to a lack of adequate preparation—not only in terms of how to respond practically to a victim of violence seeking immediate help during a crisis situation, but also in terms of how to relate their theological understandings to the abusive family situations within their congregation. The obvious problem is that precisely because of their lack of training, evangelical pastors may attempt to serve as amateur counselors or therapists rather than make a referral.[4] They may offer marriage counseling to the couple in an abusive relationship, or they may advise the victim to be more obedient to the demands of the abusive spouse, or they may frame the problem in purely spiritual terms by urging prayer and forgiveness and reconciliation without addressing

---

3. Trothen, *Linking Sexuality and Gender,* 129.
4. Nason-Clark et al., "Building bridges," 216.

the abuse. These strategies not only put victims in greater danger and empower the abuser, but they also ignore the dynamics of domestic violence as illustrated by several specific instances in Scripture and they show a poor or overly simplistic understanding of such important theological concepts as repentance and forgiveness. As problematic as bad pastoral advice is, I believe that though it is less obvious, it is this inability of evangelical pastors to understand domestic violence in a proper theological context that is the more serious problem.

This lack of theological understanding and application has two important consequences. First, many evangelical pastors may pride themselves in their emphasis on the high value of marriage and the family and their condemnation of divorce. When faced with a situation where a marriage is not living up to the church's spiritual ideals, such pastors may not be theologically prepared to know how to resolve the conflict between the safety of victims of violence and the church's desire to value marriage as an important social and religious institution. Second, evangelical pastors may be quick to urge that repentance, forgiveness, and reconciliation take place in the face of violence. Once the perpetrator has apologized and expressed regret, the victim is urged to forgive and forget. Such an emphasis plays into the hand of the perpetrator, who is often quite willing to express sorrow and repentance for the violent acts that have been committed. People properly trained to respond to domestic violence realize that an abuser's apology and resolve to change may be quite sincere—abusers typically express genuine remorse for their violent acts and promise not to repeat them—but they also know that problems of power and control run much deeper. Untrained pastors often do not (or will not) understand that a sincere apology is not only an inadequate expression of genuine change, but that it may be an additional strategy to maintain control over the victim: by using the victim's religious faith in order to receive forgiveness, the abuser extends control and makes future abuse even more likely.

Untrained clergy who decide to counsel couples in an abusive relationship may make the mistake of thinking that the marriage or relationship problem is one of anger or of frustration or of miscommunication—believing that once those problems have been "fixed" with counseling or pastoral advice, the abuse will stop. Once again, such a strategy plays into the hand of the abuser, who protests that the victim is the real cause of the violence—that the reason for the abuse was some frustrating act by the victim that enraged the abuser. While the pastor seeks to counsel the couple about strategies for anger management and marital compromise, the abuser is happy to cooperate because anger is seen as the real problem. The real problem, usually not realized by clergy who are inadequately prepared, is power and control. The reason for the abuser's frustration and anger that escalate to violent rage is not an incident in the home—it is the abuser's determination to control the victim.

BARRIERS TO PREPARATION

Our research has clearly documented that pastors and seminarians realize that they are not well prepared to respond to domestic violence.[5] In addition to their unpreparedness due to a lack of adequate training, there are also barriers that then prevent clergy from being adequately prepared. For example, a fear of being criticized may make clergy unwilling to attend workshops and events where they could gain information and insights. That is part of the reason why we offer the RAVE resources online so they can be accessed from the privacy of their study—it is a safe place for clergy to learn.

We know from our research that the lack of training is expressed in a many ways. Many pastors have a poor or a mistaken understanding of what domestic violence is and how prevalent it is, their lack of training often means that perhaps genuine but misguided attempts to be helpful can actually perpetuate the violence, idealistic views of marriage and unhelpful interpretations of Scripture can make clergy blind to the actual dynamics and realities of abuse, and their fear of how the congregation might be affected by the revelation of abuse in one of the church's families can make them want to ignore the problem or to provide a quick fix instead of finding appropriate ways for victims to find help and safety.

Our research has shown that the issue of fear is an important one.[6] Both in focus groups with seminary students and in interviews with pas-

5. Nason-Clark, *The Battered Wife*, 146; McMullin and Nason-Clark, "Seminary students," 234.

6. McMullin and Nason-Clark, "Seminary students," 238ff.

tors, it was repeatedly explained that pastors may find themselves in a quite different position from others who respond to domestic violence. While like others the pastor is called upon to respond to the needs of a victim of abuse, the pastor may also be called up on to respond to the perpetrator as well as to a variety of family members within the same congregation, including the children but sometimes also including the parents and siblings not only of the victim but of the abuser. When the perpetrator is a Sunday School teacher, a choir member, a church board member, or a youth leader, pastors can find themselves in extremely difficult situations, especially in small congregations with a web of family connections.[7] Because abusers may seek positions of power and control in congregations as well as in the home, the perpetrator may be a major financial donor to the congregation or a board member or a member of an influential family, and abusers may be willing to use that power against the pastor. We have heard of pastors who had been fired or otherwise attacked when they attempted to respond to an incident of domestic violence, especially when the perpetrator is a church leader or is closely related to a church leader. Pastors may fear that if they attempt to respond appropriately, it would be a lose-lose-lose situation: the victim may not be protected, the church may be damaged, and the pastor may be dismissed.

The expectation of confidentiality in the pastor's study may make it difficult for clergy to know how to respond. A victim may confide in the pastor about ongoing abuse but may not be ready either to leave or to disclose the abuse to anyone besides the pastor. Imagine being a pastor who has been told by a woman that her husband, who teaches Sunday School every week or serves on the church board, regularly beats and abuses her. Yet for a variety of reasons (such as financial dependency, or fear for her own safety or for the safety of her children if she leaves) that woman is not yet ready to leave the violent home situation and she does not want the pastor to tell anyone else until she has decided what to do.

On the other hand, suppose it has become publicly known that there is an abusive situation in a church family. In some instances the perpetrator of the abuse, while expressing remorse, may ask the pastor for help or support or forgiveness, asking the pastor to talk to his wife and tell her to return home, or to counsel the couple, or to provide spiritual counsel for the perpetrator. A pastor who does not understand

---

7. McMullin and Nason-Clark, "Seminary students," 240.

the cycle of abuse or know how to respond appropriately may unknowingly respond to those requests in very unhelpful and even dangerous ways. In other instances, the perpetrator may publicly frame the family situation quite differently from the way the pastor privately knows to be the truth. Pastors can feel torn between the expectations of confidentiality on the part of the victim and the desire to explain the actual dynamics of the abuse in the face of lies by the perpetrator.

It has been my own experience as a pastor that when a victim does decide to leave a violent relationship, she may ask the pastor to intervene in the life of the perpetrator—hoping that the pastor will be a catalyst for real change in his life.[8] One of the reasons why religious victims stay in an abusive relationship is because they sincerely love the abuser and pray for him to change, and when they choose to leave, they may have high hopes that the pastor will be able to intervene in the abuser's life. An important part of the pastor's ministry to the victim, therefore, is a spiritual ministry to the abuser. The pastor plays a quite different role therefore from others who are concerned mostly or exclusively with the victim.

In response to those needs, on the RAVE website (www.theraveproject.org) our research team has sought to include a wide variety of resources and information for clergy from various traditions. In order for pastors to know how to respond properly to incidents of domestic violence, several issues need to be addressed:

PASTORS DO NOT UNDERSTAND BECAUSE THEY HAVE NOT BEEN ADEQUATELY TRAINED

What is wrong with their seminary training about domestic violence? In most cases, there has been no training. Most denominations and churches do not require it, and the seminaries we have studied provide very little training. Most pastors do not need to be told that they have not been adequately prepared to address or respond to domestic violence—our surveys have demonstrated that most pastors know and readily admit that they are not well prepared to respond to the needs of victims. Many first- and second-year seminary students indicated to us that they expect that they will be well prepared to respond to domestic violence by the time they graduate, but most students in their

---

8. Atkinson and McMullin, "Notes from the pastor's study," 139.

final semester of seminary told us they realize that they are still not well prepared and no longer expect to be well prepared when they graduate.[9] Our study of more than 400 seminary students has made it clear that seminary-trained pastors are not prepared by such education to respond to the needs of victims and their families and that most are unaware of how to refer victims to other qualified professionals or agencies.

It is not that seminaries are not making attempts to train pastors to respond adequately. When we have met with seminary administrators and made presentations to faculty meetings, we have found them to be receptive and even eager for our help and for resources to be made available. Administrators and faculty members have expressed deep concerns about the ill-preparedness of their graduates to respond to the needs of victims of violence. The problem is that there are barriers at seminaries also.

For example, we have discovered in our research that the single most effective strategy for training seminarians is for the students to visit a battered women's shelter and meet with the staff,[10] but seminary professors told us that shelters are not always cooperative. In particular, some shelters refuse to allow male seminary students to visit. Seminary faculty members and administrators also told us of the pressures they feel to squeeze course content requirements into a very restricted time frame. Unrealistic congregational expectations that seminary-trained pastors must be experts in every area of theology and church life means that too much curriculum is squeezed into too little time, and the result is that family violence can easily be ghettoized in the seminary curriculum. Instead of being integrated into courses in Biblical Studies and Theology and Preaching and Youth Ministry and Pastoral Care, a course about domestic violence is usually offered as a stand-alone elective for those few students, mostly those preparing for counseling careers, who are particularly interested in such topics. Meanwhile, family violence is not addressed for the majority of seminary students who will go on to be pastors because the curriculum allows for too few free electives for them to choose such a course. It should also be noted that a considerable number of pastors among evangelical denominations do not have and are not required to have seminary training, which makes

---

9. McMullin and Nason-Clark, "Seminary students," 234.

10. McMullin and Nason-Clark, "Seminary students," 237.

it even less likely that they have been exposed to the kinds of resources and training that might be helpful.

THE IDEALS OF MARRIAGE AND FAMILY

In both mainline and conservative denominations, an idealistic view of marriage and of family relationships may make pastors unwilling to admit that domestic violence is a problem for some families in their congregations. This is not a Scripture problem—the Scriptures provide no illusions about the sinfulness of humanity and the prevalence of violence among religious families (Cain and Abel, Abraham and Hagar, Joseph and his siblings, David's family). There is no shortage of families in the Bible that know the pain of abuse and violence and power and betrayal. But there are powerful forces in the church culture today that serve to hide those troubled aspects of family life in the church. Christian bookstores and websites are filled with books and resources that idealize marriage and family in ways that have little to do with the Scripture s. There are religious organizations whose donation base is dependent on maintaining an idealized version of the Christian family, and those organizations have gained considerable influence in many congregations.

THE MALE PASTOR

Both male and female clergy and seminary students have mentioned their fears and apprehensions about responding to family violence,[11] but it seems that there are challenges that make it more difficult for male pastors. Our seminary study showed that the students who feel least prepared are single males, with married males not far behind.[12] While it is important that male pastors address and respond to domestic violence, the domestic violence community has not always made it easy for men to be partners. I am often the only male in meetings about domestic violence, and I am always in the minority. In those gatherings, there are often loud complaints or sarcastic comments about the lack of men, which of course is quite counterproductive because it leads to fewer men attending the next time.

---

11. McMullin and Nason-Clark, "Seminary students," 238–240.
12. Ibid., 237.

A MISTRUST OF SECULAR AGENCIES BY CLERGY

Some pastors may be concerned about protecting their members from secular influences, and they see secular community agencies and other individuals who are concerned about domestic violence as being spiritually dangerous to their congregants.[13] It may be that sometimes those concerns are justified, but in most cases the problem is that bridges have not been built between the resources in the community and the clergy. Because there are few connections between these important community agencies and the clergy, pastors may not see the resources in the community as resources to which they can turn when they need to make a referral.

A MISPLACED SENSE OF RESPONSIBILITY

Many pastors have a sense that they should be able to provide for all of the needs of the members of their congregations. Such pastors (and perhaps their church leadership also) consider it a failure when they have to depend on outside (especially secular) resources to meet the needs of church members who come to them for help. If they refer a victim to someone outside of their faith tradition, they feel like they have failed both the congregation and the person in need.

ISSUES OF SIN AND FORGIVENESS

Evangelical pastors are usually willing to address and label violence as sin. That is very helpful. However, that may be followed by an immediate push for forgiveness, reconciliation, and a mistaken presumption that the problem has been solved. Once the perpetrator has expressed remorse and the victim has extended forgiveness, the pastor believes that the problem has been solved. From this perspective, domestic violence is seen by the pastor as a sinful episode to be forgotten and forgiven, without any understanding of the complex issues of power and control that underlie the abuse, or of patterns learned by the abuser while perhaps being raised in an abusive home, or of how spiritual language may be misused by the perpetrator to silence the victim. This problem illustrates why it is important that training about domestic violence is integrated with theological preparation.

---

13. Nason-Clark et al., "Building bridges," 219.

On the other hand, mainline pastors may be reticent about labelling problems in the marriage as sin.[14] The desire to maintain the illusion that "those things don't happen in this congregation" may leave the victim to suffer in silence, blaming herself for not being able to live up to the ideals which are expected of church members.

CONFUSION ABOUT CAUSES

Some pastors equate domestic violence with alcohol abuse and think that by addressing alcoholism they are addressing the abuse. While it is certainly true that abuse often takes place when alcohol has been consumed by the abuser, domestic violence is not the same as alcohol abuse. They are two problems, and they may be related in some ways—people may be abusive when they drink, and they may drink when they know they have been abusive. Sometimes the partner of someone who drinks becomes abusive, either against the person who has been drinking or against the children. However, addressing alcoholism is not sufficient for addressing the abuse. Many people are not abusive when they are drinking, and many perpetrators are abusive when they have not been drinking, though they may seek to use alcohol as an excuse for their violence.

As has already been mentioned, some pastors may equate domestic violence with anger and frustration, or with marital problems, without understanding the deeper issues of power and control that more adequately explain the violence. In healthy relationships, anger does not lead to violence.

"IT IS NOT MY GIFT"

Some pastors would say that they are not counselors; that their job is to preach the good news and to lead the church and to provide vision and Biblical teaching and spiritual leadership. They may hope that another congregation in the community or area would offer ministries to victims of domestic violence so they do not have to address the issue. The problem of course is that all congregations are affected by domestic violence, and victims need to know that their pastor will respond to their spiritual needs when they seek help.

---

14. Trothen, *Linking Sexuality and Gender*, 129.

Even more seriously, such pastors may see the response to domestic violence as a very limited aspect of ministry, because they don't see a link between domestic violence and the wider mission of the church. This is a problem on several levels. It means that clergy may see a response to domestic violence as a good thing, but optional. It affects their understanding of pastoral care, which they see as an extra service that churches may or may not offer, as opposed to such ministry as a necessary aspect of the discipleship process in a congregation where people's lives are affected by sin.

Such a minimized understanding of the role pastoral care is not necessarily the fault of the pastor. Expectations of church leadership have changed—many pastors are expected to act like the congregation's CEO, and the pastor is expected to provide ministries for members as if those ministries were consumer products. In such a secularized church environment, spiritual aspects of community and care can be thwarted by the pressures of performance that are placed on pastors who are expected to lead the congregation to ever-increasing numbers of people and more generous offerings.

DOMESTIC VIOLENCE AND THE MISSION OF THE CHURCH

Because of its pervasiveness both in society and among families in congregations, in each church and in the mind and heart of each pastor the response to domestic violence should be seen as a vital aspect of the church's mission. The strategy to make that happen is not to make the response to domestic violence the central aspect of church life. In fact, advocating for such a strategy would be counterproductive because pastors would push back: they know that the mission of the church must encompass all of the members and the entire community to whom the church ministers, not only those who are abused. Instead, it is important to provide a clear link between domestic violence and the church's overall mission. When I am addressing pastors, I always try to link the pastor's response to domestic violence to the church's witness in the community and to the importance of justice. In both evangelical and mainline congregations, witness and justice are central to an understanding of the overall mission of the church.

PASTORS FEEL LEFT OUT OF THE COMMUNITY RESPONSE BECAUSE OFTEN THEY ARE

The community needs to so some of the work of building bridges—it is not only the responsibility of churches and clergy. Rather than complaining about the response of churches and clergy, community responders can seek to collaborate with clergy. I have talked with pastors who have tried to make connections with the local shelter, and the response has been unenthusiastic except for soliciting donations from the church. When a victim is part of a congregation, it would be very helpful for the pastor to be part of the team of people who are responding, and that means developing that team relationship before the response begins. When community responders know and understand the pastor, trust can be built among people.

Such collaboration may not always happen easily, but it is worth the effort. When I first became involved in a community response to domestic violence, I had no training or expertise—that is why I wanted to get involved—and I was sincere in my desire to learn and to be part of the solution. Unfortunately, it took six months of dogged work and considerable grace on my part. While I was sitting at the table I often had to endure negative comments about clergy and snide remarks about men. I did not remain a member of that group because I was so enjoying the experience of being rejected, but because I believed that it was important for me to learn how serious the problem was in our community and how it was affecting people in our congregation, and I was determined to find partners in the community so that we could respond effectively together.

If we want pastors to understand, we must make room for them at the table and we must welcome them with their faults and with their misunderstandings and with their lack of training. They do not need to be lectured; they need to be trained. If pastors are to be part of the solution, they must be welcomed at the table. Until they are, the church will continue to be a place where domestic violence takes its toll.

WAYS THAT CLERGY CAN RESPOND

Pastors have an important role to play in the response to domestic violence. That role is not to replace therapists or shelters or community agencies that in most cases are much better trained and equipped to respond to the violence. Instead, the pastor should play a vital role in providing spiritual care and Biblical guidance throughout the process of healing and in providing a safe and caring environment within the congregational setting. By addressing and condemning domestic violence from the pulpit, by offering resources for victims including information about community agencies that the pastor can recommend, and by educating the congregation and its ministry leaders about the prevalence of domestic violence, the pastor breaks the illusion that church marriages and church families must pretend to be perfect and gives permission for victims to seek help.

When religious victims of violence seek help, and especially if they choose to seek refuge from the violence and even to leave the violent relationship, they will need much spiritual support from their pastor and from their church community. Throughout the process of change that the victim will face, the pastor can offer prayer and scriptural guidance. The pastor can also help to establish and encourage support networks within the congregation so that survivors of violence do not feel that they are alone. Some very practical help from the congregation may be needed by victims who are seeking to escape the violence, things like clothing and food and financial assistance or finding employment. In some cases where perpetrators have socially isolated their spouses for years, the pastor can seek to facilitate new social ties for victims, especially including ties that are not based on their status as a survivor of abuse.

CONCLUSION

As a sympathetic critique of the pastoral response to domestic violence, this chapter has outlined ways that clergy have often failed to provide the kind of response that religious victims have needed, while at the same time this chapter has argued that pastors can and should play a key role in the response to abuse. By developing the RAVE website, our research team seeks to educate pastors about domestic violence and to equip them to respond appropriately by providing needed pastoral care and appropriate referrals. We have also begun to partner with seminaries in order to better understand how best to prepare ministry students for the realities of domestic violence that they will face in the pastorate.

There is progress. There is a greater awareness of domestic violence both in society and in congregations, and there is an awareness among pastors that they are not well-equipped to respond. Still needed are coordinated ways to provide both practical and theological training for pastors so that they can both address the violence and respond appropriately, and ways to facilitate more and better partnerships between clergy and community agencies.

BIBLIOGRAPHY

Atkinson, T. and S. McMullin. Notes from the Pastor's study" in *Responding to Abuse in Christian Homes*, edited by N. Nason-Clark, C. Clark Kroeger, and B. Fisher-Townsend, 138–146. Eugene, OR: Wipf and Stock, 2011.

McMullin, S. and N. Nason-Clark. "Seminary students and domestic violence—applying sociological research" in *Responding to Abuse in Christian Homes*, edited by N. Nason-Clark, C. Clark Kroeger, and B. Fisher-Townsend, 231–246. Eugene, OR: Wipf and Stock, 2011.

Nason-Clark, N. *The Battered Wife*. Louisville: Westminster John Knox, 1997.

Nason-Clark, N., S. McMullin, Fahlberg, V., and Schaefer, D. (2011). "Building bridges between clergy and community-based professionals" in *Responding to Abuse in Christian Homes*, edited by N. Nason-Clark, C. ClarkKroeger, and B. Fisher-Townsend, 215–230. Eugene, OR: Wipf and Stock, 2011.

Sterling, M. L., C.A.Cameron, Nason-Clark, N., and Miedema, B. *Understanding Abuse: Partnering for Change*. Toronto: University of Toronto Press, 2004.

Trothen, T. J. *Linking Sexuality and Gender: Naming Violence against Women in the United Church of Canada*. Waterloo, ON: Wilfred Laurier University Press, 2003.

13

Preparing Congregations for Collaborative Work

The Role of the Mennonite Central Committee in Strengthening Families

Linda Gehman Peachey and Elsie Goerzen

MENNONITE CENTRAL COMMITTEE: RELIEF, DEVELOPMENT, AND PEACE IN THE NAME OF CHRIST

MENNONITE CENTRAL COMMITTEE (MCC), a worldwide ministry of Anabaptist churches, shares God's love and compassion for all by responding to basic human needs and working for peace and justice. MCC envisions communities worldwide in right relationship with God, one another, and creation.

MCC's priorities in carrying out its purpose are disaster relief, sustainable community development, and justice and peace-building.[1] For over 90 years, it has partnered with churches and local communities to respond to the suffering caused by war, injustice, and natural disasters. As a ministry of Mennonite/Anabaptist denominations known historically as "Peace Churches," MCC has upheld a special commitment to peace and nonviolence. Nevertheless, these churches and its institutions have been slower to recognize the reality of violence within, and have struggled to articulate a theology of peace,

---

1. http://www.mcc.org/purpose-vision-statements.

which is life-giving to all, especially to those who are most vulnerable. It is in this context that MCC addresses the issues of violence and abuse in the home. In fact, the genesis of the Women's Concerns desk at MCC grew out of a challenge from women that peacemaking must focus not only on international issues and conscientious objection to war, but also address discrimination against women, as well as violence in Anabaptist homes and churches. Otherwise, the church's public witness on peace and nonviolence has little integrity. Words and deeds must be consistent.

This chapter will therefore address the reality of violence in this community of faith, some of MCC's work with churches and communities to respond to these realities, and finally theological questions which need further attention.

PART ONE: THE REALITY OF VIOLENCE IN MENNONITE HOMES AND CHURCHES

The reality of sexual violation

Tragically, in 2007, there were more than 600 sexual assaults on average per day in the United States. Women are eighteen times more likely to be victimized than men.[2]

Peace churches are not immune from this violence. In 2006, an Anabaptist research center conducted a Church Member Profile, which included a question related to "sexual abuse or violation." According to this study, 21 percent of women in Mennonite Church USA and 5.6 percent of men experienced "sexual abuse or violation," with most of this occurring when they were a child or teenager. This means that in a congregation of one hundred members (fifty women/fifty men) there are likely more than ten women and two men who have experienced sexual violation.[3]

One Mennonite woman described her abuse this way:

---

2. *The facts on Domestic, Dating and Sexual Violence,* Family Violence Prevention Fund, at http://endabuse.org/content/action_center/detail/754.

3. This study was conducted by the Young Center for the Study of Anabaptist and Pietist Groups at Elizabethtown College (PA) and included responses from a representative sample of 2216 Mennonite Church USA members and 685 Brethren in Christ members. The analysis was done by C. L. Kanagy, and paid for by the MCC US Women's Advocacy Program.

> I was groomed to accept verbal, physical and sexual abuse over a long period of time. So when the rape happened at age twelve by my brother it was just a slight alteration from the normal pattern.... Over the course of my young life I learned to accept inappropriate sexual touching from my grandfather, father, and brothers, punishment for things I did not do, and unexpected and unexplained violent outbursts from my father. I worked hard to become smaller and smaller so I would not be noticed and mistaken for a target. Many years later I discovered that the times I was not targeted the abuse was aimed at my younger siblings. No matter what I did, I couldn't stop it.[4]

Women in marginalized groups are even more vulnerable, since they are often afraid to call for help or use social services. For instance, immigrant women can be violated by abusive employers because they fear being deported. Even when they have a legitimate work visa, it is tied to a particular employer, so that a woman cannot leave her workplace without risking her immigration status. This can lead to situations of sexual servitude, or even the selling of women to others as prostitutes.[5]

Young women who run away from home are also in danger. Sometimes they run away to escape abuse from family members. Whatever the reason, pimps look out for these girls, pretend to befriend them, and then lock them up and force them into prostitution or sell them to others.[6] But the problem is not just in homes. It also exists in the church. In 2008, the Social Work program of Baylor University conducted a national, random survey on clergy sexual misconduct with over 3,500 respondents. They found that more than 3 percent of women who had attended a congregation in the past month reported they had been the object of clergy sexual misconduct at some time in their adult lives.[7] This means that in a congregation with at least thirty-five women,

---

4. From "Surviving my Childhood—Katherine's Story," http://abuse.mcc.org/family-violence/child-abuse/child-abuse-stories#Katherine.

5. Immigration Policy Center, at http://www.immigrationpolicy.org/special-reports/reforming-americas-immigration-laws-womans-struggle#danger, *Exploitation in the Workplace* section.

6. Kristof, "Seduction, Slavery and Sex," New York Times, July 15, 2010.

7. Clergy Sexual Misconduct Study; see http://www.baylor.edu/clergysexualmisconduct/.

there will likely be at least one who has experienced an inappropriate sexual advance by a pastor or leader.

The reality of abuse by an intimate partner

On average, more than three women are murdered by their husbands or boyfriends every day in the United States.[8] At least one-fourth of all women report violence by a current or former intimate partner.[9] Dating violence is also an increasing problem: one in three adolescent girls is a victim of physical or emotional abuse from a dating partner.[10] According to Dr. Nancy Nason-Clark, the incidence of abuse in Christian homes is similar to general society; the only difference is that Christian women tend to remain in an abusive relationship longer.[11] Men also report intimate partner violence, but women make up 85 percent of victims, and their injuries are generally more severe and life-threatening.[12] A Mennonite woman described her experience this way:

> Whenever people share a living space they run into little problems. . . . These are things you can talk about, problems you can solve together. But in our house the problems would not be solved. . . . His anger and his criticism of me would grow. I would try harder to please him but he would not be soothed. . . . Once he threw his brush at me in anger and accused me of breaking it. He threw his plate when he didn't like what I had fixed for dinner. . . . Physical and verbal abuse became a regular pattern. He would grab me or push me if he thought I wasn't listening to him. He would throw things and tell me that I was a lousy wife or mother or housekeeper. . . . A beating is a hard thing to describe. It's a hard thing to remember, not because the memories have faded, but because they are so clear and painful. I felt an inexpressible fear, my arms pinned immobile to a bed by the knees of the man I loved, his fist coming toward my face. I have looked in the mirror and not recognized myself. . . .

---

8. *The Facts on Domestic, Dating and Sexual Violence*, Family Violence Prevention Fund, at http://www.endabuse.org/content/action_center/detail/754.

9. Centers for Disease Control and Prevention, 2008, at http://www.cdc.gov/mmwr/preview/mmwrhtml/mm5705a1.htm.

10. *The Facts on Domestic, Dating and Sexual Violence*, Futures Without Violence, at http://www.endabuse.org/content/action_center/detail/754.

11. See Nason-Clark and Kroeger. *Refuge from Abuse* and *No Place for Abuse*, 2010.

12. *Family Violence in Canada* and *Family Violence Statistics*.

> I finally realized that I was living in a kind of hell, and that it surely couldn't be God's will for anyone to live like this. So I ran away, to the Crisis Intervention Centre in my town. That's where I began to learn to be alive again.... No one deserves to be abused and submitting to such abuse is not the way for us to be God's peacemakers."[13]

The consequences of this violence are severe, not only emotionally, physically and spiritually, but also in terms of major disease. Women who have experienced domestic violence are 80 percent more likely to have a stroke, 70 percent more likely to have heart disease, 60 percent more likely to have asthma, and 70 percent more likely to drink heavily than women who have not experienced intimate partner violence.[14]

The reality of child abuse

In 2008, 1,740 children in the United States died as a result of abuse or neglect, over four per day, and three-quarters were less than four years old.[15] This too is a problem in the church. Although there is no specific data, the 2006 Church Member Profile indicated that only 7 percent of Mennonite Church USA members believe that spanking children is always wrong. This compares to 25 percent who felt that "copying a music CD for a friend" is always wrong and 38 percent who would not buy "government lottery tickets."[16] A church which preaches peace and even love for enemies needs to ask how it can be so comfortable with physical punishment of vulnerable children.

One woman wrote:

> Was what I did so bad that I deserved all that anger vented on me? I was only a child and I believed that I was that bad.... Dad would often go into quiet spells for one or two weeks.... Mom was often told she had turned us kids against him, that her perms were sinful, that she spent too much money on unimportant things....

---

13. From an anonymous story.

14. Center for Disease Control and Prevention. http://www.cdc.gov/mmwr/preview/mmwrhtml/mm5705a1.htm.

15. Child Maltreatment 2008 report.

16. Kanagy, *Road Signs for the Journey*, 169.

> I tried to reason that the strappings, the fights, whatever my dad ... did was right because he said he was a Christian and that he loved us. It must be okay for my dad to kick us, bruise us with the strap for whatever reason, or manipulate and humiliate us to the point where we did what he wanted, because 'it was God's will.'[17]

PART TWO: MENNONITE CENTRAL COMMITTEE'S WORK TO STRENGTHEN FAMILIES

Mennonite Central Committee has responded to these realities by collaborating with churches to strengthen families, focusing on all three of its priorities of "relief, development, and peace." The *Abuse Response and Prevention Program* of MCC British Columbia (MCC BC) provides a good example of this work, as it addresses domestic violence and abuse in church families at the local level, as well as through the network of MCC workers in other parts of Canada and the US.

Providing relief

The woman who comes to this program has somehow realized that what she is experiencing in her home is abuse. She may have been referred by her pastor, a victim services worker in the community, a counselor, or a friend who has some knowledge about abuse. She may have picked up the MCC brochure *Home Shouldn't be a Place That Hurts*.[18] The primary role of the program is to provide her with relief from the burden of carrying the responsibility for the behavior of the person who is abusive to her. This is done in several ways: through meeting her for coffee and providing her with a space to tell her story, as well as giving her some resources.

The primary resource is the book *When Love Hurts*[19], written by Karen McAndless-Davis and Jill Cory. Almost every woman responds to the information in the book by saying something like: "I looked around while I was reading; I felt like someone had been in my house watching what had been happening to me." That sense of being un-

---

17. From an Anonymous Child Abuse story.

18. Brochure available free in English, Spanish, German, French, Chinese, Swahili from http://resources.mcc.org/content/home-shouldn't-be-place-hurts-brochure.

19. Cory and McAndless-Davis, *When Love Hurts*.

derstood provides a huge relief, learning that she is not alone in this frightening journey and that it is not her fault.

In addition to hearing her story and providing written materials, practical resources are also offered. For some women, leaving the abusive home is the only option for safety for herself and for her children. Women often say they feel like refugees. One woman said, "I don't even have a fork of my own." In these situations, MCC BC's Rent Assistance Program has enabled women to move from an unsafe environment to safety. MCC Thrift Shops offer free basics for setting up a household. In some situations, churches help to cover costs of relocation and settlement.

Women are also invited to join a ten week *When Love Hurts* support group, joining other women in the journey of understanding the crazy-making experiences she has been going through, in most cases for many years. The sense of relief experienced in the group is described by some of the comments women make at the end of the ten weeks:

- "It is helpful to realize that I am not alone. Others walk this path too."
- "Being in this group has literally saved my life—physically and spiritually."
- "I was free to go to the depths of pain and grief because it was safe and there was care provided."
- "*When Love Hurts* is a place to which you can carry your wounded self and find healing, burdens released and acceptance by those who truly understand."
- "At long last I had a voice—and you all understood the painful and lonely life I'd been living for forty-one years."
- "This group has helped to restore my relationship with God."
- "I began to understand the depth of how emotional abuse had affected me. This group has educated and equipped me to make better decisions, and given me courage and clarity of mind. I'm not crazy; I will be OK."[20]

After women have completed the first ten weeks, they have the option of joining a second ten week group: *When Love Hurts, Phase*

---

20. Quotes from Evaluations participants fill out after the *When Love Hurts* sessions complete.

Two. Further healing takes place in Phase Two. The themes for the sessions are the issues the women choose to work on. These usually include boundaries, forgiveness, managing anger, supporting children who have been impacted by the abuse, understanding how scripture can be misused, self-care, healthy relationships, and more.

Further growth takes place, and friendships are forged. There is healing in being supported, and also in giving support to other women.

All these aspects of the work of MCC BC that support the Abuse Response and Prevention Program are funded and supported by the wider Mennonite Church community. In addition, partnering with other community agencies gives strength to the program. Participating in inter-agency committees that ensure a coordinated response to women's safety creates connections that enhance the work of MCC. Referrals are made to assist women in gaining access to other support services, counselors, and places of safety. These other agencies also refer women they encounter in their work to the MCC Abuse Response and Prevention Program.

Development of healthy families and communities through awareness and education

As awareness of the reality of abuse grows in the Mennonite faith community, opportunities for education are welcomed. There are a number of ways to develop capacity to respond helpfully when disclosures of abuse are made within the church setting.

Publications and website

Publications have been an effective way to distribute materials to churches across Canada and the US. These have been developed collaboratively by the MCC Abuse Network, comprised of several staff in Canada and the US. Telephone conference calls and emails have been the primary mode of working together.

The thirty-two page booklet *Abuse: Response and Prevention: A Guide for Church Leaders*[21] is available free from Mennonite Central Committee, and was sent to all Mennonite Churches in Canada and

---

21. Available free from http://resources.mcc.org/content/abuse-response-and-prevention or as a pdf download from abuse.mcc.org/system/files/page/2011/08/Abusepercent20Responsepercent20bookletpercent202010.pdf.

many in the US when it was first produced in 2008. This guide is now available in English, Spanish and German.

Copies of *Home Shouldn't be a Place That Hurts*, the brochure referred to earlier, is also distributed free to any church or agency that requests them. Holders are also supplied to enable the church to place the brochures in washroom stalls, for safety and anonymity. Churches are encouraged to place the brochures in men's washrooms as well as women's.

Another excellent MCC resource, the thirty-six page booklet *Created Equal: Women and Men in the Image of God*[22] by Linda Gehman Peachey, promotes Biblical equality and mutuality between women and men. This booklet helps congregations rethink assumed beliefs of male dominance in leadership in the church and home. Research shows that 81 percent of couples in egalitarian marriages, where power is shared, consider themselves to be "happily married," whereas 82 percent of couples where both perceive their relationship to be "traditional" and the husband is in authority over the wife, considered themselves to be "mainly unhappy."[23]

Understanding Sexual Abuse by a Church Leader or Caregiver,[24] a thirty-eight page booklet, was revised and updated in 2011 by the MCC Abuse Network to address misuse of power in the church family and prevent clergy sexual misconduct, and is also available free.

The MCC Abuse Response and Prevention website[25] provides information and stories to support those experiencing abuse in relationship, as well as professionals and others responding to situations of domestic violence and abuse. All forms of abuse are addressed: intimate partner violence and abuse, child abuse, elder abuse, sexual abuse, and professional sexual misconduct. Worship resources and prevention tools for churches are offered. New articles and stories are added regularly.

22. Available free from http://resources.mcc.org/content/created-equal-women-and-men-image-god, or as a pdf download from bc.mcc.org/system/files/reference/47/Createdpercent20Equal.pdf.

23. Survey published in *Priscilla Papers*, Winter 2005, conducted by Olson through University of Minnesota, 2000, based on 21,501 married couples.

24. Available free from http://resources.mcc.org/content/understanding-sexual-abuse-church-leader-or-caregiver or as a pdf download from abuse.mcc.org/system/files/page/understandingpercent20sexualpercent20abusepercent20bypercent20apercent20churchpercent20leader.pdf.

25. http://abuse.mcc.org.

Training and workshops

Regular workshops and training events are offered through MCC BC, often in collaboration with other agencies and institutions. The workshop 'Relationships With Integrity' is provided to persons in pastoral leadership roles, addressing right use of power in the church and home. 'Sexual Ethics,' a one credit course required for graduation at Columbia Bible College in Abbotsford, BC, is taught several times a year, and addresses abuse of power in the church and home.

'Understanding Abuse in Relationships,' an annual two-day training event offered by MCC BC, equips counselors, pastors, advocates, and shelter workers to respond more effectively to those suffering abuse by their intimate partner, as well as to those misusing power in abusive ways. A third day of facilitation training is offered for those interested in becoming qualified facilitators of *When Love Hurts* groups. Following this training, learning facilitators observe *When Love Hurts* group, and then participate in a second group, taking more responsibility in leading the group under the guidance of a fully qualified facilitator. *When Love Hurts* facilitators then become part of a network that meets twice a year for encouragement, supervision, and skill development. Karen McAndless-Davis, co-author of the book *When Love Hurts: Understanding Abuse in Relationships,* leads these meetings, which are hosted by the MCC BC Abuse Response and Prevention Program. Most of these facilitators are volunteers.

Conferences

The Abuse Response and Prevention Program participated in sponsoring and planning the Fifth Conference of Peace and Safety in the Christian Home. 'Emerging from the Shadows: loving, reflecting and pursuing justice together' which took place May 12–15, 2011. 195 people from many parts of the US and Canada, as well as from other parts of the world, gathered in Abbotsford, BC to consider ways of bringing healing to families impacted by abuse and to equip pastors, counselors, advocates and others who support those families. Fifty pastors came to a breakfast to hear Dr. Nancy Nason-Clark speak about the reality of abuse in Christian homes.

Following the conference, the local organizing committee met to determine what the next steps should be in promoting peace and safety in the Christian home at the local level. Two themes emerged from the discussion: the need to establish faith-based groups for men who have abused and the need for seminary education on domestic abuse and violence.

MCC BC and WINGS[26] Fellowship Ministries are collaborating to establish faith-based support and accountability groups for men who wish to address their abuse of power and learn healthier ways of being in relationship. A steering committee is giving guidance to this process, and curriculum has been developed by several professionals who have over twenty years experience working with men who misuse power. Eleven counselors and restorative justice workers have been trained by the curriculum developers for facilitation of these groups.

The ACTS[27] Seminaries Executive Certificate Program was launched at the May 2011 PASCH Conference. 'Domestic Violence and Abuse in the Christian Home,' a twelve credit course designed by Dr. Catherine Clark Kroeger in 2009, is being delivered by course mentors Lorrie Wasyliw of WINGS Fellowship Ministries, and Elsie Goerzen, MCC BC Abuse Response and Prevention Program.

Other MCC programs addressing domestic violence and abuse

Voices for Non-Violence (VNV) is a program of MCC Manitoba, that serves as a resource to faith communities and individuals by promoting positive family life and empowering individuals and groups to respond effectively to domestic violence and abuse. VNV raises awareness about abuse through workshops and presentations in churches, support groups, consultations and referrals.[28]

MCC Ontario coordinates the Sexual Misconduct and Abuse Response Resource Team (SMARRT), a cooperative resource of several Mennonite denominations. SMARRT offers services and support for persons and congregations in constituent conferences who find themselves in the midst of sexual misconduct or abuse.[29]

The Restorative Justice Program of MCC US works to respond to and prevent violence and sexual abuse in families and communities,

---

26. Women In Need Gaining Strength (WINGS) is an arm of the Pacific District of Fellowship Baptist Churches.

27. Associated Canadian Theological Schools (ACTS) is located at Trinity Western University, Langley, BC.

28. http://manitoba.mcc.org/programs/vnv.

29. http://ontario.mcc.org/restorative/smarrt

to support healing, and to promote mutuality through biblical reflection and practices which create life-giving spaces in communities.[30] The program offers consultation, referrals, presentations, training, and written resources.

MCC British Columbia, MCC Manitoba, MCC Ontario, and MCC United States collaborate together as the MCC Abuse Network.[31]

Peace and safety in the Christian home

The peace theology of the Anabaptist churches that form the constituency of Mennonite Central Committee gives a call to reject violence. Yet it also requires that power be acknowledged and used for the well-being of others. Power must be used to resist evil and violence as Jesus did. James 4:17 insists, "Anyone then, who knows the right thing to do and fails to do it, commits sin."[32]

The focus in Part Two of this chapter has been how the MCC Abuse Network collaborates to provide educational materials and resources, and how MCC BC collaborates with the church at the local level in addressing intimate partner abuse. There is much additional work to be done in the other two areas of abuse named earlier: sexual violation and child abuse in church families.

Several principles help to promote peace and prevent violence of any kind, making homes and churches safer for those with less power. How God is understood in churches and homes must be considered. Having only images of God as judge, king, omnipotent, and sovereign may be dangerous, as these images can be used to justify the misuse of power over others. It is important to also use Biblical images of God which are nurturing and life-giving, such as light, healer, redeemer, mother eagle, midwife, shepherd, guide, comforter, advocate, sustainer, and shelter.[33] Abuse happens when those with more power believe they have the right to control and manipulate those who are considered weaker or less worthy.

In addition, promoting equality and mutuality in marriage relationships will strengthen families and create more safety and peace in homes. Including women in all positions of leadership in the church

30. http://us.mcc.org/programs/restorativejustice
31. http://abuse.mcc.org
32. *Abuse: Response and Prevention*, 11.
33. Ibid, 12.

brings balance to decision-making and shared wisdom between men and women, for the well-being of the entire church family, both collectively and in the individual families of the church.

Teaching children healthy boundaries and ownership of their bodies, the temple of God, can do a great deal to prevent child abuse and sexual violation. Excellent curriculum is available through the Dove's Nest website,[34] a Christian network formed to equip faith communities to keep children and youth safe in homes, churches and communities.

Youth groups can use curriculum that explores the characteristics of healthy relationships and teaches warning signs of abuse of power in relationship. Women who come to *When Love Hurts* often comment that youth need to be given the information they are gaining in the group, before decisions are made that have long-term consequences.

Jesus gives a model for right use of power in Matt 18. His strong words in verses 1–6 to those who would harm the little ones, those with less power, must be taken seriously. Further, the model set out for community confrontation and accountability in verses 15–20 is meant for situations where a person in the community has been seriously harmed by another. As Ched Myers and Elaine Enns explain,[35] this process is designed to empower victims and their moral authority, and marshal ". . . the support and accompaniment of the whole community. . ." in seeking justice and restoration.[36]

When a person experiencing abuse by her partner comes to the church for support, this model can guide the process of response, holding the one who has harmed her to account, and providing safety and support to her and to her children. This process can offer hope for healing from the wounds of abuse, and hopefully bring about repentance in the heart of the one who has done the harm.

PART THREE: FORGING AN UNDERSTANDING OF PEACE FOR VICTIMS OF DOMESTIC VIOLENCE AND ABUSE[37]

As described above, MCC workers and church leaders have done much to provide relief and provide resources to build healthy, peaceful fami-

---

34. http://dovesnest.net.
35. Myers and Enns, *Ambassadors of Reconciliation*, 65–71.
36. Ibid, 66.
37. From a paper presented by Linda Gehman Peachey at *Emerging From the Shadows*, May 12–15, 2011, Abbotsford, British Columbia.

lies and communities. In the process, the traditional emphasis on peace has been both helpful and problematic. On the one hand, it is a great resource in that these churches teach and try to practice peace. But there are also difficulties, in that these beliefs have often been formulated and taught by powerful leaders, who have not always been aware of the experiences of victims of violence and those who are most vulnerable in our communities. Many have had to ask how Anabaptist peace theology addresses the realities of abuse described earlier.

Following are some of these challenges. This is not comprehensive, but rather an illustration of many o the essential issues that need to be confronted more carefully.

The emphasis on suffering and the cross

Growing up in the Mennonite Church, one hears over and over that a Christian must "take up their cross" and follow Jesus; one should be willing to suffer harm rather than defend oneself against violence; one must love enemies and do good to those who mistreat others.

Unfortunately, this emphasis on suffering love has too often led to passivity in the face of evil. It may encourage victims of violence and evil to simply "bear their cross" rather than seek safety and justice. It may glorify sacrifice and even death rather than promote the life and wholeness God intends for all. This is especially true for women, who over the generations have been told to bear a "cross" of abuse from their husbands or other family members.

For instance, listen to this voice:

> I am a survivor of childhood sexual abuse. The man who abused me attended our church. My father was the pastor. When I came to the church with my story many years later and asked for help in my healing process, I was treated as a threat, a liability and a nuisance. I was asked to share a story of healing and victory. The man who had abused me was sheltered by the church institution. I was instructed in the various techniques of forgiveness and "moving on." I was even told that everyone was called to suffer, and that included me."[38]

---

38. From "Through a Clouded Glass" at: http://abuse.mcc.org/family-violence/child-abuse/child-abuse-stories#Glass.

What then did Jesus mean by urging believers to "take up their cross?" What should be done in the face of evil and violence? Here it is important to affirm several truths.

First, taking up the cross does not mean meek submission to evil. Jesus was not passive in the face of injustice and violence. He was active and assertive. That is why he was crucified. His actions and preaching threatened the ruling authorities and their control over the people. The cross did not result from timidity but from resistance to evil. Secondly, suffering itself is not redemptive. Suffering is not God's will, not for anyone. Indeed, by raising Jesus from the dead, God acted to undermine such violence. The resurrection affirmed that it was not Jesus who disobeyed God's will, but those who tried to silence him, those who sought to punish him.

The resurrection also provides assurance that God desires healing and life, and promises to be with each person even through the most difficult times. This is what is redemptive. It is not suffering but God's love that has the power to bring good out of distress, healing out of pain, redemption out of sin, resurrection out of death. Still, God does not guarantee one's safety. God desires that everyone be safe and whole, yet does not always intervene, does not always rescue people from danger. Herein lies a profound paradox. Choosing life may involve risks. One may feel called to leave what is familiar and face the unknown, or be led to challenge evil and its power over oneself or others. This is what Jesus meant in urging his followers to "deny themselves and take up their cross" (Mark 8:34–37). It is not that one should seek suffering and death but that there be courage and freedom to follow God's call, even in the face of danger. That God can be trusted, no matter what, and that fear need not bind and destroy.

Finally, God does not excuse sin or evil. Jesus urged repentance and change, not only in beliefs and attitudes but in actions and relationships with others. He urged people to take responsibility for their behavior, change their ways and follow him.

Too often the church has insisted on love and grace from its weaker members yet has been unwilling to require accountability from those in positions of power. Jesus did just the opposite. Although he expected repentance from everyone, his strongest words were for religious leaders who abused their power and exploited others. Those who claim to follow him must also find ways to urge repentance and accountability from those who abuse and mistreat others. And just as Jesus did, deeds must be emphasized over words. Indeed, church leaders should make clear that "bearing the cross" is not a call to submission and death. Rather it is an invitation to life and faith. It is a call to take risks, trusting that God's love and justice will prevail.

The rush to forgiveness and reconciliation

Forgiveness and reconciliation are important, crucial tasks for healing, yet sometimes they can be used to stop the process, before there is enough understanding of the harm done. If urged too soon, forgiveness can dis-empower those who've been wronged and allow the status quo to continue without addressing what needs to change. Before seeking forgiveness, it is essential that perpetrators recognize the harm they have caused and take responsibility for their actions. Such repentance prepares the way for true accountability and transformation in the relationship.

One woman explained her journey this way:

> As I found myself, three things happened. First, I began to experience Jesus' love in new ways. I found that even though there were many holes in my life, Jesus was slowly healing them through people, events and dreams. Second, I began a lifelong process to retrieve the many losses which come with abuse, and third, a desire began to grow in me to learn about and tell the truth to the perpetrators as a way of reconnecting with my family. This was/is extremely painful and, in many ways, has been more painful than the actual abuse, as family members close their eyes and ears to my story, take sides with the perpetrators and continue cycles of abuse into the next generation. . . .

I wasn't interested in revenge, or peace at any cost, but in hearing and being heard, no matter how painful the event. The mantra I began to hear from my family was, "forgive and forget." Marie Fortune [of the FaithTrust Institute[39]] says, "forgive and remember."

> Remembering helped me not to be re-victimized, empathize with others who were/are suffering, start new rituals of healing and do all I could to remain in the family and in the
> church. Jesus invites us to break bread as a way to remember or re-member him. As I pray, seek guidance and healing, I imagine

---

39. http://faithtrustinstitute.org

a day when God will set the table before me and my "enemies" and we will be anointed with oil and be re-membered as we experience the goodness and mercy of God.[40]

The belief in entitlement

In the United States, there is a strong belief that some people have the right or even the duty to use or control others. This concept of entitlement encourages a dynamic of exploitation which uses some people to satisfy the needs of others. In international relations, it allows powerful nations to justify taking the resources and labor of others. It's also the dynamic which misuses and destroys the earth.

But this dynamic also shows up in gender relations, as women have often been used as servants or play-things, rather than recognized as full human beings. This is clearly evident in pornography which is becoming much more violent, normalized and accessible in our culture, including among Christians.[41]

It is important to return to Gen 1:27–28 and recall that God created both men and women in God's image and gave them the joint task of caring for the earth. It is also crucial to recognize that God did not give this task to a king or emperor but to an ordinary human couple, who can represent all people.

Images of God and God's power

As already mentioned, one of the most common images of God is of a supreme ruler with power to do whatever God wants. Certainly, God is strong and mighty and it is helpful to think of God as an alternative to powerful rulers like Caesar. But it is also essential to make sure these images of God match who Jesus was. Jesus revealed God as One who has endless capacity to love, to empower, to encourage and to heal. And power is not primarily coercion and domination, but the power of love and the capacity to nurture and strengthen others. Too often, God is pictured more as Caesar than like Jesus. And if Caesar is wor-

---

40. From "Surviving my childhood — Katherine's Story" at: http://abuse.mcc.org/family-violence/child-abuse/child-abuse/stories#Katherine.

41. Information and statistics about pornography are available at: http://stoppornculture.org/stats-and-studies/ and http://www.blazinggrace.org/cms/bg/pornstats.

shipped, then the ways of Caesar will be reproduced in one's life and relationships.

It is therefore important to use many images for God, just as the Bible does. For instance, in addition to images of God as king, rock, father and eagle, the Bible pictures God as a mother, a woman in labor, a midwife, a mother bear, and a mother hen.[42] Using more diverse and comprehensive images for God will assist in staying rooted in a Biblical picture of God. It will also aid in seeing all people as created in God's image, and worthy of full respect.

Expanding the understanding of sin

Sin is not only what one does, but also how one is sinned against and/or trapped by sinful forces. It is not only personal but also structural and built into the fabric of life together. So too, salvation is not just personal and future, but also needs to challenge and change the way people live together on a daily basis. New leadership patterns, new ways to understand peace and reconciliation, new ways of acknowledging pain and brokenness, and new ways of finding hope and deliverance can be discovered.

Attention to victims of violence and oppression

As work is done by the church in all these areas, there must be continued close attention paid to those who have been hurt and impoverished by individuals and oppressive systems. They indeed are the ones closest to the situation of Jesus and the prophetic tradition he embraced, and the church desperately needs their perspectives in order to faithfully understand and articulate faith today.

Key questions need to be asked, such as:

- Who is missing from the discussion?

- Who is most vulnerable in this situation and how would they hear this message?

- Does this path lead to life and wholeness? This does not mean avoiding all risk, but asking if the path being taken is life-giving, or whether it enables and supports the forces of domination and death.

---

42. Deut 32:18, Job 38:29, Hos 11:3–4, Isa 49:15 & 42:14, Ps 22:9–10, Hos 13:8, Matt 23:37.

- To whom is one accountable and how? This question is especially important when one is in a position of privilege and authority.

Embracing courage and nonviolent resistance to evil

All of this will require courage as well as humility in the face of evil. Again, this does not mean rejecting peace or nonviolence, but working for peace that is robust and full of justice, and not just an absence of conflict.

One helpful image is from a stained glass window in the 16th St. Baptist Church in Birmingham, Alabama. The church was bombed in 1963, killing four young girls. The window was given by people in Wales to replace one that had been destroyed in the bombing. Initiated and designed by the Welsh artist, John Petts, it shows a black Jesus, his arms stretched out as on a cross. The right hand is held up in resistance, "pushing away hatred and injustice," and the other is open in hospitality and forgiveness.[43]

A similar image comes from Eastern Congo, where women are raising one hand to denounce the violence committed against them, while at the same time holding a hand over their hearts, as a symbol of holding onto love and dignity. After participating in a recent march to recognize the many women who had been ". . . raped, beaten or forced to flee their homes," Fifi Pombo Madikela, a Mennonite Brethren pastor, declared, "We will never forget the joy of standing together to resist evil and we will continue the work."[44] These images of resistance and welcome, of defiance and love, can give courage for the ongoing work of speaking truth to power.

Truly, God desires that everyone follow the way of Christ: to show love to all people, work for justice, care for the suffering, empower the weak, and hold to account those who harm others. Proverbs 31:8–9 urges us to "Speak for those who cannot speak, for the rights of all the destitute. Speak out, judge righteously, defend the rights of the poor and needy."[45] In this way, Christians can participate in building safe, healthy families and communities which honor God and all whom God created.

43. Younge, "American civil rights" guardian.co.uk, 6 March 2011.
44. Will, "MCC supports Congolese" December 3, 2010.
45. *Abuse: Response and Prevention*, 12, MCC, 2008.

BIBLIOGRAPHY

Baylor University. *"Clergy Sexual Misconduct Study,"* http://www.baylor.edu/clergy sexualmisconduct/.

Center for Disease Control and Prevention, 2008:http://www.cdc.gov/mmwr/preview/mmwrhtml/mm5705a1.htm.

Cory, J. and K.McAndless-Davis. *When Love Hurts: A Woman's Guide to Understanding Abuse in Relationships.* New Westminster, BC. WomanKind Press, 2008.

Family Violence Prevention Fund, *The Facts on Domestic, Dating and Sexual Violence.* http://endabuse.org/content/action_center/detail/754.

Immigration Policy Center, *"Exploitation in the Workplace,"* http://www.immigration policy.org/special-reports/reforming-americas-immigration-laws-womans-struggle#danger.

Kanagy, C. *Signs for the Journey, A Profile of Mennonite Church USA,* Herald Press, 2007.

Kristof, N. D. *"Seduction, slavery and sex,"* New York Times, July 15, 2010.

Kroeger, C. Clark and N. Nason-Clark. *No Place for Abuse: Biblical and Practical Resources to Counteract Domestic Violence.* Downers Grove, IL: InterVarsity Press, 2nd edition, 2010.

Mennonite Central Committee. *Abuse: Response and Prevention: A Guide for Church Leaders,* MCC, 2008.

Nason-Clark, N. and C. Clark Kroeger. *Refuge from Abuse: Healing and Hope for Abused Christian Women,* Downers Grove, IL: InterVarsity Press, 2004.

Statistics Canada. *Family Violence in Canada: A Statistical Profile 2002,* Ottawa: Canadian Centre for Justice Statistics, Statistics Canada, 2002, www.swc-cfc.gc.ca.

"Surviving my Childhood—Katharine's Story,"
http://abuse.mcc.org/family-violence/child-abuse/child-abuse-stories#Katharine.

U.S. Dept of Health and Human Services, *"Child Maltreatment 2008 Report,"* http://www.acf.hhs.gov/programs/cb/pubs/cm08/.

U.S. Department of Justice, Family Violence Statistics, Bureau of Justice Statistics, 2005, http://bjs.ojp.usdoj.gov/index.cfm?ty=pbdetail&iid=828.

Will, E., "MCC supports Congolese women calling for an end to the violence against women," December 3, 2010. Retrieved 5/5/2011: http://mcc.org/stories/news/mcc-supports-congolese-women-calling-end-violence-against-women.

Younge, G., "American civil rights: The Welsh connection," guardian.co.uk, Sunday 6 March 2011, 21.00 GMT.

14

Preparing Seminaries for Collaborative Work

Steve McMullin and Nancy Nason-Clark

INTRODUCTION

This chapter asks a rather straight-forward question: are seminaries equipping their students to respond to domestic violence in the church and within the community? To address this question, we discuss data we have collected from seminary students in four different locations. As this chapter demonstrates, the story of preparing seminaries for collaborative work is challenging. We outline several features of challenge, focusing most specifically on the results of a study we conducted that involved four seminaries. To contextualize this data, we offer observations drawn from our experiences of working within the seminary environment with administrators, faculty, and students.

Recent sociological research that we have conducted at accredited theological seminaries in North America demonstrates that although administrators, faculty, and students are in agreement that there is a need for seminary students to be better trained to address the issue of family violence in congregations and to respond to the needs of religious victims, much work needs to be done in order for graduate-level theological education to provide the kind of preparation that students will need as pastors and church leaders. Although administrators expressed fears that their graduates are unprepared to respond to the abusive family relationships that they will face in pastoral ministry, and although faculty members invited us to conduct our research on their campuses and in their classrooms, the research results make it clear that in these educational institutions there are structural barriers that prevent the training of seminary students to respond adequately to the needs of victims of domestic violence. Until these structural barriers and their causes are understood and addressed, it is unlikely that seminaries can provide the kind of training that will prepare their graduates to address and respond to the violence that characterizes many families in society and within congregations. We conclude that seminaries are unlikely to be able to make the necessary changes to their core curriculum without partnering with other organizations in a collaborative effort.

When we met with them, seminary leaders expressed to us their concerns about the unpreparedness of their graduates and the need for better training. Some suggested possible solutions, yet real change seemed unlikely in the short term. The vice-president of a mainline seminary told us that because of the institution's emphasis on social issues, their graduates think they are more prepared to respond to domestic violence than they really are, and she expressed her concern that the fact that they think they are prepared may make the problem of their unpreparedness even worse. At an evangelical seminary, the interim president proposed to the seminary's academic leadership team that faculty would be instructed to include in every course at least one assignment that relates in some way to domestic violence. The proposal was never carried out. At all four seminaries, faculty members expressed to us their frustration that they are unsure of how to include instruction about domestic violence in the core curriculum. In many cases, the faculty members themselves have received little instruction and are not certain about how church leaders should address the issue or respond to the needs of victims; like their students, the faculty members at seminaries are also unprepared. At every seminary, students expressed fear and anxiety about knowing that they will face crisis situations in ministry without adequate preparation.[1]

The concerns of administrators and faculty were more than academic. One senior administrator spoke to us about his brother who had been fired as the pastor of his first congregation when he attempted to confront a church leader who was battering his wife. Another leader discussed the problem of violent families in the seminary's student housing. A senior faculty member talked about an academically gifted

1. McMullin and Nason-Clark, "Seminary students."

former student who had gone on to serve on the faculty of another seminary and who turned out to be a wife batterer. Faculty members mentioned that some victims of domestic violence enroll as part-time students so they can take pastoral care courses, presumably in an attempt to find help and support in a seminary class that they could not find in their congregation or community, yet those seminary courses are neither designed nor intended to provide such help and support for victims. Neither administrators nor faculty disagreed with us that domestic violence is a serious problem that seminaries need to address. Yet in spite of these genuine concerns and good intentions, the seminary students reported to us in surveys and in focus groups that they do not feel adequately prepared for the situations they will face in ministry, and the seminaries have no plans in place to address that deficiency.

IDENTIFYING THE ISSUES—WHY SEMINARIES MATTER

Theological seminaries provide formal post-baccalaureate training for ordained pastoral ministry in the Christian church. The *Association of Theological Schools in the United States and Canada* (ATS) included 260 member institutions in 2011, of which 240 were fully accredited. In total, these seminaries enroll more than 74,000 students, most of whom are preparing for some form of church or denominational leadership[2]. Several denominations require a seminary education for ordination to the Christian ministry, and even among denominations without such a requirement, many individuals who intend to serve as pastors or as congregational leaders desire seminary-level training in order to be adequately prepared to provide church leadership in a complex world. Although seminary enrollment has declined somewhat in recent years and although not all denominations and congregations require seminary training of their clergy, with more than 74,000 students enrolled in 260 ATS-related theological schools across North America, seminaries are important and influential institutions when it comes to the training and preparation of church leadership. The problem of inadequate preparation among Church leaders will not be adequately addressed if seminaries are not a vital part of the solution.

---

2. Detailed information about 2011–2012 North American seminary enrollment is available online on the ATS website at http://www.ats.edu/Resources/Publications Presentations/Documents/AnnualDataTables/2011–12AnnualDataTables.pdf.

There are other reasons why the theological seminary is an important setting for learning about domestic violence. First, the student can learn in seminary *before* facing actual cases of domestic violence. Too often, the circumstance in which a pastor seeks guidance about how to respond is in the midst of a crisis—a victim has come to the pastor for urgent help and the pastor either does not know what to do or makes a serious error and provides advice that further endangers the victim or that leads to a troubled outcome. The time to learn how to respond is not in the moment of crisis in a home or when under pressure from an abusive church leader, but at a time and in an academic atmosphere when alternatives and their outcomes can be considered and when practical questions can be asked and answered. A theological seminary can provide that atmosphere for thoughtful learning that is free of the personal dynamics that can cloud the crisis situation for someone who is unprepared to respond to immediate needs.

Second, the theological seminary provides an important opportunity to integrate an understanding of domestic violence with the study of theology, Biblical studies, and the practice of ministry. It is this integrated understanding that allows the pastor to contribute to the safety and healing of the religious victim in ways that other professionals cannot. Such an integrated understanding also prepares the pastor to address the issue effectively among the whole congregation and with congregational leaders, with both a Biblical and a practical understanding, so that the congregation becomes a safe community in which those who are being or have been abused may disclose that they are victims. Instead of domestic violence being addressed only when the need becomes apparent due to an immediate crisis, a pastor who has been well prepared can address domestic violence in the church with knowledge and understanding.

Third, seminaries emphasize the importance of equipping the pastor to train church leaders. The pastor is not the only person in a leadership role in the church who may be called upon to respond to the needs of victims. Clergy who have been well prepared in seminary will be more likely to equip ministry leaders such as youth leaders and women's ministry leaders to recognize and respond to signs of abuse. Those church leaders will also be less likely to ignore such signs or to deny that abuse is happening if they are confident that they have a pastor who will know what to do when asked to respond to an abusive situation.

Barriers to overcome (Evidence from the data)

In 2009–2010, the RAVE research team at the University of New Brunswick carried out a study of 412 students at four ATS-accredited seminaries in the United States and Canada. Three seminaries describe themselves as evangelical, while the other identifies as a mainline seminary. Members of the team met with seminary administrators and members of the faculty at each seminary and a researcher conducted a survey among the students and met with focus groups of students.

A. Seminary students

In light of previous research[3] regarding the unpreparedness of clergy, it is not surprising that the seminary students in this study expressed a lack of preparedness to respond to victims of domestic violence. Their lack of preparation was manifested in several ways:

1. WRONG INFORMATION AND ASSUMPTIONS

We have previously documented ways that students in all four seminaries consistently underestimated the rate of domestic violence among church families.[4] A more detailed analysis of the data from the student surveys indicates not only that there is a lack of understanding of the numbers, but that there is a lack of understanding of the dynamics of abuse. First, although abusers in church families are often adept at using spiritual language and concepts to maintain control, the seminary students rarely made a connection between any religious or spiritual aspect of family life and the domestic violence that is experienced in church families. When the survey asked the open-ended question, "In your opinion, why are some men abusive toward their wives?" only 14 respondents (3 percent) identified any connection between spiritual factors and abuse. As documented below (Table 1), 35 percent of respondents correctly identified issues related to power and control as a factor, but two thirds of respondents did not. Mainline seminary students were more likely to blame alcohol and drug use, while evangelical seminary students more often attributed spousal abuse to feelings

3. Nason-Clark, *The Battered Wife*."
4. McMullin and Nason-Clark, "Seminary students."

of insecurity or frustration in the abuser. Some answers demonstrate that at all four of the seminaries at least a few students have serious misconceptions:

> "I think also that men have had leadership roles taken from them and do not know how to respond correctly (male 1:198).

> "Their wife might be stubborn or like to push their husband's buttons" (male 1:264).

> "Never learned how to really love someone" (female 2:43).

> "Women may also persistently push the men's buttons even when some may have asked them to stop or leave them alone and when that does not work the man loses his control and becomes abusive" (female 2:49).

> "They have verbally abusive/frustrating wives" (male 2:55).

> "Maybe comes from misunderstanding of what women need" (female 2:223).

> "The usual complaint of the men is that their wives do not respect them" (male 3:171).

> "Lack or understanding of woman nature" (male 4:337).

> "They have not learned how to express their emotions in a healthy manner" (female 4:339).

> "Our society does not allow men to be vulnerable. I think there have been unrealistic expectations put on men emotionally" (4:354).

> "Wife getting stronger and more assertive" (female 4:386).

The students' most common answers are summarized in Table 1:

TABLE 1: WHY ARE SOME MEN ABUSIVE TOWARD THEIR WIVES?

Reason for Abusive Behaviour (students' answers)	Mainline Seminary Students N=95	Evangelical Seminary Students N=317	All Seminary Students N=412
Power and Control Issues	30 (32%)	114 (36%)	144 (35%)
Abuse in Childhood	30 (32%)	90 (28%)	120 (29%)
Inability to Manage Anger	23 (24%)	80 (25%)	103 (25%)

Reason for Abusive Behaviour (students' answers)	Mainline Seminary Students N=95	Evangelical Seminary Students N=317	All Seminary Students N=412
Stress (job, finances)	11 (12%)	43 (14%)	54 (13%)
Alcohol and/or Drugs	14 (15%)	30 (9%)	44 (11%)
Feelings of Insecurity	5 (5%)	32 (10%)	37 (9%)
Maleness, Masculinity	4 (4%)	27 (9%)	31 (8%)
Feelings of Frustration	3 (3%)	27 (9%)	30 (7%)
Low Self-Esteem	8 (8%)	20 (6%)	28 (7%)
Bad Communication Skills	7 (7%)	18 (6%)	25 (6%)
Mental Disorder/illness	4 (4%)	10 (3%)	14 (3%)

2. Poor Biblical/theological integration

Although the seminary plays a key role in providing future clergy with an integrated Biblical/theological/practical understanding for ministry, many students struggled to understand possible reasons for domestic violence in Christian homes. In focus groups, students repeatedly attempted to integrate their Biblical/theological understanding with the reality of abuse in Christian homes, but the attempts rarely met with agreement from all of the group members. When asked how pastors might effectively address the issue in a congregation, students did not have clear answers:

> "As far as raising the issue in a church I think preaching good Biblically based sermons on how God wants us to live in community with each other in peace and harmony and that outside of that it's not the way God wants us to live" (male 1:1).

> "Some pastors really don't want to admit that church people can do these horrible things" (female 1:2).

> "I just feel completely helpless, I have no idea, I don't know, like I just don't know, I don't even know what I would do, that might be why some people do ignore it because they feel completely helpless and have no idea what to do that they just, they're frozen, I can't even get words out, I don't know what to do so you don't do anything" (female 1:1).

> "I'm not sure the pastor alone doing something, he's going to be as strong as if somebody above him or her [in the denomination] is giving the direction as well" (male 1:7).

> "I think one of the things that's missing in a large majority of churches is the acknowledgement that though we're saved, there still exist evil influences in our lives and we bring that with us when we come to the Lord and we can be right in the midst of it, we can have come out of it but not have been healed of it, we can see it going on around us but not draw alongside the people who need the help because it is not an issue that has been addressed in the church" (female 2:3).

> "As a whole, trying to steer the congregation into understanding what domestic violence means, how it can rear its ugly head sort of thing, using Scripture I think—it's the basis of our faith, and talking—I would hope pastors are talking about social issues anyway that are going on and relating it to how Christ would deal with it. So I would hope that domestic violence is on the list of important things to talk about" (female 3:1).

One female student at an evangelical seminary suggested that a pastor should *not* attempt to integrate a Biblical or theological understanding of domestic violence, but instead to address it more from a secular viewpoint:

> I think that really staying away from spiritualization, the concept of marriage or family, because it only brings in ideas of guilt, of shame, of 'why did God do this to me?' and it also means that you're not in touch with that person's feelings, when really the last thing they need to hear about is the faith and so forth. The very first thing which Christ tells us is to love and to be there for another person. You don't always have to bring God into it immediately so the most effective thing for a pastor to do is to step out of his pastoral role (female 2:4).

Her argument that "you don't always have to bring God into it," which resulted in considerable discomfort among the other focus group members, suggests a conviction on her part that it may not be possible to integrate a Biblical worldview with the realities of violent church families. Her belief that spiritual affirmations lead only to guilt and shame demonstrates that the lack of preparedness among these students is not simply one of technique (knowing what to do in a crisis) but, more seriously, a deep lack of understanding of the dynamics of abuse and of the spiritual needs of religious victims. Victims of domestic violence who approach their pastor for help are not looking for the pastor to step out of the pastoral role; they are looking for spiritual guidance, for prayer that God will guide and help them, for an understanding of how Scripture applies in their situation, and for practical (pastoral) guidance about how to find help and safety while being faithful to their Christian commitment. Pastors need to be equipped to provide effective spiritual guidance and to be able to assure victims that the Christian faith is a resource on which they can rely as they seek shelter and safety from violence.

It was noteworthy that in the majority of cases, the members of the student focus groups chose to respond to the question about addressing domestic violence in a *private* sense. Even though the question clearly asked about addressing domestic violence in the church, most did not consider the possibility of addressing the issue with the whole congregation, but thought about how to talk about it with specific individuals. It apparently did not occur to most seminarians that the topic would ever be addressed in a sermon.

3. Immediate need

To an extent that we had not expected, the data demonstrates that seminary students need preparation now, not later. For example, 109 of the 412 seminary students indicated in the survey that they currently serve as a pastor in a congregation. A high proportion of those students indicate that they have been called upon to provide counseling in situations of relationship violence, and since many seminary students serve as youth pastors, most frequently they have been called upon to counsel youth who are in abusive relationships or to counsel children who have been abused by a parent. What was surprising, however, was that many of the students who are not yet serving as pastors also have considerable experience in seeking to respond to victims of relationship violence (Table 2):

TABLE 2: SEMINARY STUDENTS' EXPERIENCE WITH VICTIMS OF DOMESTIC VIOLENCE[5]

Have Counselled:	Students Already Serving as Pastors N=109	Students Not Serving as Pastors N=29[A]	All Students N=400[A]
A child abused by a father	58 (53%)	146 (50%)	204 (51%)
A child abused by a mother	44 (40%)	88 (30%)	132 (33%)
A youth with an abusive bf/gf	62 (57%)	117 (40%)	179 (45%)
A violent couple	32 (29%)	72 (25%)	104 (26%)
A woman with an abusive husband	52 (48%)	119 (41%)	171 (43%)
A man with an abusive wife	23 (21%)	39 (13%)	62 (16%)
An adult being abused by children	31 (28%)	25 (9%)	56 (14%)
A. 12 students did not indicate if they serve as a pastor or not.			

Although they have much experience, many feel woefully unprepared. One seminary student explained in some detail the frustration of trying to respond to a report of domestic violence without having been trained to know what to do:

> And so I reached out to the ... officer on duty and reported what I was aware of. After that night, there was much turmoil as the police were pulled in on a situation in which was later determined that physical abuse was going on. The couple was angry ... and it caused many difficult and uncomfortable situations for those parties involved in the situation. The couple's name who reported the situation to me was shared with the husband and wife who were in the abusive relationship and it only created more strife. In the midst of all the anger and finger pointing as to who handled things poorly, something was lost. I felt that the fact that a woman had been beaten was forgotten and I felt that a sick husband in need of God's redemption and restoration was also in need of healing attention. The wife needed healing

---

5. To compare the experiences of these seminary students with the experiences of clergy, see Nason-Clark, *The Battered Wife*, 69.

and restoration to be whole again. The problem is, I didn't know what I was doing (male 2:6).

In light of the students' own assessment of themselves as unprepared to respond to the needs of a victim of domestic violence (McMullin and Nason-Clark 2011), the data shows that seminary students not only need to know how to respond after they complete their seminary education, but because they are often involved in congregational leadership while they are students, it is important that resources and information begin to be made available as soon as students begin their seminary training.

Among the 257 seminary students who reported that they have provided counsel for a victim of family violence, only fourteen believe that they are well prepared to do so and 101 believe they are somewhat prepared. Two students rated themselves between "somewhat prepared" and "poorly prepared." The majority (55 percent) of these students who have provided counsel to victims believe that they are either poorly prepared (106) or not at all prepared (34) to do so.

Summary of student data

In summary, the data demonstrates that the problem of students' unpreparedness is more than one of students being unaware of resources, referral options, and best practices. Many seminary students do not understand the dynamics of abuse, they cannot integrate a Christian worldview with the reality of domestic violence among church families, and they are already being called upon to respond and provide counsel even though they know they are not well prepared to do so. These students need more than a seminar about how to react in a moment of crisis; they need to understand how to apply a Biblical understanding of marriage in a world of painful relationships. They need to know how to address domestic violence in sermons so that the secrecy of abuse is challenged. They need to have a sufficient theological framework to be able to provide pastoral guidance in the midst of crisis and also during the prolonged time of change and healing that victims must face. They need to know how and to whom they can confidently refer religious victims. And they need to understand how to mobilize the congregation not just as a social organization but as a spiritual community in order to support those whose lives have been damaged by abuse and its effects.

B. Faculty

There was little if any resistance from faculty to our research and our presence on the seminary campuses. Several faculty members expressed strong support of our research and indicated that they believe it is important that students be better prepared. In spite of those genuinely supportive attitudes, barriers to change were observed in three areas:

1. Zealous Advocates on Faculty

At the seminaries, certain faculty members (who in most cases are female) may see domestic violence as *their* issue. While the interest and concern of such faculty members is welcome, they may be perceived by some other faculty members and by students as being on a campaign to make domestic violence a central concern on the campus, which results in resistance and even an adversarial response. The issue becomes political and tends to divide the faculty. These zealous faculty members would identify to us others on faculty as being either *for* or *against* the issue of domestic violence, without understanding that what they perceive as opposition may represent either a lack of agreement of how to prepare students or a concern that the issue of domestic violence would hijack other issues that the other faculty members were seeking to raise among faculty. Faculty members see the seminary as having very limited resources (class time, finances, personnel) and are worried about any issue that will remove some of those resources from their own areas of interest.

Seeing domestic violence as a political issue may also affect ways that students are perceived as *for* or *against* advocacy for victims of domestic violence. For example, at one seminary I [Steve] was invited to provide a presentation about domestic violence to a class comprised of fifteen male and two female students. The instructor, a capable advocate for victims of domestic violence, assured me there would be students who would not be supportive and expressed concern that some might even be argumentative during my talk. I chose to make a presentation that expressed that the congregation's response to domestic violence is an important aspect of the witness of the church—a presentation that intentionally attempted to integrate the conservative theological understanding of the seminary with an appropriate response to domestic violence. During the time for questions and discussion that followed, the students were very engaged and enthusiastic and displayed no opposition whatever. After the class, the lecturer expressed her shock at the class discussion—she said the very students whom she expected to disagree most strongly were the ones who participated most enthusiastically, asked the most engaging questions, and seemed most appreciative of the presentation. She had misjudged a lack of understanding and a lack of theological integration among the students as a lack of support for the issue.

Ghettoization of the issue of domestic violence

A second problem that became apparent on each of the campuses was a division between the courses that are included in the core curriculum for the *Master of Divinity* degree (the degree designed to prepare students for ordained pastoral ministry) and what might be considered specialty courses or electives. Because there are so many required core courses, students have very few options for other courses.

Three of the four seminaries currently offer a full course about domestic violence. In each case, faculty members told us that only a small percentage of the seminary students take the course and that those who do take the course are rarely the students who are preparing for pastoral ministry. One of the seminaries offers a master's degree in counseling, and another offered a social work degree; most of the students who choose to take the Domestic Violence course are in the counseling or social work program. The unintended result is that the problem of domestic violence is disconnected from preparation for pastoral ministry.

In focus groups, the way in which the "Domestic Violence and Abuse" course was separate from the core curriculum was discussed:

> "I don't think there are any particular classes here that I've taken that spoke directly about the issue or the.... I learned about the practicalities of how to deal with the issue. I don't know if the [counseling degree] classes offer any courses on it but I do wish I had more opportunities to take more of the counseling courses along with my MDiv degree" (female 2:5).

> "As a [counseling degree] student I want to elaborate a bit on it, there is a 'Domestic Violence and Abuse' class. The professor that taught it shared with us that this issue, I think it's in the pastoral counseling class, I'm not really certain, but he only has three hours to address this whole issue within that, and in that is perhaps maybe the only training in class that is provided for those who are not in the [counseling degree] program" (male 2:7).

Since the quantitative data from the student questionnaires do not distinguish between the students who were in the Master of Divinity (pastoral ministry) program and the students in the counseling or social work degree programs, it is quite conceivable that the students who felt better prepared were more likely to be those in the counseling or social work programs. If that is the case, then those pursuing the Master of Divinity degree may be even more poorly prepared than the total numbers suggest.

Structurally, opportunities must be found to include training about domestic violence in the core curriculum of seminaries. We saw some isolated examples of professors who were making an attempt to do this, but even those faculty members expressed an interest in receiving help. At all four seminaries, it was made clear that there is no room in the core curriculum for any additional required courses, including required courses that address domestic violence. Because congregations expect their pastors to have expertise in a wide variety of areas, Biblical, theological, and practical, seminaries struggle to fit all of the requirements into the core curriculum and instructors feel pressure to provide a comprehensive understanding of the material in limited class time.

2. UNPREPAREDNESS OF FACULTY AND ADMINISTRATORS

Conversations with faculty suggest that seminary faculty members and administrators may also be quite unprepared to respond to domestic violence. As seminary graduates themselves in most cases, they also received little if any instruction about the issue. Faculty members who teach theology, Biblical studies, ethics, preaching, mission, and church history have likely had little if any training themselves, which leaves domestic violence to be seen as a "pastoral care" issue. Yet the small amount of class time allocated to the core pastoral care course is already filled with everything from hospital visitation and funerals to issues like depression and suicide. In focus groups, the students indicated that usually no more than one three-hour class was allocated to the problem of domestic violence. One concerned and supportive faculty member was very polite in getting the point across that most faculty feel they do not have nearly enough class time as it is to deliver their courses, so it will be important to find ways to encourage them to provide domestic violence training without sacrificing what they are currently including in their classes.

This issue of unpreparedness became particularly clear when one administrator stopped to read through the questionnaire that the students were completing and said, "I cannot understand why any woman would go back to an abusive relationship after she leaves." Not only do students not understand the dynamics of abuse, neither do some members of the seminary leadership.

Because seminary faculty may not be well equipped to provide training in how to address and respond to domestic violence, it becomes important for seminaries to be part of a collaborative process that brings together the resources that will be necessary in order to provide training for the students. Some of the resources may be in the seminary, but other resources may be in the community, in local congregations, and in advocacy organizations. A web-based resource such as the RAVE website may also be incorporated into the seminary curriculum.

THE POSSIBILITIES: A STRATEGY FOR MOVING FORWARD

The need is great for pastors and church leaders to be able to address domestic violence and to know how to respond appropriately to the needs of victims in a congregation. Yet pastors have made it clear that they realize that they are not well prepared to respond and the reason for their unpreparedness is linked to seminary training that does not adequately address the issue. Since part of the reason that seminaries have largely ignored domestic violence is because they perceive congregations to be asking their students to be well prepared in other areas, it is important that congregations and religious denominations communicate with the seminaries that they expect their graduates to be better prepared to respond to the needs of victims of domestic violence.

The fact that faculty members may also be uncertain about how to provide training means that collaboration will be essential, and the internet provides a helpful opportunity for such collaboration. First, internet-based training may help faculty members better understand the dynamics of abuse so they can find ways to include domestic violence in their course content. Second, the modular use of internet-based resources in the seminary classroom may provide opportunities for students to learn from a wide variety of resources. We have seen such use of the RAVE website in a Doctor of Ministry program at one seminary. The RAVE team is interested is in partnering with seminaries to prepare seminary students.

Preparing seminaries for collaborative work: Celebrations and challenges

For quite a few years now, I (Nancy) have been working collaboratively with colleagues affiliated with the Doctor of Ministry program at Gordon Conwell Seminary, Dr. David Currie and Dr. Ken Swetland. Together with them, I have offered one day workshops for cohorts of their DMin students—at their main campus and their sister campuses—on the subject of domestic violence.

This has been an especially rewarding experience for me. I have learned a tremendous amount as I listen to students struggle with the interplay between domestic violence, faith, and religious concepts of family living. The chasm between our theological notions of gender and family coupled with the reality of abuse in so many families of faith is hard for any committed believer to understand. There is a great need for pastors to respond with compassion and best practices to those who suffer in the aftermath of domestic violence, and to do so without hesitation and with the full knowledge of both spiritual resources and practical links to community-based services.

There is a lot of information to be shared, a lot of soul-searching to do, a lot of skeletons in the closet to reveal, and an enormous ministry challenge to accept. Most of the students are eager to learn, receptive to the research and its potential practical application, and desirous of concrete suggestions that will enable them to enhance pastoral care for those they serve in their own congregation and within the community where it is located. A few students each year are resistant—to either the content, or the pedagogy, or both. We often learn most from the experiences of challenge. This is certainly true for me.

Based on my experiences over the last seven years, I would like to identify five recurring challenges. I offer each, with an illustration, to outline what I see as the road-blocks on the journey to working together with seminaries and seminary students in cooperative partnerships.

Challenge # 1—Keep the focus on the data and best practices

Many religious leaders do not want to come face to face with the reality of abuse in families in their own denomination or even more specifically, their own congregation. They want to talk about the issue in vague generalities, and keep the discussion at the level of condemning divorce, increasing marital communication, and keeping men and women spiritually strong. Amongst those who are most resistant to any highlighting of the issue of abuse are those who dismiss it outright as a sign of weakening family ties, the impact of the women's movement, and the infiltration of feminism into church circles. For me, the best strategy is to stay clear of these important but sidelining discussions and keep us on track where we focus on the data and abuse-response best practices. Those most resistant will do everything in their power to try to hijack the discussion. They will want to focus on stories of women who were violent, stories that they believe have been exaggerated by victims, or the problems of divorce for children, or families, or congregations.

It happens almost automatically: as soon as I discuss the general prevalence rates of domestic violence across the country and its severity within families connected to churches, a hand goes up and a voice says, "I have a man in my congregation...."

It is true—some men are victims of domestic violence; some women are perpetrators. But within the first few minutes of a day workshop, things can get derailed if this is not acknowledged in a careful and therapeutically-enhanced way. Given my years of experience in working with pastors and other religious leaders, I name this up-front. As soon as I discuss the statistics, I immediately explain that some of those present will have had experience in offering support to men who have been victimized. I spend a few minutes talking about the male victim—either during his childhood or as an adult man. I attempt to deliberately diffuse the possibility of derailing the broader context of the gender dynamics of domestic abuse in families across the nation, or within congregational life. And the data we have been collecting over the years points out that while scores of church women look to their pastors for help in the aftermath of domestic violence, few church men do.

This focus on the data serves several purposes: it acknowledges that there are a great variety of victims of intimate partner abuse and family violence—elders, children, spouses, and teens in dating relationships; it acknowledges that not all pastors will have the same experience—such as those working with immigrant populations, or those who minister in predominately urban or rural areas; it brings all the seminary students into the conversation of the day very early on—even those who are very resistant to the notion that family life can be dangerous to your emotional or physical health; and it proclaims that we can all be part of the solution—or part of the problem—and that the choice is ours to make.

Challenge # 2—Minimize the messenger

For religious leaders in very conservative traditions, the question of women in leadership is always present. While it might be too strong—misleading even—to call it the elephant in the room, it certainly lingers around the edges, and ultimately reveals itself in unusual but important moments. At the end of a recent training, a middle-aged seminary student who was male, someone that had been quite attentive throughout the day workshop asked a probing question of me: "Do you think you would have been more effective in your life work if you had been male?" Not exactly sure what to say, and a bit taken-aback by the question, I turned to the rest of the class and said, "What do you think?" "Would today's workshop have been more impactful for you if I had been a man?"

The issue of the messenger is not new to me. Over the course of my career, it surfaces from time to time. "Does your husband know the kind of work you do?" a young pastor once asked of me. Others have asked: "Who looks after your children when you are away on speaking engagements?" or "Does your husband help you with your research work?"

Often seminary students and current religious leaders are overly inquisitive about the credentials of my husband, or his productivity, with questions such as: "Has he written more books than you?"

While I give little thought to these matters most of the time, in writing this section of our chapter, I have given it some sustained attention. I think the crucial issue has to do with gender hierarchy: who is in the position of power; who is the most important; and who is in control.

The subject of abuse is all about control. It raises questions for some about the "messenger" as well as the "message."

In the seminary context in particular, I try to de-politicize the message as much as it is possible (and, of course, it is never really possible to do so completely) and focus on understanding and responding to abuse as behaviour. But let there be no doubt about it, the subject of domestic violence is grounded in a political reality and talking about it challenges some taken-for-granted gendered notions of family life. Concern with the dynamics of the family of the messenger then becomes important to some seminary listeners. If my husband is understood as smarter, with more publications, and a broader profile, then my role as messenger becomes "safe."

Challenge # 3—Offer real-life examples where seminary students themselves may be excluded

In Doctor of Ministry seminary classes that I have taught men always outnumber the women and sometimes there are no women present at all.

A few years ago, the instructors for the course decided in consultation with me that one idea for a very good assignment would be to have the students contact the transition house, or shelter, in their local area—where they live and minister, not the location of the school. They were to complete this exercise before they came to the two-week residency for that particular term.

Some of the seminary students—pastors themselves—were rather outraged when they discovered that the director of the local transition house would not let them visit the premises and showed little or no interest in getting to know them or having any connection with their church. While I do not applaud the indifference on the part of some secular agencies toward religious leaders, for directors of shelters, sometimes that reluctance is based on prior negative experiences with clergy members. The point that I wish to make is that for some ministers engaged in further training at seminary this is one of the first times that they have been denied access to a resource from which they had sought help. It indeed is a very good learning experience. This enables us to talk in class about the very reasons why shelters have certain policies in place, and why such policies are not uniform across the nation.

The experience of exclusion—and it is a minority who have this experience—offers a great teachable moment. It enables me to say that this is exactly the experience of many women seeking help from a religious leader in the aftermath of domestic violence at home. They too are turned away, or offered a deaf ear to their cries for help.

Challenge # 4—Overcome the notion that one person cannot make a difference

One pastor can make an enormous difference on the issue of violence in families of faith. Think about it for a moment. If a minister was to preach a sermon condemning abuse once a year (or even highlight the issue within a sermon that focused on other matters), mention abuse-prevention or abuse-response as a priority within the regional ministerial association, have posters, or information, or shoe-cards in the bathroom(s) at church about the local transition house, and raise the issue in their pre-marital counseling classes, this would touch countless people in their own congregation and others who come as visitors, or who use the church facilities for other events in the local community.

It is true that when the issue of domestic violence is first raised in a seminary context, there can be a collective sigh—a feeling that the prevalence and severity of the problem is so much greater than the resources of an individual pastor, or the congregation, or the denomination to respond to it. But relatively small steps make a big difference. Not every pastor will become well acquainted with the statistics or the dynamics of abuse. Not every pastor will know the criminal justice or therapeutic responses to the problem. But every pastor should know when to refer a woman who comes in crisis and to whom a referral should be made. Every pastor should be able to hear a cry for help and know the first steps in offering a safe response—one that will help to ensure the safety of the victim and the children. Every pastor should be able to bring to account a person who acts abusively in the home—and there too to understand what resources are available in the community to help. Every pastor can do something to offer safety, ease the suffering, and bring spiritual help to a very deep emotional wound.

Challenge # 5—Draw links to the broader challenges facing the contemporary church

How can the contemporary church be mission-minded in the local community and beyond? Are there gaps in service delivery where a cup of cold water might be needed? To whom can newly immigrated men, women, and families turn when they need help? Where is there a safe place to disclose all the angst and anxiety of life? Does anybody care? Does anyone have answers?

I think it is very important to help seminary students, as well as religious leaders, see that there is a broader context into which to place their work to offer help to those impacted by domestic violence and to work together with others to decrease its prevalence and severity within individual families and the wider community. To be sure, the implications of this vary depending on the region of the country in which you minister, the context of the ministry, size of the congregation and its staff resources, and the constituency with whom you serve. But notwithstanding these differences—real as they are—is a very profound possibility of making connections to others in the community to support initiatives that condemn domestic violence in all its various forms—from elder abuse to teen dating violence—and to be part of the coordinated community response to those whose lives have been impacted by it, as abuser or as the abused, or both.

CONCLUDING COMMENTS

Seminaries are training grounds for pastors and pastors are often the first stop on the long road to healing, wholeness, accountability, and change for a religious victim, perpetrator, or family impacted by domestic violence. As a result, seminary administrators and faculty are an important resource in offering their students both the challenge to respond to domestic violence in an appropriate manner and the skills to employ best practices as they do so. In this article, we have examined some recent data collected by our research team that has involved four seminaries, their administrators, faculty and students. And the results give us little cause for celebration. In a similar vein to the research we have collected amongst pastors over the last twenty years, large numbers of seminary students feel ill-equipped to respond to domestic violence and indeed are fearful of their lack of preparation as they approach the completion of their training and the dawn of full-time ministry responsibilities. The later section of our chapter focuses on some of the direct challenges to preparing seminaries and seminary students. Yet awareness of domestic violence and the knowledge of the process of collaboration with community resources are vital to every religious leader. Together we must address the needs of families touched by violence—both those inside and outside congregational life.

The time to act is now: seminaries are a central spoke in the response of faith communities to this critical issue. We ignore their partnership potential to our peril. Every pastor can challenge their alma mater to do something about domestic violence and our RAVE Team are happy to provide any resources that may assist along the way.

BIBLIOGRAPHY

McMullin, S. and N. Nason-Clark. "Seminary students and domestic violence—applying sociological research," In *Responding to Abuse in Christian Homes: A Challenge to Churches and their Leaders*, edited by N. Nason-Clark, C. Clark Kroeger and B. Fisher-Townsend, 231–246. Eugene, OR: Wipf and Stock, 2011.

Nason-Clark, N. *The Battered Wife: How Christians Confront Family Violence*. Louisville, KY: Westminster John Knox Press, 1997.

15

Project Esther in New Zealand

The Challenge of Working with Women at Risk

Daphne Marsden

Editor's Note: Project Esther was begun by Rev. Daphne Marsden under the umbrella of Spreydon Baptist Church in Christchurch, New Zealand. It is an example of what happens when one pastor decides that domestic violence has no place in the lives of women and that the faith community where she pastors needs to be part of the solution.

PASTORAL REFLECTION

A few years ago I didn't know that some women who are battered sedate their husbands in an attempt to gain short term relief from the violence. Apparently, children's cough medicines, some antihistamines, and codeine-based pills added to a cup of coffee are useful for such causes, especially if one's partner, or husband, is already a little intoxicated.

I learned about this method of respite from women inmates in our local prison. It was to this prison that one of our congregation's current members—and neighbor of mine—had been sent for fourteen years on a charge of murder. Unfortunately, the father of her children didn't wake up after his "aided sleep." On discovery of this, amidst her anguished state of mind and with panic and fear for the wellbeing of her children, she buried him in the backyard. For the next year she attempted to manage her life in the context of this horror, all the while living with her six children, including a new baby, in the house where they had once lived together as a couple.

I well remember the court case and the media hype as this woman was tried and convicted for murder. These were the years when research around battered women's syndrome, or even post natal depression, was not as well understood. The public learned of these issues mainly through the grid of sensational local TV news. As a result, there was little public mercy as she was sentenced to fourteen years in prison. Her children, in some sense, were sentenced also—to navigate her absence as their mother for an extended period of time.

Prior to the events which captured national media exposure, I remember her coming to church on a Sunday, arriving with two black eyes and a split lip. Looking back I am astounded by what little she asked for in the way of help. Her only request: six mattresses, plates, knives and forks, and prayer! She never told us she was being abused.

As she was a close neighbor of mine, we would take meals and baking and leave them on her doorstep knowing she was home and feeling puzzled that she didn't come to the door when we knocked loudly. Like others, I did not understand the whole story of her life or the pain and devastation of domestic violence.

This woman calls herself Project Esther's 'first woman.' Our group began investing in her and her children for many, many years, throughout the time she served her prison sentence and even beyond. Each weekend for all these years, Project Esther volunteers would gather up her six children from different parts of the city and make the long journey out to the prison so that mother and children could spend time together. Our desire was to help to keep their severed connection intact. Our relationship with her, in God's providence, opened wide the prison doors for our organization to serve and invest in the lives of many women in our local prison.

THE GROWTH AND DEVELOPMENT OF PROJECT ESTHER

For over seventeen years we, the Project Esther staff and volunteers, have provided assistance at the prison by taking chapel services, providing and funding grief counselling, and supplying clothing for inmates, as well as small gifts that women could send to their children on their birthdays and for Christmas. At times we have paid for inmates' child care. We have run small groups in the prison, including a support group for women who were coping with their childhood sexual abuse. We have helped to fund, and provide entertainment and food for 'family days' where many families have come for a day to the prison and meet together with the woman inmate. In some cases, this has meant paying for travel for children to actually get to the city where the prison is located. Project Esther has provided study fees and books for some inmates that are working towards graduate level education and beyond. It is worth noting here that family violence is a very common aspect in the backgrounds of the women prison inmates.

Project Esther is not only about women and prison. Our activities include a fun weekly preschool music and movement class that attracts hundreds of local families. Women who are at risk or impoverished mutually connect relationally with other families, find information, and ask for and offer help and support to each other. Our services also include a small residential emergency accommodation facility for women and their families, where a family support worker is able to assist them. We run programmes and support groups focusing on anger and abuse as well.

Our Single Mums Support Service caters to a wide range of needs from teen mums to older mums. There are support groups, a drop-in service, activities, and trips away for mums and children, mums and daughters events, mums and sons events, parenting classes, and school holiday programmes. Also available are second-hand clothing and household goods from our very visible and accessible location. Home visits from a family worker can be requested by women or referrals are received from their family doctors, social workers, community nurses, and other professionals or services working with the family.

An example of support

Early on in the life of Project Esther I stumbled upon a young woman who became very influential in the development of our work. I had met her in a shop and admired her toddler; she told me that her new baby of 6 weeks had died a few days earlier. As I was inviting her to come to a local mother's support group a young man joined us in the shop. She turned to this young man and asked him, "Can I please go to a mother's group? This person has just invited me." He didn't reply. She asked again, and he ignored the question. The third time, with a tone of exasperation, she said, "Just tell me if am allowed to go or not!"

Project Esther continued to journey with this woman. She had been pregnant three times during her teens by the young man I met in the shop. He was the older brother in the foster family with whom she lived. The encounter with her left us at Project Esther with questions about her background, her present plight, and her future. What was to be our response as a local Christian community to a woman like this? What could we do to help? We knew our Bibles told us that God cared deeply for this young woman and her children. Immediately we knew that we were called as Christians to reflect this truth to her and others like her who shared similar plights. The time for action had come.

Stories like these abound within Project Esther. The women and their families offer us insights as to why there need to be programmes in our communities for women at risk. In their adult lives many women carry very heavy loads of unresolved childhood pain and their adult lives bear the fruit—of theft, intrusion, and inadequacy from their younger years.

For women at risk who come to Project Esther there is a need to listen and give them voice to speak their present pain. Offering strength to those who have yet to find their voice and then honoring their words when they do, is no small feat. The consequences of abuse and neglect in childhood have left many women who come to Project Esther at the mercy of others. These 'others'–people from the past, the present, and into the future include parents, partners, husbands, schoolteachers, police, pastors, health professionals, judges, social workers, and friends. Some of the women do not have the resources or capacity to make choices of their own agency—choices that are safe, constructive, and life-giving. As an example, I think of a teen sex worker on our local city streets who once asked me how much she should charge for a particular sex act. Many of her life issues, as well as the issues with which we deal at Project Esther, could be wrapped up in her one question. The need for money, for self worth, for safety and shelter, and for longer-term planning—these are the things we think about and offer programs for at Project Esther.

As is probably clear by now, the needs of Project Esther women are not usually isolated, nor are they simple. For a homeless woman, prisoner woman, teen mother, poor woman, woman addicted to alcohol or drugs, low educated woman, battered woman, trafficked woman, or refugee woman, the needs are complex and multiple. They overlap in her life and often are intergenerational in nature.

Many of the women we serve come with multiple and many layered issues that intersect, but the common themes revolve around gender, abuse, lack of community or family support, fear, insecurity, and poverty. None of these presenting problems have an easy or straightforward solution.

PROJECT ESTHER AND THE VISION OF THE CHURCH

The presenting needs at Project Esther are often practical—someone wants a second hand stroller, or clothing, or shoes for a baby, or financial help for interventions regarding learning challenges for their children who are not keeping up at school. Many women need accommodation; others require advocacy and support to navigate the publicly funded rigid social service sector to access their entitlements for income, housing, or disability needs. Some women ask for assistance to gain protection orders from abusive husbands, or partners, and others require legal help. In New Zealand, our community has been struggling through the long, hard grind of recovery from recent earthquakes. People are displaced; stress levels and outcomes related to trauma and loss go into the kaleidoscope of lives already loaded with difficulty and disadvantage. The poor of our community are the most impacted and our poor are very often women and children. As a member of OECD,[1] New Zealand is not doing well in the stakes of child poverty and family abuse, even without earthquakes. But now things are much, much worse.

Project Esther is one of several community-based ministries seeking to live out the dream of a local church whose vision is to be a redemptive community, sharing the love of Christ in the world by word, sign, and deed, and in so doing, to help people become lifelong followers of Jesus Christ.

Project Esther, like many other related ministries in our congregation, is financially independent from our local church and is responsible

---

1. The Organisation for Economic Co-operation and Development. The OECD provides a forum in which governments can work together to share experiences and seek solutions to common problems and works with governments to understand what drives economic, social and environmental change.

for its own funding, running expenses, staff management, and business practices. However, Project Esther is in mission partnership with the church to express tangibly the compassion of Christ. As described earlier, a variety of services and programmes are offered with goals of creating opportunities for women and their families to connect and make relationships with each other and with families from within the church community. Our staff and volunteers are connected to the local church and share the dream and work of being in mission together. We are heading towards 20 years of service. Over this time, we have had a lot of opportunities to reflect on what it means to work together in the lives of women at risk.

PARTNERSHIP AND THE LOCAL CHURCH[2]

Being in partnership with the local church brings blessings and challenges for both the community/social ministry and the congregation. Other such community ministries serving our congregation's mission and vision include a preschool, a ministry working with youth at risk, residential mental health respite care, budget advice and debt management, after school care, and an accommodation project for the elderly. With such a range of services sharing common goals it has meant that together with the local church at times we have the opportunity for comprehensive involvement in the lives of families over long periods of time. For instance a woman may come to the church asking for help with budget or debt issues and then discover she can attend a playgroup or a support group for women parenting alone. An ex-inmate from the women's prison can access the food bank, get help with debt, arrange preschool care for her children, or come to a parenting class—all of these services offered in the context of a shared vision and common values. When we refer women or families to each other's social ministries we know we can expect common compassion and professionalism.

Another exciting trend is to see young adults who, with their families, came through the programmes from early childhood (for example, the music and movement classes or the preschool) and are now working in the afterschool care, or holiday programmes, or on Sundays in the children's Sunday ministries. This work experience has been helpful for launching several people into training as teachers, social workers,

2. Spreydon Baptist Church in Christchurch, New Zealand.

and other professional occupations. We have a volunteer who came as a child to preschool music and movement classes and now that she is in her twenties she is on our prison team and is training as a social worker.

Because relationships develop in Project Esther programmes women and their families are invited and often find their way to the Sunday church gatherings. The scenario might develop like this: a woman comes to a preschool music and movement class, referred by her doctor, social worker, or counselor, and then attends a support group like our healing journey course for women survivors of childhood sexual abuse. In these settings she may connect with a woman who comes on a Sunday to church and who extends an invitation to join along. By using the church café during the weekly activities, women and their families are noticed and made welcome by church folk who inform them of other options and additional Sunday services. Additionally, the church website promotes our community services as well as the Sunday happenings.

Our church draws its congregation from across the city of Christchurch, but it has a strategic plan for connecting people to their local neighborhood. This means, for instance, we can direct a teen mum asking for help to others on her street or in a local neighborhood who have an affiliation to the church. This is invaluable for an isolated depressed young mum who comes to Project Esther to participate in a support group for parenting. We can also direct her to the pastoral care team of her local neighborhood who may invite her to social events like family picnics and/or to join other young mums who will befriend her. This way the church and community/social ministry works with local initiatives so isolated or vulnerable women and their children can find community, a worship context, and specific need-based help. This is so much more resourcing and empowering than sending her off with a food parcel only.

A significant blessing in Project Esther has been when church members become a source of willing, inspiring volunteers. This has resulted from preaching and the use of Scripture that has oriented people towards a mission perspective over a long period. Another source of blessing has been the church's generosity in sharing and making available its rich resource of facilities for offices, meeting rooms, a gymnasium, toilets, kitchens cafes, and auditoriums. The church also provides a reception hub where community folk drop in, phone, or email with a need. That person is then referred to the appropriate community ministry and local neighborhood church contact.

Since our church is comparatively large, and well known for its commitment to the wider community, Project Esther is able to obtain the advice of professionals, or specialists, whose work is offered free, or at low cost, for people on low incomes. And there are those from the congregation who have given financially because of their own backgrounds—their mother struggled with family violence, or their father drank too much, or they had a sister who struggled with mental health. In other words, many in our church give generously from a base of empathy. Another blessing that our collective church culture has developed over decades is the desire to reach out and embrace the local community. We respect, value, and seek out the interaction and approach of people who come with need, whether or not they share our Christian faith.

We are able to ask a local home group to dig over the garden of a sick single mother, to paint a fence, or to perform maintenance work for Project Esther's emergency accommodation. Blessings abound—presently and historically—in our partnership as community/social ministry and our church works together serving, reaching out, and responding to those in need. Alongside the blessings, however, naturally come multiple challenges.

The challenges of partnership between the church and its social ministries

We have experienced specific challenges related to the area of abuse. Here there has been a combination of good intentions, ignorance, biblical illiteracy, and uninformed theological interpretation. Any plan for action to strengthen families and end abuse, the theme of this edited collection, will need to include intentional investment to reduce the negative influence these issues have on family violence.

New Zealand is the place where two oceans collide, the Pacific and the Tasman. On a calm day, one can stand and watch the waters gently merging and absorbing one another, but on a windy day the choppy swells clash against each other. Like the oceans on a windy day, the world of family violence does not always merge easily, or smoothly, with the theology or expectations of the general congregation. As a result, we are a long way from dealing consistently well both with our responses to abuse victims and with our contribution to preventing domestic violence in the first place. However we want to do better in both response and prevention.

One of Project Esther's services is *Te Whare Atawhai* (The House of Kindness), the emergency accommodation offered to women and their children, including those dealing with abuse. As mentioned earlier, we have the blessing of a committed group of volunteers and a wider supportive church network. As a Community Ministry Pastor, I sometimes personally feel a pressure from statements such as "if these people would just give their lives to Christ everything will be fine." For some in the congregation, a simple conversion is what they believe is required to resolve the multidimensional factors contributing to family violence.

From another perspective there are those with the view that the success of the whole ministry ought to be measured by how many souls are saved and that ought to be the criteria for resourcing or supporting various ministries. These challenges include the tendency to assume that when certain Christian principles are applied to family violence, such as praying, turning the other cheek, or forgiving seventy times seven, a safe solution will be forthcoming. For some, when these principles are applied, they are interpreted as markers of growth in the discipleship of the woman dealing with abuse in her life.

Basically the challenges to which I am referring have arisen as particular people in the church do not appreciate the complexity of men's violence and or the misuse of certain Scriptures. Education and training is the key to change these misperceptions.

The stories of two women help to illustrate the collision of different expectations between a community ministry and a Christian worshipping community. These are the challenges of which I write.

One woman came to Project Esther after prosecution for benefit fraud; she was to work out her judiciary sentence by doing community service with us. We had her working as a volunteer at our music and movement sessions for parents and their pre-schoolers. This led to her developing relationships with others, attending some support groups, and eventually coming to church and making a decision to become a follower of Jesus. We celebrated with her as she made these positive choices.

Then there came a time where she needed to flee from her husband's abuse and she was offered a place in *Te Whare Atawhai*, our emergency accommodation. Some of her newly found Christian friends were most concerned and insistent that she return to her husband. He became a target for overt evangelistic efforts, which included being accompanied to an Alpha course. He too made a decision to become a Christian and, on the basis of this, some folk pressured the woman to reconcile with him and continue in the marital relationship. The sanctity of marriage was proclaimed and promoted. Some people praised God for her husband's salvation, which they saw as the salvation of the marriage too.

The happily-ever-after scenario was short lived. The complexity of abuse was not appreciated. The perspective held was unrealistic and not rooted in any evidence of transformation and changed behavior. Nothing was ever asked of the husband in terms of his abuse, as people claimed God had forgiven him for everything in the past. If he continued to abuse and his wife continued to forgive, this scenario was considered by some as progress and the formula for their spiritual maturity.

In another unrelated case, a church member took refuge in our emergency accommodation and the husband 'came to the Lord' in a dramatic conversion experience. There were many tributes given to his marvelous turnaround and his decision to live in a different way. As in the first story, told above, a little party was held to celebrate the successes of dramatic conversions.

Both men were in some ways deceived by the church, its culture, and its messages as much as they deceived the people of the congregation and its leadership. Both men believed their violence would cease since God was now part of their lives and they both embraced fully the view that their wives would have to forgive anything they might do in the future, including abusive acts, since they were now believers.

Both women's lives deteriorated in quality as did the home environment for their respective children.

As a pastor, I was caught in the middle, in a very awkward place. I offered words of caution. I stressed the need for more understanding about the complexity of abuse. In response, I was asked why I was "not committed to the sacrament of marriage and didn't I have faith in God's power to change these men's lives?" The phrase "It takes two to make a marriage work" was repeated to me on several occasions! The underlying view that was expressed to me as pastor was that the women had to do their part, be forgiving, be submissive, turn the other cheek, and not provoke the men whose anger might rage against them.

So the challenges were related to church people unintentionally misusing Scripture, particularly teachings around issues of forgiveness, suffering, God's will, headship, and marriage for life. These Scriptures were highlighted for both women. They were proclaimed from both folk who supported the women and from the support the husbands received. Success in evangelism was considered paramount to a woman's safety. The complexity of abuse, or the long road of accountability, or the need for women's journey towards healing was never fully understood. Essentially, church people espousing these teachings did not understand issues of safety as it related to domestic violence in the family context.

At times there has been resistance when church women want to use our emergency facility for respite and safety or to be referred to an alternative safety shelter. Some church members are not convinced it is appropriate for a Christian woman to flee her abusive husband. They hold marriage in high regard and want the church to be seen to model this. As a result, Project Esther has drawn criticism from some people.

Fortunately, in our particular congregation there is enough support and insight to provide such emergency accommodation when asked, despite the criticism of some. Like the two oceans, we still have our days of tension and mutual resistance but ultimately those oceans do merge. We can both be concerned about family violence and celebrate church fellowship and new believers. But, we all look forward to consistent settled weather conditions!

Another challenge for a ministry working with women and families at risk relates to teachings on the family that are highlighted both on Sunday and within the wider culture of the local church. This surfaces in a variety of ways, from the way the Sunday service is conducted to the explicit content of the teaching. There can be tension when certain well-known and promoted male-focused ministries advocate and model relationships of headship and submission.

As churches we aim to connect compassionately within our church walls and beyond. In New Zealand, as church congregations, we have our own particular contributions to make to strengthen families and end abuse. Together with the wider community we collectively groan at the persuasiveness of family violence, which is highlighted by our media and that which we know is hidden and silenced even within our congregations. We, along with the secular community, continue to observe and ask questions about attitudes, morals, values, and practices that have been modelled, taught, and fostered in our church cultures, which are hampering safety within families. We can ask where and why have we applied Scriptures and theology that has enabled violence to exist unchallenged. For our part in ending violence we can ask from the pulpit on Sundays: in what ways will we seek to counter domestic abuse within leadership and governance?; how we serve and connect with our communities to counter domestic abuse?; and what would God want our churches to model?

Voices are being raised and are asking what influence and role our church culture and practice has on promoting, allowing, and even silencing any mention of family violence. It is not pain free to critique such issues. Church culture and practice does not seem to appreciate or consider important of dealing with the issue of violence in the family context..

As church communities we would prefer to focus and be known for the good things we are doing. However, we can be reminded, as Amos said to the people of God, "*you* are selling the righteous for silver and the needy for a pair of sandals." We too, as church communities, have and do contribute in various ways to family abuse—albeit, at times, unwittingly and unintentionally.

Prophets of old, like Amos, articulated to God's people exactly how they were expected to model God's standards of justice: by letting justice roll down like rivers and righteousness like an ever flowing stream. We too as church communities are called to our particular work, like the cessation of family violence.

Of any people group we have the resources, mandate, and guiding principles, which when applied, will strengthen families and end abuse. God's intentions are clear in the original creation account—that man and woman were made in the image of God. There was mutuality and egalitarianism and oneness. On the other hand, violence and inequality are consequences of the fall, consequences which Jesus came to redeem along with all other sin-induced suffering and pain. As churches we are the people of God to act out God's story, God's intentions, and the beautiful outcomes of redemption.

The modelling of male-dominated church leadership is tolerated, accommodated, promoted, and valued. Some churches validate such bias using Scripture and its impact is detrimental and influential on family abuse. Within this framework, women and issues of importance to women are minimized. Good intentions—combined with ignorance, skewed biblical interpretation and theology, and modelling of gender biased church leadership—is reflected in Sunday church gatherings. Serious thought must be given to the negative consequences of this. As a pastor working with Project Esther, there is another hurdle to ending abuse. It concerns valuing and maintaining treatment work as more critical than the work of prevention. Churches are especially vulnerable to this as it makes us look good and important when we offer accommodation to a victim, raise money, cook or bake for refuges and shelters. These are good actions and required of us. But it is an incomplete response and a more comprehensive one is invited by Jesus, "In your kingdom come, your will be done, in earth as it is in heaven."

But "bringing this kingdom" to family abuse means reversing and stopping abuse. This calls us, within the church, to the enormous and costly multifaceted task of challenging and dismantling all that encourages and fosters the abuse of power within our churches. Then comes the task of envisioning and rebuilding, employing the designs of God's original intentions.

This is hard work.

There are further tensions when inviting the church to consider patriarchal strongholds as contributing to abuse. A ministry working with and serving women who are abused wants and yet does not want to sabotage the benefits of witness, support, prayer, and any help the local church has to offer. Sometimes by resourcing and serving victims of abuse both within the walls of the church and in the community our churches hinder on some levels the means to work towards ending abuse.

Strengthening families and ending abuse cannot only be about giving a woman and her family a safe place. The concept of "strengthening the family" must also include the goal of bringing about the cessation of the injustice of family violence.

This chapter started by recounting the relationship Project Esther had with a woman who went to prison for a number of years for killing her abusive partner. Earlier this year a young woman arrived at the church reception office wanting to see me. Our receptionist came to find me and said these words, "A young woman is waiting to see you; she said if I told you her name you would help her and she says she needs help."

As soon as I heard her name, I went with much enthusiasm to find her, and embraced this youngest daughter of the mother who had gone to prison when she was just a baby.

What help did she want? Her life has been lived through the grind—it was the story of a child and young person whose mother has spent most of her daughter's life behind bars. She has had to navigate the separation from her mother, and the separation from her older siblings. She, and one of her brothers, went to live with, and be raised by, their elderly grandmother, a woman who was reluctant at the time about inheriting the role of raising a baby and another pre-schooler. At no point has this young woman's life journey been easy. And there she was in my office, asking for help about how to access counseling. In her words, she was having trouble with life. Together with her young boyfriend, both unemployed, they wanted to know if "the church" could help them.

Since that time, they have been coming on Sundays for several months, and have joined a small midweek group. They have decided, at least for now, to join our community of faith. But, what will we be for her? How will we be part of her journey? In what ways will we be empowering, life-giving, and respectful? She has dreams, she wants to study, she has pain, she has need, she has gifts, experience, wisdom, and her boyfriend has his story as well. How will our congregation meet their needs, encourage their journeys, and assist with the healing process? As they come to church, Sunday by Sunday, I feel a mixture of hopefulness and tentativeness about the role our church community and our church culture will play in her continued development. I celebrate the kindness of the small life group that has made them welcome each week and the delight of standing next to her in church and hearing her young voice singing, proclaiming God's great love for her.

It is important that what is being expounded and practiced from the pulpit is helpful and valuing of her gender, complex history, and forward life journey. Such practices as inclusive language, as well as women and men modelling egalitarianism with spiritual gifts (in preaching, leading, teaching) will be sowing seeds in her young mind and heart. She will be making many conscious and subconscious conclusions about herself, and about God as she comes and listens, and sings, and prays in our midst. It is important that as her trust grows and she begins to articulate and speak of her life and issues that those who listen will respond with wisdom and use of Scripture which is well informed, sound, and constructive.

God trusts us with her: can we serve her well?

There is also her boyfriend: what is he absorbing as he journeys as part of our community. What is being modelled to him Sunday by Sunday and during the week? What is he learning and absorbing about relationships and gender as he journeys with us? Will some well-meaning man invite him to a men's ministry popular with some that promotes headship, submission, and male entitlement? There are so many questions, and so many concerns. As a pastor, I think on these things.

CONCLUSION

In conclusion, let us bear in mind and heart women who face the anguish of family violence who are within the walls of church communities, on its edges and beyond. Any plan for action must include all of these groups of women. This invites church communities to take seriously woman abuse in all its varied forms, to work with women, men, and children who are victims, and abusers, but also to consider what we might do to stop the violence in the first place.

A most influential dimension of our faith journey as we respond compassionately is how we talk about and apply scripture to the problem of abuse. And then we must consider issues such as how we resource each other, and our faith communities, to do that with integrity. We need to make good use of existing, honorable, exegesis of Scripture, and to work towards God's intention for oneness, mutuality, and respect in all aspects of individual and corporate relationships.

Let's not get trapped into the adulation of being popular or famous as a congregation for doing good works and by-pass the very hard and costly work of prevention. Let's own how the modelling of power bias in church leadership and culture is failing to follow Paul's model of neither slave, nor free, Jew nor Greek, male or female. Let's maximize our advantage of faith and resource in our God who did everything possible to turn the kingdom of darkness on its head and bring a kingdom of love and peace and safety to all, especially to those who are the most vulnerable.

16

The Story of Restored

Mandy Marshall and Peter Grant

EDITOR'S COMMENTS:
The reader will note that the format of this chapter differs from others in this volume. We wanted to include the story of Restored in part because Catherine Clark Kroeger was such a strong supporter of this new initiative and longed to see work around the world that supported peace and safety in the Christian home as a reflection of the Biblical message.

RESTORED GREW OUT OF Tearfund. Tearfund is a British-based, Christian international development agency that began in 1968. After 2005, Tearfund adopted HIV and AIDS as one of its corporate priorities. This led to important work on tackling stigma in the church and to test out whether attitudes and behaviours within families and communities could be changed on the basis of a biblically-based approach. This work in Burkina Faso and Zimbabwe was led by Mandy Marshall, Tearfund's Gender Adviser. The case study can be found here: http://tilz.tearfund.org/webdocs/Tilz/Topics/Gender/Gender%20HIV%20and%20Church%20web.pdf.

In 2008 both Mandy Marshall and Peter Grant, the International Director of Tearfund, joined a delegation to the World AIDS conference in Mexico City. As the result of attending this conference, Mandy and Peter realized that the problem of abuse of women across cultures needed to be addressed. Here they provide the process by which they formed and developed Restored and also review Restored's mission.

BECOMING AWARE OF THE NEED

On 1 August 2008 at the Mexico City Conference we heard a Namibian woman tell her story of being raped three times as a teenager. God spoke powerfully that day. How had we allowed a world in which women could suffer so much, and men could commit acts of violence with such apparent impunity? Also at the conference was Lyn Lusi from Goma, who spoke about the appalling sexual violence in Democratic Republic of the Congo and the work of HEAL Africa[1] both to undertake restorative surgery for women, but also to challenge the culture and beliefs that made such violence possible. We were confronted by two questions: where is the church, and where are the men when it comes to ending violence against women? We knew that we needed to do something in response to what we had heard.

Researching and praying

When we returned to the UK, we expressed our desire to do something and consulted widely with other Christians involved in social development about the issue. We communicated what a response by the church, including men, might look like. We then entered an extraordinary period in which God opened numerous doors and spoke to us very clearly about the extent to which the issue of violence against women was on His heart. People started to pray for us, some with great prophetic insight and encouragement. We have many prophecies and Scriptures that were given to us in this period, which provided a precious foundation for the work. We met an amazing range of people who were called by God to work on these issues with men, soldiers, prostitutes, young people, and survivors of domestic violence. We were confirmed in our

---

1. Founded over a decade ago during the peak of the conflict by Congolese orthopedic surgeon Jo Lusi and his social activist wife Lyn, HEAL Africa is a direct response to horrific conditions. HEAL Africa partners proactively with communities to transform the status of women and bring village life back into balance. Through its full-service training hospital in Goma and its community-based initiatives in public health, community development, and conflict resolution, HEAL Africa works with individuals and communities to restore health, build hope, and help create a better future for all people of the DR Congo.

focus on the church and on men—violence against women cannot be just a women's issue. Jan Ransom from Flame International summed it up when she said that "it is the attitudes and actions of men that have to change."

Our research suggested that there was no organization bringing together the efforts of Christians working on violence against women worldwide. Whilst there were pockets of good practice going on these were often under resourced and over utilized. We wanted to help bring people and information together to resource Christians globally. We also felt that there was insufficient high-profile challenge to some of the attitudes and teaching within the church, which we feared were exacerbating the problem and making it very difficult for women to disclose their experiences. When we spoke at events and met people we got very powerful responses, which convinced us that this was God's time for these issues to be addressed. A group of people formed to encourage us and direct the work, including Elaine Storkey, the President of Tearfund. There was an increasing conviction that God wanted us to establish an alliance working in this area and in October 2010 the group agreed to establish a new organization. Restored was born.

Development and launch of Restored

This meant changes for both of us. Tearfund allowed us to work on the development of Restored within our existing roles, but it soon became clear for Peter that he should leave his role as International Director of Tearfund to become Co-Director of Restored. Wise advice from friends led to Peter combining his Restored work with a move into consultancy. Mandy was able to combine her role in Tearfund with Co-Director of Restored until she left Tearfund in June 2012. We both continue to work as Co-Directors of Restored on a half-time basis. Restored is about men and women standing together to end violence against women. We have two Co-Directors and a Board of Directors, chaired by Jill Garner, with equal numbers of women and men.

We have been very encouraged by Restored's progress so far. Our original vision for churches and men to be mobilized to end violence against women is beginning to be realized as we see the growth of a global Christian alliance committed to transforming relationships and ending violence against women. Restored was registered as a company in May 2010 and as a charity in July 2010, through the excellent work of one of our trustees, Matthew Hutton. At our launch event, the "Bringing Hope" Conference held in June 2010, we had the privilege of listening to Catherine Clark Kroeger as the keynote speaker, who passed on her wisdom and reflections from a lifetime of working to end violence against women. She remains a huge inspiration to us all at Restored.

THE WORK OF RESTORED

Since that time we have developed a church pack which provides basic information to equip local churches to respond to domestic abuse (see www.restoredrelationships.org). We have had the opportunity to speak at a range of conferences and church events and on TV and radio to raise the profile of these issues. Natalie Collins, officer and an indispensable part of the team, has been able to share her story of living in an abusive relationship powerfully in many locations and led the work related to domestic abuse in the UK, including writing the church pack. She has developed training materials for young people and is developing a training strategy for UK churches.

In our men's work, we have collaborated with Christian Vision for Men[2] and have hugely appreciated the encouragement and support of its General Director, Carl Beech. In June 2011 we launched First Man Standing, a campaign challenging men to "Respect all women, challenge other men, and join the cause to end violence against women." Regular follow up with several hundred men has helped to start a movement for change on which we can build for the future.

We have seen that violence against women is found in all societies around the world. In the UK one in four women will experience violence in their lifetime; internationally, one in three women will experience violence. In Bangladesh, over fifty percent of women experience domestic violence; in Kyrgyzstan women are kidnapped and forced into marriage; in many parts of Africa cultural practices (including female genital mutilation, initiation rites, and widow cleansing[3] exacerbate the

---

2. "CVM is a movement. It is made up of thousands of men who believe the message of Jesus is true, relevant and much needed in the UK today. CVM exists to serve the local church to engage with men in every village, town and city in this country. CVM supports and equips anyone who believes the Christian message can still radically change people's lives today." See: http://cvm.org.uk/about.php.

3. "Widow cleansing gives a nod to a man from the widow's village or her husband's family, usually a brother or close male relative of her late husband, to force her to have sex with him—ostensibly to allow her husband's spirit to roam

vulnerability of women; in Latin America churches are often dominated by "machismo" culture. Restored is a member of the We Will Speak Out Coalition, which is focused on ending sexual violence with and through the church. Mandy has particularly been involved in delivering training and resources through the coalition to church leaders and communities across Africa and in Russia and Central Asia. This work continues.

Since its inception, the Restored alliance has grown to fifty-seven members (including PASCH) in over fifteen countries. We are continuing to seek ways to support members in their work and to help them to work together at national and international levels. This includes "28 Too Many" led by Ann-Marie Wilson, who works closely with us, which is dedicated to ending the practice of female genital mutilation across Africa and in diaspora communities worldwide.

CHALLENGES AND OPPORTUNITIES FOR THE CHURCH

Working with and through the church brings both great opportunities and great challenges. The Christian church is one of the biggest global communities with millions of members. In many countries there is a church in most villages and towns. Indeed, churches can be found in the smallest of communities in some nations. With this global reach at the community level the church is centrally placed to bring about cultural change, support, encouragement, prayer, and social action with advocacy. The church remains highly influential in many communities and can be the pillar of support when help is needed. Many people flock to the church in times of crisis and look for help from within. This high level of trust needs to be rewarded through safe, practical advice and support on issues of relationships and how to end violence against women.

Sadly the church sometimes does not, because of human failure, give the best advice nor support. In some cases we know the church has contributed to women remaining in violent relationships because they have been told they are 'not submitting enough' or 'need to pray more.' This misuse of the Scriptures can lead to devastating effects on women. We need to use Scriptures with caution when we are pacing the lives

---

free in afterlife. It is also rooted in the belief that a woman is haunted by spirits after her husband dies or that she is thought to be unholy and 'disturbed' if she now is unmarried and abstains from sex." See: http://isiria.wordpress.com/2009/04/13/the-appalling-practice-of-widow-cleansing/.

of women and children at risk. Part of Restored's church pack gives an overview of helpful and unhelpful theology to assist in clarifying some of the Scriptures related to women and men that are often debated. The church also needs to grapple with difficult issues such as divorce and remarriage. The covenant relationship can keep women in situations where the husband is choosing to abuse a lot longer than is safe to do so. Barbara Roberts states in her book, *Not Under Bondage*, that when abuse occurs the person choosing to abuse has broken the covenant. Divorce, as a result of abuse, is making public this breaking of the covenant. The church needs to address some of these thorny issues if we are to both support victims of abuse and confront perpetrators of abuse in ways that bring men to account for their actions and to full repentance.

HOPE FOR THE FUTURE—THE STORY CONTINUES TO UNFOLD

Where do we go from here? We remain convinced that God is behind this work and that He longs to see an end to the violence that brings fear and suffering to so many women around the world. We continue to pray regularly alongside the practical action convinced that we need to be led by God every step of the way. One important part of the bible for us has been Isa 61. God promises to bring ". . . a crown of beauty instead of ashes, the oil of joy instead of mourning, and a garment of praise instead of a spirit of despair." Our prayer is that this might be more and more true in the lives of women and that churches and men, standing together with women, will demonstrate an increasing commitment to ending all forms of violence.

We are beginning to see impact in the lives of women given new hope by the launch of Restored and the early signs that both churches and men are willing to respond. Our model is Jesus himself, who demonstrated what life and relationships could be like. We are committed to this work in the long term and believe that God will bring change and restoration. We look forward to working with others to see this come about. If you want to know more about Restored do contact us at info@restoredrelationships.org and please use the free resources on our website at www.restoredrelationships.org. You can keep in touch with Restored on Facebook at www.Facebook.com/RestoredRelationships and on Twitter @Restored.

17

Caring for the Caregivers

The Efficacy of a Centred Meditation Practice within a Secular Setting

Irene Sevcik, Nancy Nason-Clark, Michael Rothery and Robert Pynn

INTRODUCTION

The work of the FaithLink program, spanning a decade, confirms research findings by Nason-Clark (1997) that when religious communities and secularly-based service agencies work collaboratively they each benefit from the collective wisdom and expertise of the other. The FaithLink program grew out of work by key religious, social services, and justice leaders in Calgary, Alberta (Canada) to create a broadly-based and coordinated response to intimate partner violence (IPV). Not only did this group recognize that IPV occurs as frequently within religious communities as it does within the general population, their desire for a broad-based and coordinated response required that religious communities be included.

To explore how religious communities could be engaged, a small committee was formed and therein FaithLink was born. It took as its vision this statement: *Spiritual/religious communities and service providers working together to prevent domestic violence and to provide healing and hope to all those affected by it.* To fulfill this mission five areas of focus were identified:[1]

- With religious communities, to raise awareness of the issue of IPV and enhance response capacities.
- With secularly-based service providers, to raise awareness of the importance spirituality holds for women of faith who access their services.
- To build collaborative working relationships between religious/ethno-cultural leaders and service providers.
- In recognition of the effects of vicarious trauma, to offer opportunities to those who are first responders to traumatized individuals opportunities to enhance their self-care; and
- To conduct relevant research that explores the interface between the religious and the secular regarding IPV.[2]

It is the fourth focus—which we labelled 'caring for the caregiver'—that is the focus of this chapter. The research project which we report here emerged from two unique events in 2004, sponsored by FaithLink, which introduced the concept and practice of a centering contemplative meditation practice to the Calgary community's family and sexual violence service sector. The first event was a week-long series of workshops in which the focus was on contemplative meditation as a self-care technique. The resource person was Dr. Cynthia Bourgeault.[3] She met with small and large groups in sessions that ranged from an hour over lunch to a full day. Front line service providers and Executive Directors of service agencies availed themselves of this opportunity. The second event occurred in the fall of 2004 and took the form of a one day conference, the theme of which was again centred meditation and collaborative work. As with all of the conferences sponsored by FaithLink, attendees included both secularly-based service providers and religious leaders. Following the spring workshops

---

1. For a more complete description of the FaithLink project and its work see Sevcik and Reed, "It's everybody's business," in Kroeger et al., *Beyond Abuse*, 146–166.

2. See Sevcik et al., "Finding their voices," in Kroeger et al., *Responding to Abuse*, 169–189.

3. Dr. Bourgeault is an Episcopal priest, Christian contemplative and Wisdom teacher, author on the spiritual life, retreat Leader and conference presenter on Centered Meditation.

a group of agency directors began discussing how they could utilize this meditation practice within the context of their work and agency environments. After the fall conference this committee asked FaithLink to take a leadership role in conducting a piece of research that would examine three primary questions:

- What effects, if any, a centred meditation practice would have for front line service providers in managing work-related stress.

- What effects, if any, a centred meditation practice would have in increasing the capacity of counselors to 'be present' with clients; and

- What effects, if any, a centred meditation practice would have on collaborative work among colleagues within one's own agency and with colleagues from other agencies.

IMPLEMENTING THE RESEARCH

There is growing recognition of vicarious trauma—'the cost of caring' as Figley (1995) termed it—borne by first responders to those impacted by traumatic events, including IPV. These impacts are a result of both the stress and often crisis nature of the work, and repeatedly hearing and being empathetic towards victims who tell their traumatic stories. There is also a growing body of research on the effectiveness of various forms of meditation practices, also referred to as 'mindfulness,' to alleviate symptoms arising from a variety of illnesses and psychological conditions; improve general health, well-being and emotional balance; and reduce stress.

The research proposed by the agency directors was in recognition of the risks to which their staff members were exposed and the realization that a meditative practice may well prove efficacious in enhancing staff well-being, enhancing the effectiveness of the work, and strengthening working relationships among colleagues.[4]

---

4. Bonadonna, "Meditations' impact"; Bourgeault, *The Wisdom Way of Knowing*; Clemans, "Life-changing"; Figley, "Compassion fatigue," *Treating Compassion Fatigue*; Finley, *Christian meditation*; Iliffe & Steed, "Exploring the counselor's"; Kabat-Zinn et al., "Effective of meditation-based"; Newberg & Waldman, *How God Changes Your Brain*; Majumbar et al., *Alternative Complementary Medicine*; Mason & Hargreaves,"A qualitative study"; Reibel et al., "Mindfulness-based stress reduction"; Rosenzweig et al., "Mindfulness-based stress reduction"; Unger "Web extra"; UCLA Psychoneuroimmunology Center "Mindfulness research"; Way et al., "Vicarious trauma."

The research project comprised two phases: training and support, data collection and analysis. Developing a meditation practice requires instruction and discipline. To facilitate the implementation of such a practice with research subjects, training and support were offered over a six week period. Full-day training sessions in the theory and implementation of a contemplative meditation practice were offered in weeks one, three and six. Weekly, thirty-minute support groups were arranged for the intervening weeks. The training sessions were led by Dr. Cynthia Bourgeault and The Very Reverend Robert Pynn.[5] The intent of the support groups was to encourage a disciplined practice. A designated leader arranged time, place, space and facilitated practice and discussion.

Thirty-one research participants, recruited through general advertising within family violence service and general counseling agencies, completed the three days of training and availed themselves of the support groups as their schedules allowed. They also committed themselves to private meditation practice.

Research data were collected utilizing a number of instruments and methods that were employed over the course of a three month period. An initial survey questionnaire was administered to participants on the first day of training. Two semi-structured interview sets were conducted, the first immediately following the training and support phase, the second set six weeks following the first. The first interview focused on the general themes of the research project and the second interview captured further reflections participants had on the effects of the meditation practice within the context of their work environments. Following the initial analysis of the survey and interview data, two focus groups were held where participants responded to the general themes researchers were identifying as arising from the data.

Before presenting the research findings, it is worthwhile to clarify two key terms used in the study.

- Vicarious trauma:[6] the transformation of the therapist's or helper's inner experience as a result of empathetic engagement with survivor

---

5. The Very Reverend Robert Pynn, Dean Emeritus of the Anglican Diocese of Calgary, a practitioner of contemplative meditation.

6. Clemans, "Life-changing"; Costa, "Compassion fatigue"; Figley, "Compassion fatigue"; *Treating Compassion Fatigue*; Iliffe & Steed, "Exploring the counselor's experience"; Richardson, *Guidebook*; Saakvitne & Pearlman, *Transforming the Pain*; Way et

clients and their trauma material. It results in physical, emotional, and spiritual exhaustion and difficulty separating from one's work. These effects can be subtle or pronounced, are uniquely applicable, and can extend to all realms of the helper's life. Those working with IPV victims describe: having visual images of abusive events that have been described to them; of experiencing physical reaction (churning stomach, nausea, feeling shaken); being angry, sad,, and unsupported by the legal and justice systems. They describe becoming immune as a self-protection method. Because most IPV victims are women, vicarious trauma effects appear to be more intensely and frequently felt by female counselors.

- Contemplative meditation: Meditation is a spiritual practice common to all religious traditions, which hold a vision of human transformation. Within the Christian West meditation is most commonly identified with the Christian tradition of contemplation. Contemplative meditation is intentional silence, the fostering of an attitude of listening and receptivity; a listening within, a function of consciousness, not intellect. Bourgeault (2004) describes meditation as the deliberate effort to "restrain the wandering of the mind, either by slowing down the thought process itself or by developing a means of detaching oneself from it."(8). Centering Prayer is described as a preparatory method for contemplation by "reducing obstacles caused by the hyperactivity of our minds and of our lives."[7] The meditative stance is that of being present, open, and awake to thoughts (including feelings, memories, interior dialogue, physical sensations, and/or stimulation), not clinging to or rejecting anything as it may arise, and maintaining a nonjudgmental and compassionate attitude towards oneself and others. The goal is to develop a detached attitude towards one's thoughts, letting them go as they are noticed, not engaging in self-reflection. This 'letting go' of thoughts is also referred to as 'surrendering.'

---

al., "Vicarious trauma."

7. Keating, *Intimacy with God,* 11.

FINDINGS:

Vicarious trauma is a reality

The majority of both front line and management personnel who participated in this study describe effects of their work, which are consistent with experiencing vicarious trauma. They spoke of their own experiences and their observations of colleagues. Specifically, they noted the cumulative effect of vicarious trauma and offered personal, relational, and workplace based examples, including:

- A high level of stress.
- The inability to 'leave work at work' (sleep disturbances, nightmares).
- Relational tension (edginess, denial, rudeness, anger), including a mistrust of and a skewed perspective of men.
- Hyper-vigilance about their own safety.
- Ill health.
- The need to vent frustrations.
- Desensitization to client situations (as a defense mechanism); and
- Staff turnover as a result of being 'burned out.'

Participants credited the study's focus on vicarious trauma for heightening their own awareness of its negative effects on their work. They also noted that through their meditation practice they became more aware of their own feeling states and of the impact working with traumatized individuals, and within a crisis oriented environment was having on them. They recognized that by participating in the study they were gaining the advantage of being able to recognize the symptoms sooner and to more readily take action to relieve the stress and limit the traumatizing effects.

The nature of the work, its inherent danger, and the demands of the workplace combine to increase the risk of vicarious trauma. The workload carried by participants, its nature, and demands were identified as significant contributing factors to their level of stress: "*. . . the workload is so high, and we're into it, and meeting goals and meeting deadlines. . . doing so much that sometimes we forget about us.*" The constancy of being available takes its toll: "*You cannot not respond to a crisis call or someone arriving at the door.*" From the perspective of someone who had had experience responding to the crisis line in an emergency shelter, one participant noted: "... *but that front line office, forget it. I've been in there and it is go, go, go, go.*" With the tight budgets many agencies experience, workloads tend to increase during times when regular staffing is decreased, (e.g., vacation times, on statutory holidays).

The element of danger is an ever-present preoccupation, whether working within a shelter or within a community-based counseling program with victims of violence. A shelter worker remarked: "*We are a secure site, [but] I still remind myself that I am working in a high risk situation.*" Those working in community-based counseling programs identified the level of vulnerability they feel when visiting victims: "*We are working in family violence. So I may not talk about it, but I am very mindful. Depending on the day, anything can happen.*" "*[When you do home visits] you're always on guard, and you're always at risk. It's one thing to be in the building [i.e., the shelter]—it's another thing to be in the home. . . . Maybe there's a restraining order, but whoop-dee-do.*" The reality of the danger inherent within the work is heightened when a victim is murdered. "*I thought it was one of my clients and it triggers so much. . . . I was really conscious when I was going out from the office yesterday because I was leaving the grounds at 7 pm and I started to be more conscious of my surroundings. . . .*"

The need for constant vigilance for one's safety also takes energy and becomes, as one participant noted, "*normal for us. . . . Because we know the work we do . . . we need to be alert. . . . I didn't realize that I'm always [alert for my safety] . . . but now I'm more conscious . . . I have to watch.*"

All research participants identified self-care practices they and their colleagues use in maintaining personal well-being. The specific practices are as varied as individual interests and abilities. There is, however, a common theme—they find themselves in a "Catch 22," struggling to maintain the very practices they know they need. It seems that as the demands of the workplace increase, their ability to implement self-care practices decreases.

The busyness of the work place, with its 'multi-tasking' demands contributes to the crisis atmosphere and stress-inducing impact. The comment of one participant captures her struggle, as a supervisor, to implement helpful management techniques. "*It's just that everybody's so busy, in terms of the job, it's like: 'Wow, there's so much to get done, and there's so much to do.' And it's like, 'How do you take care of your staff when all this is happening, and how do you check in with your colleagues, when all this is going on?' and you hear mostly the same thing: 'Going good, really, really busy, gotta go.'"

Even when there is support for staff members to take time to meet with colleagues at worksites, the demands of the work hinder consistent attendance. Time demands squeeze out self-care intentions. When workers do access on-site opportunities or take time for themselves, they find it hard to 'turn off' the immediacy of the situation and to become centered and calm. "*So when push comes to shove, your self-care in the work place just is a lower priority.*"

Contemplative meditation proved a mitigating practice

Having identified the reality of vicarious trauma and the high degree of stress encountered in their work environments, we were particularly interested to know what, if any, effects the meditation practice had in mitigating the deleterious effects identified by participants. Participating in the research project raised participants' awareness of the importance of self-care and the need for intentional and consistent implementation of self-care habits. Many identified the contemplative meditation practice as an additional self-care tool. One management group participant, who came to the research project with an established meditation practice, spoke of her experience:

> *[It's] just that calmness . . . a feeling of control, more power, for myself and my own decisions. . . . I feel so much more able to deal with larger . . . issues because it's been a clarity for me . . . when we've had . . . conflict, I've had to go to the person and maneuver or facilitate it. I did a meditation on that, to get some answers on how to approach that situation. And I write that down and so before I go in, I take that time, I just take a minute or two to have my paper, think about it, get grounded, and deal with it. It's become much better, for myself, because I walk into those meetings and I've had some where it just works. It's so successful.*

Despite its advantages, only a few participants noted they have made it a priority to practice daily by scheduling a regular time and intentionally maintaining the routine. With this disciplined approach, it becomes easier to be consistent with the practice. Most, however, experienced difficulty in finding the time to fit it into their day. They spoke of not having enough time in the day, of being too tired, and of the busyness of life as factors that limit their meditation practice.

Even given a rather sporadic utilization of the meditative practice, participants still reported significant and positive effects. They spoke of an increased sense of well-being and the influence on their work environments.

> "It has [had an impact on how I handle the work.] I think I'm able to step back, I'm able to be more objective and to allow people their own process. . . . That's really freeing. I've changed a lot. . . . I find myself doing a lot more asking questions and less information giving, letting people find their own solutions. . . . It's trusting that everybody's capable. . . . I don't have to run around trying to fix it all by myself."

> "I think I'm dealing with things a lot better. I think I feel a lot more grounded and calm. I'm not having as many jaggedy edges around my mind, my emotions. . . . I don't feel as anxious."

> "I feel more present, particularly after the support group. I feel in a better place."

> ". . . the protective shell we all develop is a little less hardened."

The themes that emerge from these and other comments suggest that a contemplative meditation practice has beneficial effects for those working in highly stressful situations and with traumatized individuals. Participants identify an increased sense of calm, of being more emotionally grounded, of increased objectivity, and trust that others have capabilities. With 'permission' to acknowledge the stress they experienced came also the permission to take time to reflect—even—if for only a few minutes. Participants credit the meditative practice with giving them a more objective perspective, of being able to let go of their own anticipated outcomes and to hear the perspectives of others. They are more able to be present with others and to allow decisions to flow from the collective discussion. With an increased sense of awareness and well-being, participants also gained a broader perspective of their work situations and their own place within it. They felt their own work was more effective.

Another common theme reported by participants was their ability to better handle the stresses they encountered. They attribute this to their changed perspective, particularly as it relates to the importance of self-care. They reported being more conscious of finding ways 'in the moment' to better shield themselves from the effects of constantly working with people experiencing multi-layered distress and the potential danger to their own person. They spoke of using meditation techniques to 'become centered in the midst' of handling a crisis; of giving themselves permission to 'not need to know everything;' of creating space and time to take a few minutes to 'slow down and re-group.' Some spoke of consciously assessing situations relative to the impact they felt they could have and of not assuming responsibilities that may be better assumed by others.

Most participants identified a number of specific personal changes which attributed to their increased ability to handle work environment stress:

- An increased ability to set boundaries, which decreased the impact of clients' situations and experiences.
- An increased ability to accept their own limitations.
- An increased awareness of the good intentions of colleagues.
- An increased awareness of one's own feeling and physical states 'in the moment,' of having become able to step back from the situation, of meditating 'on the spot' to lessen frustration and stress levels, of utilizing the meditative technique of surrendering thoughts.

Respondents also identified changes within their agency's culture. As one participant noted, "*When workers can deal better with stress, it has a positive effect on the work place environment.*"

How the meditation practice affected work with clients

The second area of interest to us as researchers was that of the counselor-client relationship and whether a contemplative meditation practice affected how counselors worked with their clients. In responding to this set of questions participants made a correlation between their own self-awareness and their work with clients. They credited the meditation practice with an increased self-awareness and effectiveness within the work setting. When asked to be specific about the effects within the counseling context they spoke of an increased ability to 'be present,' of being more aware of the client's attitude 'in the moment,' of their own sense of calm and confidence, and of a decreased tendency to 'rescue' the client. With increased ability to 'be present' their work with clients shifted in focus. The following statements are representative.

> "I've noticed that . . . I'm not as tense; I'm not as results-oriented. . . . I'm calm with it and I think things get processed faster, somehow, or certainly more effectively."

> "I think it helps me stay more focused, more available."

The meditation technique of surrender or letting go of thoughts, which a number of participants identified as helpful in their handling of the stress they experience, was also identified as an important factor in work with traumatized clients. As one respondent put it this way: "[I can] be more open to my clients' abuse experiences because I know I can 'surrender' the effects after the sessions." Others commented on an increased objectivity and awareness of the agenda they bring into the relationship. A few felt they had an increased confidence when handling difficult situations. A number of respondents noted that they were more conscious of the spiritual component and more comfortable in discussing spiritual issues with their clients.

Some workers noted their attempts at introducing some aspects of the meditation practice into their work with clients: some introduced times of quietness; others were working with the centering and surrender techniques.

> ". . . I had an opportunity [with a colleague to do] some teaching of [a mindful meditation practice] to a senior that I work with and it was one of the coolest things that I've seen, because this woman had huge resources and just had all sorts of insights. . . . That was one of the places, with a client, I saw that it was really helpful."

For some participants, their own meditation practice and learning shifted the perspective they took in working with clients. Not only were they viewing their clients more holistically, (i.e., there is more to the person than the experience of intimate partner violence), they had deliberately shifted their counseling focus. Rather than a focus on mourning the past, they were now placing a purposeful and intentional focus on the future. As one respondent noted, *"hope leads to empowerment, which in turn leads to action."* Others noted a shift in how they viewed the work itself: *"There is a creative and spiritual component to working with traumatized individuals. This work cannot be grounded only in the intellectual. To be effective we have to connect with our core components."*

Not all respondents felt that the meditation practice had impacted their work with clients. Some noted that there had been no discernible impact they could identify. There was an assumption by some that because they went into their counseling sessions more relaxed and calm, there would have to be an effect, but they were not able to identify specific changes. Others noted that it was too early to tell—they needed a longer period of time to practice the meditation before they could expect to notice any differences.

How the meditation practice affected relationships with colleagues

Given the effects of the meditation practice participants experienced relative to their work environments and their work with clients, it was not surprising that they also identified positive changes in their relationships with colleagues. Their increased self-awareness made them more flexible within their collegial relationships. Some participants identified a change in perspective, noting an increased ability to 'hear' colleagues as opposed to a former tendency to take a defensive posture. Of note were comments that suggested that conflicts were more easily resolved as former grievances were surrendered. An increased willingness to move away from their own agendas, to be more patient and accepting of colleagues was noted. They were now more accepting of differing approaches presented by co-workers. Participants also identified that having ways of dealing with stressful situations helped them better cope with stressors arising from relationships with colleagues. Their increased sense of personal 'authenticity' allowed for more genuine relationships. The following comments reflect these attitudinal changes.

> "I think so . . . just letting something go. I'm getting to the point where I can see the value in living a life where you don't have to be right. You don't have to agree. You can have an opinion and you can express that opinion and that's okay. And so I think when I go forth like that, I get that back. And that makes for much nicer relationships— where it's not the power, the control, one of [us] has to win, one of us has to be right. You can talk about what you're thinking and feeling and believing and that's okay. And I think the [contemplative meditation] will really help with that."

> "No, I have great co-workers. Let me think. I guess maybe again, being able to hear what they're saying, to listen more, more intently, than having to figure out what I'm going to say next."

A few respondents did not identify any discernable changes in their collegial relationships.

How the meditation practice changed workers personally

Throughout our discussions with participants it was evident that the changes in how they dealt with work related stressors, their work with clients, and their relationships with colleagues were grounded in changes, insights, and learning they experienced on a very personal level. As we worked with the data from our first set of interviews it became clear that the meditation practice changed participants in very personal ways—emotionally, spiritually, intellectually, and relationally. To explore these effects in more detail with participants we first inquired as to their pattern of, and general experience with, the practice. We then turned to understanding the impact it had on them as individuals. In an effort to apply some structure to these latter inquiries, we asked participants to comment on insights that were 'intellectual,' 'emotional,' and 'spiritual' in focus. We recognize that these are arbitrary demarcations and the data bears this out, particularly across the 'intellectual' and 'emotional' categories; the 'spiritual' was more distinct. There were, however, some very common themes that emerged. It was also evident that learning took place on more than one level. It is worthy to note that, although most participants reported positive personal changes related to the meditation practice, a very few did not. Rather they spoke of being uncomfortable with the inward focus of the practice and the potential that it could result in emotional crises.

Patterns of practice

How participants actually implemented the discipline of meditation was particular to the individual. Most participants reported patterns of practice which varied in frequency from several times a week to daily. They identified a more consistent practice during the training phase of the project than during the weeks following. The support offered by the groups during the six weeks of training was helpful to this end. When this support ended, some found it difficult to incorporate a regular practice into their schedules and life patterns. A few participants reported that they were not practicing at all or were doing so 'on an as-needed basis' (e.g., when feeling particularly stressed).

Participants spoke of the importance of developing a disciplined meditation practice. They related feeling better and having 'better days' on the days they meditated. A repeated comment was the value of the technique of surrendering thoughts. Through the conscious exercise of this technique—whether part of the formal meditation practice or 'in the moment'—participants noted they were able to 'let go' of 'stuff as it arises.' Some used the surrender exercise to deal with sleep disturbances and nightmares when the stress of work intruded on their ability to get proper rest. They described the effects of this technique as freeing, even as having a sense of 'cleansing.' By 'letting the little things go,' the ability to handle stress increased.

The importance of Self-care

Most participants noted an increased awareness of the importance of nurturing and caring for themselves—to not burn out; to be prepared for crises; and to be mindful of how one responds to crises. They also identified giving themselves 'permission' to care for themselves—to take personal time. A few spoke of implementing a disciplined practice.

> *I've certainly learned and made that commitment to be kind to myself. That's very, very important. No matter how busy my day gets . . . [it's important to take] some form of time out for me.*

> *[I'm] a lot more intentional [about self-care]. I've made it a priority. I'm less apt to abandon myself, which is kind of wonderful.*

A different perspective of themselves

Throughout their responses there is a consistent theme that the meditation practice had a positive effect on how they felt about and viewed themselves. Participants spoke of:

- Being more accepting of themselves—their value, equality, that they had something to contribute.

- Being more in control of themselves—their time, how they saw themselves, their responses to situations;

- An increased awareness of the importance of one's inner self and of acknowledging that some difficult issues may need to be addressed.
- An increased awareness of the need to maintain boundaries between their own emotional states and those of their clients.
- The need to respond to others from a less defensive position.

Changes in self and impact upon others

Participants spoke of the calming effect the practice had and the accompanying sense they gained of being more centered and grounded within themselves. They used a variety of phrases to describe their emotional experiences, such as a sense of peace and serenity, being more relaxed, the enjoyment of 'being quiet,' and an increased ability to regulate their level of activity—to deliberately 'slow down' the pace of their lives. Accompanying these changes were corresponding decreased levels of anxiety, anger, and stress. Some spoke of gaining the ability to 'let go' of fear, of self-judgment, or always feeling they have to 'perform.'

Some participants spoke of gaining awareness that they had been assuming responsibility for situations that rightly belonged to others or for which they could not effect change. With this awareness came the capacity to view situations within a broader perspective and an ability to set limits on the degree to which they took on unrealistic responsibilities. They identified the importance of setting stronger boundaries between their 'work lives' and their 'personal lives.'

> ... I'm very aware of limits now, and I'm very aware that. . . . I tend to think about [difficult cases] quite a bit. So I'm aware, even more so, about going home and trying to shut it off. I don't pick up my cell phone, like I used to, on weekends. I realize there's got to be a balance between home and family and so the little time I have off, I have to put it towards the family.

Participants reported that by participating in the research project they gave themselves 'permission' to pay attention to their feeling states. With this self-granting and the meditation practice came a deeper self-awareness. Participants noted an increased awareness of their ongoing coping level and the ability to take quicker action to self-correct when their level of stress escalated. Others spoke of being less 'self-driven'—of placing fewer expectations upon themselves, of gaining increased clarity of thought and ability to concentrate, of an increased openness to the perspectives presented by others. Out of this awareness came the realization that, for some, there was a need to make changes in their lifestyle. They spoke of a heightened awareness of the busyness of our culture (and their lives) with a focus on 'doing.' They expressed a desire to consciously take time 'to be' and to 'be with,' to move away from the need for intellectually-based answers by allowing other options to emerge through quietness and contemplation.

For some, there was a realization that they are not alone in experiencing stress as a result of their work. The 'learning' that others had similar experiences broke their sense of isolation. Others spoke of the importance of the trust which exists among colleagues and that this level of trust only develops when people are prepared to be vulnerable with each other.

The insights and emotional changes participants reported had influences beyond their work environments. A number spoke of positive changes in their personal relationships and lifestyles as well. They noted that as they themselves became more aware of, and dealt with, their 'own stuff' they were able to respond differently to others. *"And once I started looking more inward and acknowledging the feelings and emotions that were happening, I think I had more patience as a mother, I had more patience as a co-worker and more patience with my husband. . . . Knowing, acknowledging who we are, and we can't be everything to everybody. . . ."* Others spoke of an increased ability to handle stressful events within the family setting. Some reported that when both partners made a practice of taking personal time and space their marital relationship was enhanced.

Finally, a number of participants mentioned an increased sense of the spiritual as a result of the meditation practice. They spoke of being more conscious of the spiritual journey they were on; of a deeper spiritual awareness; of a sense of connectedness to a transcendent power— the divine, the creator, God, a higher power. *"Spiritually? Oh, now I'm tingling. What have I experienced spiritually? I feel a sense of confidence and a sense of guidance and I'm not alone. . . . I feel like I'm connected to something bigger, I'm not frantically searching in my head for this."* Others identified a confirmation of an established spiritual foundation, a validation of personal beliefs, of an awakening quest to re-establish religious practices. *"A sense of coming home. They're [the trainers] speak-*

ing in my language. They're talking about the stuff that's influencing me, my values."

DISCUSSION

The findings of this research study suggest that a contemplative meditation practice can significantly enhance the well-being of service providers, positively affect the efficacy of their work with clients, strengthen collaborative working relationships with colleagues, and change the perspective in which they view their work. As such, contemplative meditation can be viewed as an important practice for those responding to traumatized individuals.

The cost of caring

That there is an emotional cost borne by those who work with IPV victims is confirmed by this study. Although the body of research examining the effects on service providers working with this client group is limited, the personal testimonies provided by the participants of this study leave little doubt that they are impacted in significant ways. These effects are consistent with the findings of other studies and with the general symptoms associated with vicarious trauma.[8] The variation of effects reported by participants is also consistent with the findings of Saakvitne and Pearlman[9] who conclude that not all first responders to traumatized individuals are affected to the same degree. Rather it is the interplay between the personal and the situation that determines the specific impact. Mitigating factors include: the strength of one's professional identity; personal history; current life circumstances; one's coping style; the number and type of clients and their trauma; the length of time working with traumatized individuals; and the nature of the trauma.

The emotional cost arising from the nature of the work—its constant demand for compassionate responses, crisis-focused work environments, the implicit danger in IPV—is also seen in the struggle service providers have in caring for themselves. The more the demands

---

8. Clemans, "Life-changing"; Figley, "Compassion fatigue," *Treating Compassion Fatigue*; Iliffe & Steed, "Exploring the counselor's experience"; Way et al., "Vicarious trauma.."

9. Saakvitne and Pearlman, *Transforming the Pain*.

of the work indicate the need to exercise consistent self-care regimes, the less time and energy they have to actually implement these practices. To maintain their emotional well-being it is critical for service providers to exercise self-awareness as to the risks, self-assessment as to the on-going impacts of their work, and to be diligent for their self-care to both prevent and ameliorate the effects of vicarious trauma.[10] Without consistent monitoring and attention to the personal effects experienced as a result of their work, service workers are at risk of withholding or limiting their emotional availability to clients. As Iliffe and Steed[11] found, this self-protective stance can manifest itself in the tendency for counselors to 'avoid hearing' traumatic material and thereby limit the effectiveness of their therapeutic work.

The impact of contemplative meditation

The meditation practice had the effect of increasing practitioners' awareness of their own feeling states, making them more alert to the impacts of their work environment and to the symptoms of vicarious trauma they were experiencing. They were then in a position to more quickly take action to relieve stress and thus decrease the overall impact of their work with traumatized clients and the demands of the work place. That participants were more aware of their feeling states as a result of the meditation practice is not surprising. Keating,[12] speaking of Centering Prayer, notes that positive effects can be realized soon after starting the practice. Finley[13] notes that:

> You do not have to meditate very long to begin experiencing more interior, meditative states of awareness. There is something about simply sitting still, quietly attentive to your breathing, that tends to evoke less agitated, less thought-driven modes of awareness."

Similarly, Newberg & Waldman[14] report that even a few minutes of meditation can be beneficial to one's health.

---

10. Richardson, *Guidebook*; Saakvitne and Pearlman, *Transforming*.
11. Iliffe & Steed, "Exploring.."
12. Keating, *Intimacy with God*.
13. Finley, *Christian Meditation*, 42.
14. Newberg & Waldman, *How God Changes Your Brain*.

With increased awareness also came changes in how participants approached their counseling role. As they experienced increased internal calmness they were able to be more emotionally available to their clients, more alert to the client's presentation, more 'in the moment' with the material presented by the client. They found themselves approaching the counseling forum with a more positive and future-oriented perspective. As they experienced more confidence, and moved away from a 'rescuing' position with clients, they felt the effectiveness of their work increase.

A similar pattern is seen in how participants described changes in their relationships with co-workers. As they themselves gained self-awareness they were able to move away from more rigid positions resulting in more co-operative and flexible working relationships. Not surprisingly, they reported less conflict and more open decision-making processes.

In describing the changes they observed in their work with clients and their relationships with colleagues, participants spoke of the benefits they gained through the meditative technique of surrender. Within the context of contemplative meditation, surrender is the 'letting go' of issues, thoughts, hurts, anxieties as they arise. Keating[15] describes this 'relaxation of attention' as a purification process at work. Bourgeault herself identifies this gesture of release as the central power of the contemplative meditation form. The effects are realized in daily life: increased calmness and ability to cope with life circumstances; increased emotional and spiritual strength; and increased flexibility and compassion towards oneself and others.[16]

The meditation practice was also identified as affecting how service providers viewed the work of responding to IPV and their part in it. They reported moving from a more subjective to a more objective and broader perspective. This shift allowed them to see themselves as part of a larger whole and to place their contribution and responsibility within this broader context. With this shift also came a more holistic frame of reference, a decrease in personal agendas, defensiveness and need for control, and an increased confidence in the capabilities of others. This shift is exemplified in the challenge some participants ex-

---

15. Keating, *Intimacy with God*, cited in Bourgeault, *Centering Prayer*, 92.

16. Bourgeault, *Centering Prayer* and *The Wisdom Way*; Finley, *Christian Meditation*.

perienced in changing their perspective towards individuals who have acted abusively.

Proponents of contemplative meditation would explain this broadening of perspective as a shift in awareness—from an 'ordinary' or 'egoic' awareness to a more 'spiritual' or 'unitive' awareness. Ordinary awareness is described as a way of perceiving which arises from the functioning of the mind—our sense of identity, our thoughts, memory, associations, sensations. This way of perceiving is dualistic, self reflective, separating self from others, win-lose subjective-objective in nature.[17] Spiritual awareness is also a way of perceiving, but one which arises

> [t]hrough an intuitive grasp of the whole and an inner sense of belonging. . . . And since spiritual awareness is perception based on harmony, the sense of selfhood arising out of it is not plagued by that sense of isolation and anxiety that dominates life at the ordinary level of awareness.[18]

Notwithstanding the significant changes reported within the work setting, perhaps the more significant are those which occurred on the more personal level of participants' lives. It would appear that these personal changes in fact underpin the more overt changes in how participants handled the stress of their work environments, and relate to clients and colleagues.

Yet there is need to be cautious to not overstate this correlation. Although meditation is a "transformative process of shifting from surface, matter-of-fact levels of consciousness to more interior, meditative levels of awareness of the spiritual dimensions of our lives"[19] it also is a discipline requiring commitment and consistent practice. Finley further states that "it is in committing yourself to daily meditation that you stand to benefit the most from the ways in which meditation can revolutionize your life."[20] And Bourgeault[21] notes that the transformative process is not necessarily an easy one: "Centering Prayer is a psy-

---

17. Finley, *Christian Meditation*; Helminski, *Living Presence*; Keating, *Intimacy with God*.

18. Bourgeault, *Centering Prayer*, 13.

19. Finley, *Christian Meditation*, 5.

20. Ibid., 72.

21. Bourgeault, *Centering Prayer*, 98.

chological method and will produce results in that realm, some of them initially painful. . . .

But the changes research participants describe are consistent with, although not as profound as, the transformative changes arising from a cultivated habit of contemplative meditation. Keating, Finley, and Bourgeault[22] attest to this psychological transformation.

> The fruits of this [Centering Meditation] prayer are first seen in daily life. They express themselves in your ability to be a bit more present in your life, more flexible and forgiving with those you live and work with, more honest and comfortable in your own being. These are the real signs that the inner depths have been touched and have begun to set in motion their transformative work.[23]

In identifying the results of a dedicated practice Keating[24] speaks of the realization of new levels of freedom, faith, hope, charity, creative energy, humility and trust. The quest is that of transformation, something Bourgeault[25] refers to as

> [a]kind of sacred alchemy. And it is precisely this alchemy that defines our essential human task. The secret of our identity does not lie in the outer form or in how successfully we manipulate the outer forms of the sensible world. Rather, it lies in how we are able to set them (and ourselves) aflame to reveal the inner quality of their aliveness.

Contemplative meditation is one method of entering into this transformational quest.

CONCLUSION

What conclusions can be drawn from this research study? Meditation is an inward focused, transformative discipline, which has the effect of changing perspectives and increasing spiritual awareness. That service providers participating in this study reported positive changes in how they experienced their work, the people they worked with and them-

---

22. Keating, *Intimacy*; Finley, *Christian Meditation*; and Bourgeault, *Centering* and *The Wisdom Way*.
23. Bourgeault, *Centering*, 30.
24. Keating, *Intimacy*, 90.
25. Bourgeault, *The Wisdom Way*, 55.

selves is consistent with the emerging research regarding the efficacy of meditation in other physical and mental health fields. As participants gained congruence between their intellectual and emotional selves, they experienced increased capacities to accept themselves and others, to let go of personal agendas and control. They found their viewpoints broadening as they gained a more objective perspective of themselves, their work, and how their contributions fit within a larger whole. The changes they reported suggest that a contemplative meditation practice increases and fosters emotional health and more positive relationships with colleagues and family members. But conclusions can also be drawn within a broader perspective.

The efficacy of a centred meditation practice, as demonstrated within secularly-based services, can also be applicable to those working within other professions and settings marked by high stress, crises, and trauma. This includes Christian pastors who, in addition to their 'regular' duties in leading a congregation in spiritual growth and development, also find they are called upon to assist those—from the congregation and from the larger community—who have experienced any number of individual and/or family tragedy and crises.

The strength of transdisciplinary cooperation and collaboration is demonstrated by this research project. The FaithLink program worked to build understanding, cooperation, and collaboration between secularly-based and religiously-based communities. This research study began with recognition that intimate partner violence impacts not only family members—the direct victim, the partner who acts abusively, and child witnesses—but also those who respond to them. Recognition of the risks posed to first responders through stress and vicarious trauma is implicated in FaithLink's vision statement. In addressing this focus area, FaithLink introduced to the IPV service sector a contemplative meditation practice. The result was this unique research project with findings that strongly suggest the efficacy of the practice across several individual and work-related domains.

One final conclusion demonstrated by this research project is that there is Wisdom, vested within Christian tradition, which has applicability within a secular and professional cultural context. Its introduction requires the appropriate groundwork to be laid and must be offered simply as a gift. Those who utilize it—each in their own way—will draw their own conclusions regarding the practice's theological grounding.

BIBLIOGRAPHY

Bonadonna, R. "Meditation's impact on chronic illness." *Holistic Nursing Practice*, 17 (2003) 309–19.

Bourgeault, C. *The Wisdom Way of Knowing: Reclaiming an Ancient Tradition to Awaken the Heart*. San Franciso. Jossy-Bass, 2005.

———. *Centering Prayer and Inner Awakening*. Cambridge, Mass. Cowley Publications, 2004.

Clemans, S. E. "Life changing: The experience of rape-crisis work." *Affilia*, 19 (2004) 146–159.

Costa, D. M. "Compassion fatigue: Self-care skills for practitioners." *OT Practice*, (2005) November 7.

Figley, C. R. (Ed.) *Treating Compassion Fatigue*. New York. Brunner-Rutledge, 2002.

Figley, C. R. "Compassion fatigue as secondary traumatic stress disorder: An overview." *Compassion Fatigue: Coping with Secondary Traumatic Stress Disorder in Those Who Treat the Traumatized*. Charles Figley (Ed.). London. Brunner-Rutledge, 1995.

Finley, J. *Christian Meditation: Experiencing the Presence of God*. New York. HarperCollins Publishers, 2005.

Helminski, K. E. *Living Presence: A Sufi Way to Mindfulness & the Essential Self*. New York. G. P. Putnam's Sons, 1992.

Iliffe, G. and L.G. Steed. "Exploring the counselor's experience of working with perpetrators and survivors of domestic violence. *Journal of International Violence*, 15 (2000) 393–412.

Kabat-Zinn, J. "Effectiveness of meditation-based stress reduction program in the treatment of anxiety disorders." *American Journal of Psychiatry*, 149(7) 936–943.

Keating, T. *Intimacy with God: An Introduction to Centering Prayer*. New York. The Crossroad Publishing Company, 2002.

Majumdar, M. P. et al. *Alternative Complementary Medicine*, 8 (2002) 719–730.

Mason, O. and I. Hargreaves. "A qualitative study of mindfulness-based cognitie therapy for depression." *British Journal of Medical Psychology*, 74 (2001) 197–212.

Medscape Psychiatry and Mental Health. "Compassion fatigue: An expert interview with Charles R. Figley, MS, PHD." (2005). http://medscape.com/viewarticle/513615.

Newberg, A. and M. R. Waldman. *How God Changes Your Brain*. New York. Ballantine Books, 2009.

Reibel, D. K., et al. "Mindfulness-based stress reduction and health-related quality of life in a heterogeneous patient population." *General Hospital Psychiatry*, 23 (2001) 183–192.

Richardson, J. I. *Guidebook on Vicarious Trauma: Recommended Solutions for Anti-Violence Workers*. Centre for Research on Violence Against Women and Children in London, Ontario for the Family Violence Prevention Unit, Health Canada, 2001.

Rosenzweig, S., et al. "Mindfulness-based stress reduction lowers psychological distress in medical students." *Teaching and Learning in Medicine*, 15 (2003) 88–92.

Saakvitne, K.W. and L. A. Pearlman. *Transforming the Pain: A Workbook on Vicarious Traumatization*. New York. W.W. Norton & Company, 1996.

Tolle, E. *The Power of Now: A Guide to Spiritual Enlightenment*. Vancouver, B.C. Namaste Publishing, 2004.

UCLA Semel Institute. "Mindfulness research at UCLA Psychoneuroimmunology Center (PNI)." (2011) http://marc.ucla.edu/body.cfm?id=18.

Unger, K. "Web Extra: Mindfulness for the Masses." (2005) http://www.npr.org/templates/story/story.php?storyId=4770779.

Way, I., et al. "Vicarious trauma: A comparison of clinicians who treat survivors of sexual abuse and sexual offenders." *Journal of International Violence*, 19 (2004) 49–71.

18

The Dating Game

An Innovative Way to Engage Church Youth on Strengthening Relationships

Catherine Holtmann, Barbara Fisher-Townsend, Steve McMullin and Nancy Nason-Clark

INTRODUCTION

Engaging church youth is, or should be, on the radar screen of every senior pastor and every congregation across North America. Almost without exception, parents who are connected deeply to their faith community want their children to follow in their footsteps—to support a local congregation where they learn how to worship God collectively, and in private, understand the Scriptures, and fellowship with likeminded believers. Keeping church youth connected to their church and Christian faith is a priority for youth leaders too—whether they are on staff of a congregation as a youth pastor, or serve as a volunteer leader of a youth program. Amidst the fears that many parents and congregations harbor about their youth, scant attention is given to teen dating violence. In fact, there appears to be little thought given to helping young people develop healthy interpersonal relationships and to avoid unhealthy ones. This chapter addresses the issue of dating violence head-on. We explore why this is an important issue for youth ministries to consider in their programming and we offer one example of how to approach this delicate matter of abuse in dating relationships. In many ways our work in this area is in its infancy stage—we are still learning why so many churches and youth programs fail to address the problems that young men and women face in their interpersonal lives and we are just beginning to develop a strategy to address this critical problem. But, despite the steep learning curve we are eager to share some of our insights and to offer a glimpse into our developing interactive set of resources, called The Dating Game.

For several reasons, the church youth group can be a strategic setting for informed instruction about the problems of abuse. Because it is a setting that is trusted by devout parents and by the church leaders, it can provide freedom to discuss difficult issues that may be avoided or poorly addressed in other social contexts including the home. At an age when teen-agers are nervously preparing for or just beginning to experience dating, straightforward discussions at youth group about inappropriate relationships can be preventative at the very time when teen-agers' understandings of those relationships are still developing. Church youth who might easily be potential victims of dating abuse can be taught to recognize signs that they are being manipulated so that they will know when they are in danger. For church youth group members who, because of unhealthy relationships modeled by friends or even by parents, may think that manipulation, dishonesty, and violence are "normal" when dating, wrong understandings can be challenged and appropriate attitudes and behaviours can be taught. The youth pastor and/or youth leaders can make it clear that abuse in any form is wrong. The Dating Game, described below, will provide an engaging and interactive way to address the issues surrounding dating violence.

Devout Christian parents may sometimes question or worry about their teenagers receiving instruction about dating from secular sources for reasons that may or may not be valid, but they are quite likely to encourage their teen agers to respect and follow the teaching that they receive from trusted church youth leaders even if it might not be the advice that the parents themselves would give. Such support from parents allows the leaders to be candid about addressing issues of violence and manipulation, but it also means that youth leaders face high expectations from parents who do not address such issues at home but expect the youth pastor or youth leaders to do so on their behalf. In many cases, if instruction is not given at church, it will not be given at home (except perhaps unhelpfully in the form of warnings or prohibitions about dating certain people). By providing the Dating Game as a resource, youth leaders can use the teenagers' digital world as a platform for a discussion of important issues about dating.

A related problem is that Christian parents may be quite naïve about the dangers related to dating among Christian youth. They may comfort themselves with the thought that as long as their child is dating another member of the church youth group, there is no danger of abuse or sexual exploitation. A church youth group can become a place where manipulation takes place if parents and leaders do not recognize and address those dangers. In cannot be taken for granted that members of a church youth group have all come from homes where good relationships between parents are modeled.

Youth pastors and leaders need good resources in order to adequately address the issues. Many youth pastors have inadequate levels of education or experience in comparison to the level of expertise that churches expect. Youth pastor salaries are typically quite low yet expectations are high. With no money for the additional education that they may realize they need, they are put in the position of addressing issues like dating with little more than their own dating experiences. That makes it especially important that resources like the Dating Game can be provided. There is no guarantee that youth pastors themselves come from healthy home environments, or that their own marriage or dating relationships have been healthy and free from abuse.

There are a number of concerns that good youth pastors may have about addressing an issue like dating violence. There is the very serious issue of fear.[1] What if a discussion about dating leads to revelations of abuse, either in the youth's own dating relationships or in the family? How will the youth pastor respond? There is also the possibility that the youth pastor already suspects or recognizes abusive dating relationships between youth group members. The youth pastor will want to challenge abusive attitudes and behaviours without losing the ability to have ongoing influence.

Because youth pastors cannot be everywhere during the week, they will be interested in developing peer support among the youth regarding the development of healthy dating relationships. Youth pastors understand that it will not be enough to have youth understand what

1. McMullin and Nason-Clark, "Seminary Students."

adults think and prescribe; having the youth encourage one another to treat each other with respect is more helpful.

The youth pastor may have knowledge of abusive situations. In most church youth groups there are at least some teen-agers who come from abusive home environments where they have learned that manipulation, control, and violence are the norm. The youth pastor may be aware of such situations, but be unable (for reasons of confidentiality and trust) to address them even with the youth. Such youth need an opportunity to understand relationships differently both from instruction and from seeing good relationships modeled, for example in the lives and homes of the youth pastor and youth leaders.

Youth pastors will want to address the issue of dating in a spiritual, not purely social, way. That means that instruction about dating must be integrated with Biblical instruction with a goal to encourage not just appropriate dating but a truly Christian character that displays healthy attitudes as well as actions that are in keeping with Christian ideals. For many youth pastors, their ultimate concern is to help teenagers become devout followers of Jesus. That means not focusing on rules and prohibitions about dating, but on the development of Christian character.

The early pages of this chapter set the stage for understanding how children and teens learn about relationships—beginning with the role of fairytales. We then explore several issues that relate directly to dating violence—prior exposure to abuse, risk factors and warning signs, the difference between teen and adult violence, and emerging issues involving the use of technology, such as cell phones and Facebook. The remainder of the chapter focuses on the RAVE Project Teen Dating Game www.theraveproject.com [found under the Youth Tab] and examines in some detail what the game hopes to achieve. We close our chapter with a few examples of what every youth leader can do to highlight the problem of unhealthy relationships, or teen dating violence, in the lives of young people.

DATING AND VIOLENCE

Throughout history children from very early ages were incorporated into the daily life of work and ritual within families. This was a time of egalitarian participation in the life cycle of families where children were treated as 'little adults.' However, beginning as early as industrialization in the mid to late 19th century, a complex process in which society transitioned from agriculture to industry and from home-based work to factories, has led us to the present day family structure in which we distinguish the age category of "teenager" or "adolescent" as a person between the ages of thirteen and nineteen, with a further distinction of "tween," being those aged eleven and fourteen.[2] Another transition that began during industrialization was related to the ritual of family-based courtship between one man and one woman that often took place in the home of the young woman under the watchful eyes of her parents—with the ultimate goal of marriage—evolving into a more publicly oriented ritual called *dating* that most often involves a series of partners through the teen years and into young adulthood. Dating has become an integral part of the maturation process in young people's lives, particularly in the western world[3]—with an estimated seventy-two percent of eighth and ninth graders in the US engaging in dating.

So where do young people—teenagers—learn about dating and romantic love? Certainly for many their early ideas are formed through listening to and reading tales that have been passed down for hundreds of years—*fairytales*. These tales often have similar themes—everything is perfect; the handsome prince overcomes all obstacles to rescue the heroine; and, they live *happily ever after*.[4] The scene is set by these tales and young children begin to imagine and anticipate their own happy endings. Cinderella is saved from her miserable home life by the handsome prince; Sleeping Beauty awakes from her long sleep after being kissed, again by a handsome prince; Beauty transforms the Beast into a wonderful and desirable man—throughout the stories similar themes abound. Even though there is now a proliferation of newer fairytales written with more egalitarian themes where girls prevail—such as The Paperbag Princess by Robert Munsch—girl children are still entranced by the heroes of the classic stories. As they move away from fairytales, by age nine or ten the influence of popular culture becomes and remains much more important in their social worlds, with a plethora of music (New Direction, Justin Bieber, Selena Gomez, for example), teen magazines (e.g., Twist, Teen Voices, J-14), teen novels (e.g., The Hunger

---

2. Tanner, *Teenage Troubles*, 28.; a 2008 study by Swahn et al. found that nearly one in four 7th grade girls (24.9 percent) and more than one in five boys (21.2 percent) reported perpetrating physical violence in a dating relationship in the past year.

3. "Dating Violence Research."

4. Jackson, "Happily never after," 305.

Games, Passion, The Edge of Nowhere) and television shows such as Gossip Girl, Glee and The Secret Life of the American Teenager, that provide young girls and boys with a critical component of their worldview—entertainment and information on success in the adolescent world—fads, trends, dating, fashion, etc. The narratives found within these media often focus on romance and issues like what it takes to be beautiful or handsome, popular, and to attract and keep a boyfriend or girlfriend. They reinforce the scenario learned at an earlier age of a world of romantic fantasy in which young women may have learned that it is necessary to become submissive, dependent, and sexually vulnerable as they seek to maintain the "happily ever after" relationship and young men come to see their role as more dominant.[5] Indeed, Lisa Jackson argues that the romantic narrative learned by children and teens reinforces the fusion of love and violence wherein women "tremble" under the seductive power of men and dominating, violent behavior is portrayed as a "contorted expression of the hero's love and desire."[6]

So the idealized *happily ever after* outcome is not the reality for a large minority of young people. The numbers tell the story. Violence in adolescent romantic relationships is alarmingly commonplace, with a continuum of violence ranging from verbal abuse to rape and even murder.[7] Mulford and Giordano[8] summarize several research studies related to violence in teen romantic relationships—they note that in the US approximately 10 percent of adolescents reported being a victim of physical violence at the hands of a romantic partner in 2006 and that in terms of psychological violence the number is even higher with between 2 and 3 in 10 teens reporting being victimized. Others report even higher rates[9] related to physical and sexual abuse, estimating that 30 and 41 percent of teens experience these types of violence in their dating relationships. Of tweens (age 11–14) who have been in a dating relationship, 62 percent say they know peers who have been verbally

---

5. Jackson, "Happily never after," 306.
6. Ibid., 307.
7. O'Keefe, "In Brief: Teen dating violence"; 1. according to a 2000 special report of the Bureau of Justice Statistics on intimate partner violence, 7 percent of all murder victims in 1995 were young women killed by their boyfriends.
8. Mulford & Giordano, "Teen dating violence," 34.
9. Avery-Leaf et al., "Efficacy of a dating violence prevention program."

abused by a dating partner.[10] In Canada, more than half of teenage victims of violence between the ages of 14 and 17 were assaulted by a close friend, acquaintance, or co-worker.[11] While a multitude of conceptual issues blur the definition of dating violence, with some researchers including psychological and emotional abuse in the definition, while others include only physical violence, two definitions provided online by Violence against Women Online Resources[12] and by TeenDVMonth.org[13] help to clarify the issue:

> Teen dating violence ... is violence committed by a person who is in, wants to be in, or has been in a social relationship of a romantic or intimate nature with the victim. It occurs in both opposite- and same-sex relationships, between non-cohabiting and sometimes cohabiting, partners. Dating violence which occurs between the ages of 11 and 14 is often referred to as "tween" dating violence. Teen dating violence includes physical, sexual, and emotional abuse.
>
> and
>
> Teen dating violence and abuse is a pattern of destructive behaviors used to exert power and control over a dating partner.

While dating violence can begin as young as eleven years of age, the prevalence of violence has been found to increase with age so that by age fourteen violence rates have increased fourfold.[14] When looking specifically at sexual violence, girls are subjected to significantly more violence than males.[15]

Issues to consider

a. Prior exposure to violence

Exposure to violence appears to be a key risk factor for the perpetration of dating violence because of its link[16] to other behaviors identi-

---

10. Liz Claiborne, Inc/Teen Research Unlimited. "Study on teen dating abuse."
11. Statistics Canada, *Children and Youth*.
12. VAW online 2010.
13. Dating Violence 101.
14. VAW online 2010; Statistics Canada, The Daily, April 20, 2005.
15. Bennett & Fineran, "Sexual and severe physical violence."
16. NIJ, "Teen Dating Violence."

fied as risk factors (e.g. alcohol and/or drug use, aggressive behavior, and attitudes regarding aggression). Children who are subjected to or who witness violence within their families of origin internalize that culture of violence found at home. The intergenerational transmission of violence is often linked with social learning theory wherein children learn based on what they witness[17] and experience.[18] Certainly during our primary socialization, most often within the context of family, we gradually come to believe in the values of our family, of our culture, internalizing the norms and moral precepts.[19] The learned norm of abusive behavior is then carried into teen dating relationships and into adulthood.[20] In a research project conducted by Nancy Nason-Clark and Barbara Fisher-Townsend, the Executive Director of a large batterer intervention agency in the Northwest USA that was under study stated that her clients, who over the years have numbered in the thousands, are often second-generation batterers—she estimates about 90 percent of them, in fact. In personal interviews conducted with men enrolled in the program the men often noted that their abusive behavior began during their teen years because that was the behavior they saw around them within their family and peer groups[21] and it was all they knew.

b. Risk factors and warning signs (attitudes and behaviors)

Numerous researchers[22] have identified specific warning signs of abusive behavior. These include but are not limited to:

- Possessiveness.
- Telling you what to do.
- Isolating you from friends or family.

---

17. According to Overlien and Hydén children are not passive witnesses to violence. Rather, "they hear it, see it and experience the aftermath . . . the violence is something children experience from a position as subjects [and] . . . the violent episode is situated in a larger context, i.e. the child's living environment, and is not something to which the child can merely be a passive witness."; "Children's Actions," 480.

18. Rosenbaum & Leisring, "Beyond power and control."

19. Goldenberg, *Thinking Sociologically*.

20. Heyman & Slep, "Do child abuse and interparental violence," 867.

21. The idea of peer group support is fully discussed by DeKeseredy & Schwartz, "Male peer support."

22. For example, Foo & Margolin, "A multivariate investigation"; Himelein, "Risk factors"; O'Keefe, "Predictors of dating violence."

- Extreme jealousy or insecurity.
- Explosive anger.
- Making false accusations.
- Checking your cell phone or email without permission.
- Constantly monitoring your whereabouts.

Relatedly, a plethora of researchers have delineated risk factors for violence in dating relationships. Violence is related to certain risk factors and teens who engage in one problem behavior are likely to engage in other problem behaviors—including abuse. For example, strong correlations have been found between sexual assault and victimization and drug and alcohol use.[23] Key risks of having unhealthy relationships increase for teens who[24]:

- Believe it's okay to use threats or violence to get their way or to express frustration or anger.
- Use alcohol or drugs.
- Can't manage anger or frustration.
- Hang out with violent peers.
- Have multiple sexual partners.
- Have a friend involved in dating violence.
- Are depressed or anxious.
- Have learning difficulties and other problems at school.
- Don't have parental supervision and support.
- Witness violence at home or in the community.
- Have a history of aggressive behavior or bullying.

c. How teen violence differs from adult violence

Interestingly, power differentials do not appear to be associated with teen relationships as they are in adult relationships because young women are typically not financially dependent on young men, nor do

---

23. VAWnet.org. "Teen dating violence."
24. Centers for Disease Control and Prevention; VAWnet.org, "In Brief: Teen dating violence"; VAWnet.org, "Working with young men."

they have children to provide for and protect.[25] As well, teens have a lack of experience both in negotiating romantic relationships and with coping and communication strategies, thus without adequately developed skills their responses may involve either verbal or physical abuse.[26] Finally, the influence of peers during adolescence is very important to consider.[27] According to Molidor and Tolman[28] more than half of teen dating violence occurs when there is a third party present. "Keeping face" is particularly important to young males, so when the situation is tense and a peer is present many males respond with abusive behavior.

d. Emerging issues

Technology has presented new opportunities for pervasive forms of teen dating abuse that are often hidden. According to a 2007 study[29]:

- An alarming one in ten (10 percent) teens claim they have been threatened physically via email, IM, text, chat, etc.

- One in three teens who have been in a relationship (30 percent) say they've been text messaged 10, 20, or 30 times an hour by a partner finding out where they are, what they're doing, or who they're with.

- Nearly one in five teens in a relationship (19 percent) say that their partner has used a cell phone or the internet to spread rumors about them.

- Nearly one in five (18 percent) say their partner used a networking site to harass or put them down.

- One in six teens in a relationship (16 percent) claim their partner has actually bought a cell phone or minutes for them.

Teen abusers can easily monitor their dating partners by frequently checking in by cell phone, text or instant messenger (IM) or by requiring a dating partner to check in. Between cell phone calls and frequent texting, an abuser can exert almost constant control over a partner day and night. Interviewed for a 2007 ABC news story about this topic,

---

25. Wekerle & Wolfe, "Dating violence in mid-adolescence."
26. Laursen & Collins, "Interpersonal conflict."
27. DeKeseredy & Kelly, "Woman abuse in university"; DeKeseredy & Schwartz, "Male peer support."
28. Molidor & Tolman, "Gender and contextual factors."
29. Liz Claiborne/Teenage Research Unlimited "Tech abuse."

psychotherapist Dr. Jill Murray stated[30]: "I call it an electronic leash. . . . I've had girls come into my office with cell phone bills showing 9,000 text messages and calls in a month. This is all hours of the day and night. And it's threatening. 'Hi. How are you? Where are you? Who are you with? Who are you talking to?'"

If you are a youth leader, or a youth pastor, you might be asking yourself some pointed questions about now:

1. How can I raise a subject as sensitive as violence in dating relationships among the youth who come to our group on Friday nights?

2. What will I do if young women or young men do not want to talk about notions of violence in dating relationships? How will I handle it if they do not take the discussion seriously?

3. Is there a light hearted way to talk about matters as important as these?

These are some of the questions that we have asked ourselves. And our answer—only one idea, of course—is The Dating Game, a fun, interactive way to discuss a very serious topic—unhealthy behaviors that can occur in the context of dating relationships. Before we describe the game itself, we offer some background to its development and our thinking about these matters.

THE RAVE PROJECT TEEN DATING GAME

Personal identity construction, attitudes about relationships, and communication skills are formed through time and are continually subject to change. The teenage years are an ideal time to help young people think critically about their self-identities and relationships with their peers, to learn and practice new relational skills, as well as ways to monitor and modify thoughts and behaviours that have potential for violence and abuse.

The Religion and Violence e-Learning or RAVE Project was designed and implemented as a web-based and interdisciplinary response to the problem of domestic violence among families of faith. While seeking to equip religious leaders and congregations with the most

30. ABC News Feb. 8, 2007.

up-to-date social scientific information and best practices in order to effectively respond to victims in their midst, the RAVE Project website (www.theraveproject.org) also encourages religious groups to work together with a group of community and government organizations in a coordinated community response to family violence. The message to religious leaders is that the silence surrounding violence in families of faith must be broken so that safety can be ensured. The message to secular agencies and public services is that the particular beliefs and spiritual needs of religious victims and perpetrators of violence are an important part of the journey of change and accountability in the aftermath of family violence.

One of the potential strengths of a faith-based response to the problem of family violence is that churches are places where whole families gather. Religion has meaning and relevance for every stage of life—from welcoming newborn babies into a spiritual community, to blessing loving commitment in marriages, to mourning the death of cherished seniors. Ann Cameron's research among high school students in New Brunswick (2004) emphasizes a community-based approach to dating violence education and prevention. She acknowledges the advantages of multi-sector approach where the problem of violence in dating relationships is acknowledged by trusted adults and community leaders and practical assistance is offered. In this way, helping youth to form healthy relationships becomes a shared responsibility amongst parents, educators, advocates, community agencies, therapeutic professionals, and criminal justice workers. Every sector of the community has a role to play, including churches.

The language of faith emphasizes love, respect, honesty and compassion in relationships and these values can be drawn upon as religious communities condemn violence, offer assistance to those in pain, and help to nurture the development of relational skills and communication with youth. Religious myths, beliefs and symbols are multi-faceted and complex, filled with messages of hope for communities where justice and peace prevails, yet remarkably upfront about the tragedy of injustice and violence that so often mars human relationships. Religious stories are not neutral about the violence that occurs in relationships and consistently condemn it, calling adherents to work together for transformation and change. Therefore, it is absolutely appropriate to address issues of abuse and violence in religious contexts and draw upon the wisdom of religious traditions in seeking change. This conceptual approach is helpful when thinking about addressing violence in the lives of religious youth. Religious groups can acknowledge its prevalence with courage since they also have access to spiritual and social resources available for change.

One of the strengths of the web-based approach to providing training for communities of faith dealing with family violence is that it enables us to retell the many stories of abuse that we have collected in over twenty years of social science research. The RAVE website conveys these stories in a variety of ways—through stained glass images, graphics, text, talking circles with sound clips, podcasts, and videos. It is through the retelling of many different stories of family violence in multiple ways that online learners come to know the complexity of the cycle of violence. The purpose of telling stories in these ways is twofold. First, the use of stories helps victims and pastors come to recognize and name family violence in a religious context. This is the first step toward change since many victims do not describe their situations as violent—it is simply what goes on in their family. In listening to or reading about the stories of others, victims come to recognize pieces of their own stories and realize that the pain that they experience is not a private, shameful family secret but part of a bigger problem. Secondly, the stories are contextualized within the RAVE website with the clear message that violence and abuse are never acceptable in Christian family life. Abuse is never part of God's plan for loving relationships and needs to be addressed openly. Accompanied by the words of hope and encouragement, religious victims and pastors can take the first steps to bringing an end to violence and becoming survivors. Religious leaders can find resources on the website that help them use prayer, Scripture, sermons and symbols to proclaim the message in their churches that violence has no place in Christian families and that help is available in the journey towards restoring peace and safety.

Cameron's review of teen dating violence education programs in the province of New Brunswick[31] showed that these programs do well at increasing awareness among teenagers about the prevalence of dating violence and its many forms. After receiving information through personal stories, dramatizations and social science statistics about the prevalence of violence in the lives of youth, teens were more willing to

---

31. Cameron, et al., *Dating Violence Prevention*.

talk about the abuse taking place in their lives and among their peers. The research also emphasized that teens needed help bringing abuse to an end or intervening when they witnessed abusive behaviours between friends. Many believed that abuse, bullying or being mean were just part of being a teenager. Those that believed such behaviours were wrong did not know what they could do about it.[32] Teens needed skill development concerning forming healthy relationships in order to become empowered for making change. This is an important point in light of the additional research finding that teens are unlikely to tell or turn to adults in authority for help, such as their parents or school guidance counselors, when violence occurs. Teens prefer to talk about relationships with their peers and try to work things out for themselves as much as they can. Given these research findings and our commitment to telling stories, the RAVE Project decided to design online resources for youth ministry that were based on stories of teen dating violence and that facilitated interaction between youth.

The focus on making the stories interactive meant that youth were not simply passive recipients of information but, in using the online stories, the youth were involved in the learning process—involved with the characters in the stories, involved in face-to-face discussions with other church youth, and involved with youth ministry leaders who were conveying the message that church was an appropriate place for helping teens to deal with abusive relationships in their lives. Thus when we thought about interactive learning using online resources, we wanted to develop what is referred to as a hybrid learning environment—one that combines online resources with face-to-face learning.[33] The Dating Game, still in the early stages of development at the time of this writing, is the central component of a variety of resources designed to help those in youth ministry work engage teens in learning about relationship violence and abuse in ways that are non-threatening. There is evidence that computer games appeal to youth today and can be harnessed as a learning tool[34]. The Dating Game is primarily intended as a discussion starter—a way to begin to explore the complex dynamics of adolescent and teen relationships. The hope is that after introducing the Dating

---

32. Cameron, "Schools are not enough."

33. Holtmann & Nason-Clark, "Religion and technology"; Toth et al., "Changing delivery methods."

34. Jones & Hosein, "Profiling university students.'"

Game in a church youth group setting, the silence around the serious issues of teen violence and abuse is broken and honest discussion can begin to take place. Change may begin shortly after playing the Dating Game as youth start to relate the game to their own experiences. Then they might think about collectively exploring further ways to develop skills for healthy relationship building within their own church or in the broader community. Because of its accessibility via the internet, the Dating Game can also be used by youth groups in a secular setting, helping to raise the issue of the particular challenges that religious youth face when trying to reconcile their beliefs with the pressure from popular culture to be dating.

Change may also be set in motion as individual youth return to the RAVE Project website for further information after a meeting of their local youth group. An abused teenager, just like a battered wife, will need time and space to come to acknowledge and name what is going on in his or her life. Teens can access the website via a laptop in the privacy of their bedrooms or at the home of a friend any time of day or night. The "Exit Now" button and the "How to Cover Your Tracks" information can help a teen whose boyfriend is monitoring her internet use. In addition to providing a wealth of information on violence based on social science research, the RAVE website provides information on resources for change, including the phone number for the US national teen dating abuse helpline, contact information for shelters and domestic violence coalitions throughout North America, and faith-based resources in the US.

The Dating Game is located on the Youth tab of the website. A visitor is immediately greeted by the faces of flash characters— twelve young men and women of a variety of racial, socio-economic and religious backgrounds. After entering the game itself, the young women: Musical Mary, Spiritual Sarah, Beautiful Brianne, Wild Wendy, Brainy Becky, and Attitude Angela can potentially be paired with any of the young men: Athletic Bob, Genuine Jerome, Tough Tyson, Adventurous Adam, Sensitive Sam, or Hunky Harold via the opening screen. Clearly these are cartoon characters and a light tone is established so that youth can positively relate to any or all of the individual characters. As a collective, the characters represent the diversity that youth experience on a daily basis in society. Presently only five dates have been developed—three between Athletic Bob and Musical Mary and two between

Genuine Jerome and Spiritual Sarah. However, even with this beta version, youth ministry leaders can help their charges start to explore some of the dynamics of healthy and unhealthy relationships illustrated by the dates between these two couples.

In order to explain how the Dating Game can help individuals in church youth groups develop communication and intervention skills, one date between Genuine Jerome and Spiritual Sarah and another date between Musical Mary and Athletic Bob will be reviewed. When Genuine Jerome is chosen to date Spiritual Sarah, players are able to get a more complete image of each individual by choosing to read the bios located underneath each character. Players can learn that Genuine Jerome (possibly Caribbean-Canadian or African-American) is deeply committed to his Christian faith, does not smoke or drink alcohol, and dreams of meeting the 'right' girl at youth group who shares his dreams for ministry. Spiritual Sarah (possibly Chinese-Canadian or Korean-American) on the other hand, feels a lot of pressure from her parents to get good grades at school and to practice piano. They have 'limited her Facebook time in order to help her stay focused yet she longs to fall in love with Mr. Right.' Sarah secretly buys wedding magazines and finds church youth group meetings a welcome escape from the stress of home life.

These first impressions set the tone for giving players a sense of both the strengths and some of the obstacles that each character faces in relationships. For example, it is likely that Gerome's dedication to his faith is prized by his family but can be a source of derision from some of his peers at school who are not religious. He might be dealing with issues of self-esteem and self-confidence. Like many guys his age, starting to date is about working out his masculinity and having a girl friend can be proof that he is worthy of attention. Sarah may be fulfilling her parent's expectations for academic success but is longing for more control over some aspects of her life. Feeling trapped or smothered, she is developing a strategy for dealing with her parents and pursuing her own dreams. Having a boyfriend may give Sarah a sense of personal power and control. Gerome and Sarah's ethnic backgrounds are not explicitly developed in their biographies but they reflect the reality of multicultural societies today. Race, ethnicity, and class also add levels of complexity to social interactions. After learning a little bit about the

Gerome and Sarah, players can choose to have them go on two different dates—either to the movies or to the mall.

Once a date is chosen, the players read the thoughts and words of the Sarah and Gerome as they interact. When the Dating Game is being used in a group setting, before beginning the activity, leaders should ask for volunteers to read the scripts as they appear on the screen or read themselves so that everyone present can follow the date. For example, if players choose to send Sarah and Gerome to the movies for a date, they learn that at youth group Gerome has told Sarah that he has prayed about getting to know her better and that he feels their "hanging out" together is in line with God's plans for him. This news is so exciting to Sarah that she starts to think about how she can date Gerome when her parents have not yet allowed her to date anyone. As the date unfolds, players see how the lies that Sarah tells Gerome and her plans for manipulating her parents make her life quite complicated, all for the sake of ensuring that her dream of a relationship becomes a reality.

At the end of Sarah and Gerome's time at the movies, a screen appears asking the players a series of questions based on a key point from the date. In this case, the question is about one of the lies that Sarah told Gerome and her motivations. Players can choose one of four possible responses. After the response is chosen, a screen appears with a letter grade, depending on the appropriateness of the answer. Each letter grade is accompanied by a brief explanation about the particular relationship behavior being addressed. The final screen in the game features some "scene highlights" that explore two aspects of healthy relationships and two aspects of unhealthy relationships suggested by the dating scenario. Because each letter grade is accompanied by an explanation for the chosen answer as well as scene highlights, there is no wrong answer for those playing the game. Every answer leads to an exploration of the kinds of behaviours featured in the date and a critical response in regard to the behavior.

In the case of Sarah and Gerome, youth are invited to think about what constitutes honest communication in relationships. Sometimes youth feel pressured to agree to do or say things because they want to be liked. It is difficult to figure out what you really want and how far you are willing to do things that someone you like wants you to do. It is also difficult to juggle the expectations of your parents and the pursuit of your own dreams. Youth who feel comfortable in leadership roles, like

Gerome, are sometimes unaware of the difficulties that others have in expressing their true selves. Sarah and Gerome's characters can be discussed focusing on gender roles. Finding a balance between the developmental needs of each person in a relationship can be a real challenge yet an opportunity to develop self-knowledge as well as communication skills. These are all aspects of Sarah and Gerome's relationship that can provide the basis for a group discussion at the conclusion of the date. Youth ministry leaders could decide to facilitate these discussions either in sex-segregated groups or in co-educational groups. The former gives teens some safety, particularly when exploring gender roles, and the latter allows teens to share multiple perspectives. At the end of each date, players can choose to play again or click the link to additional youth materials on the RAVE website.

When Athletic Bob and Musical Mary start dating, players learn that sports and humor are central to Bob's identity—stereotypical for popular guys. Mary on the other hand, struggles with typical self-esteem issues for girls. Everyone likes her yet she's concerned about her weight and has to work hard to maintain her grades. Music makes her life worthwhile and she loves being part of the church's praise team. When Bob asks Mary out for pizza after youth group, Mary cannot believe her luck. Yet the entire experience revolves around what Bob wants. He shows no interest in Mary and even orders her food! Mary is somewhat uncomfortable with Bob's self-centered attitude but nevertheless agrees to come to his next basketball game. The question following the date asks youth why they think Bob acts the way that he does with Mary. In this date between Bob and Mary, youth are invited to consider power and control in relationships and ways in which the balance of power between young men and women gets distorted in unhealthy relationships. Bob's character is the epitome of masculine power and although it makes Mary uncomfortable she does not have the self-confidence to make her own desires known. Bob may very well be hiding his own uncertainties about dating behind the mask of masculinity that he feels he is expected to wear. Mary may be in danger of turning her frustrations inward and becoming more self-critical rather than addressing them with Bob.

Before using the Dating Game, youth leaders will need to become familiar with the research on teen dating violence provided at the outset of this chapter and on the RAVE website. Then after having tried out the various dates in the game, prepare a structured form of discussion for the youth following the actual playing. The additional youth materials provide some guidance in this regard as do many other resources on the RAVE website, such as the "Mending Broken Hearts" of "Stories of Hope and Inspiration after Violence" series on the Online Training tab, which provide questions for reflection based on stories of violence. Youth leaders are encouraged to think about setting up a meeting which includes playing the Dating Game in a way that makes it safe for the youth involved to ask questions about dating relationships and to talk about their own experiences in a setting that is non-judgmental, ensures confidentiality and safety, and includes the language of the spirit.

We cannot over-emphasize the importance of a strategic approach to the problem of family violence—an approach that is agreed upon by all members of a church ministry team. Breaking the silence about violence among people of faith is important but church leadership personnel need to be prepared to deal with victims who will inevitably come to them for assistance, which will include youth. Youth who have experienced violence and abuse need a listening ear from those in church leadership. Their stories of pain are real and they need help in navigating the terrain of relationships—help that is well-informed about the best practices in anti-violence work. The RAVE Project website can provide that information as well as direct users to become more familiar with the resources for referral within the broader community. Religious leaders can work together with and rely on the expertise of professionals in their local context who are trained in helping youth develop the skills for non-violent relationships.

Every youth pastor and every volunteer youth leader has an excellent opportunity to help the young men and women in their group think about—and model—healthy interpersonal relationships. The Dating Game is a tool to assist along the way. From asking individual teens to pretend they are one of the characters, and thereby explore how a young person might think or act like this, to seeking the advice of teens for one of the characters, any way that students can be involved in the game will enhance what they take away from the experience. As we continue to work on dates here at our offices, if you have some good ideas, please send them along. Perhaps this could be another activity for a youth event—writing the script, or the context, for another "date" for The Dating Game.

CONCLUSION

The Dating Game can be part of a comprehensive approach to family violence in churches that take seriously the need to speak out about violence and abuse. The stories depicted in the interactive online game, present real life dilemmas that religious teens face in dating relationships and in their own families. The RAVE Project team has plans for the development of many more dates that raise a variety of topics related to power and control in relationships including the use of cell phones, stalking, date rape, bullying, and physical violence. In playing the Dating Game in a church youth group setting, teens can be drawn into a discussion of their challenges and experiences in relationships and begin to think about how the Christian values of sincerity, love, compassion, justice, and peace can be put into practice in their daily interactions. Individual youth will be given the message that the RAVE online resources exist in order to help them end the violence in their lives. Youth will be given the message that violence and abuse, while a reality in their lives, are aspects of their journey that the church cares about. Religious leaders can make it known that they are ready to help youth live lives free of violence.

BIBLIOGRAPHY

ABC News Feb. 8, 2007. http://abcnews.go.com/Technology/story?id=2859916&page=1#.UHw5Moa8GSo.

Ammerman, N. T. (Ed.). *Everyday Religion: Observing Modern Religious Lives*. New York, NY: Oxford University Press, 2007.

Avery-Leaf, S., M. Cascardi, K.D. O'Leary, & A. Cano. "Efficacy of a dating violence prevention program on attitudes justifying aggression," *Journal of Adolescent Health*, 21, (1997) 11–17.

Bennett, L. and S. Fineran. "Sexual and severe physical violence among high school students. Power beliefs, gender and relationship." *Am. J. Orthopsychiatry* 68(1998) 645–52.

Byers-Heinlein, K. et al. "Passing the torch: Students teaching students about dating violence." In M. L. Stirling, C. A. Cameron, N. Nason-Clark & B. Miedema (Eds.), *Understanding Abuse: Partnering for Change* (297–319). Toronto, ON: University of Toronto Press, 2004.

Cameron, C. A. "Schools are not enough: It takes a whole community." In M. L. Stirling, et al. (Eds.), *Understanding Abuse: Partnering for Change* (269–294). Toronto, ON: University of Toronto Press, 2004.

Cameron, C. A., et al. *Dating Violence Prevention in New Brunswick*. Fredericton, NB: Muriel McQueen Fergusson Center for Family Violence Research, 2007.

Centers for Disease Control and Prevention. 2012. Teen Dating Violence. http://www.cdc.gov/violenceprevention/intimatepartnerviolence/teen_dating_violence.html.

Dating Violence 101. www.teendvmonth.org/dating-violence-101. Accessed February 16, 2012.

DeKeseredy, W. & K. Kelly. "Woman abuse in university and college dating relationships: The contribution of the ideology of familial patriarchy." *Journal of Human Justice*, 4(1993) 25–52.

DeKeseredy, W. & M. Schwartz. "Male peer support and woman abuse: An expansion of DeKeseredy's model." *Sociological Spectrum*, 13(1993) 393–413.

Gallagher, S. K. *Evangelical Identity and Gendered Family Life*. New Jersey, NY: Rutgers University Press, 2003.

Griffith, M. R. *God's Daughters: Evangelical Women and the Power of Submission*. Berkeley, CA: University of California Press, 1997.

Hall, D. D. (Ed.) *Lived Religion in America: Toward a History of Practice*. Princeton, NJ: Princeton University Press, 1997.

Heyman, R. and A.S. Slep. "Do child abuse and interparental violence lead to adulthood family violence?" *Journal of Marriage and the Family*, 64 (2002) 867–870.

Holtmann, C. (in press). Workers in the vineyard: Catholic women and social action. In W. Swatos & G. Giordan (Eds.), *Religion, Spirituality and Everyday Practice*. New York, NY: Springer Publishing Co.

Holtmann, C., and N. Nason-Clark. "Religion and technology: Innovative approaches to teaching and learning." *Ubiquitous Learning: An International Journal*, 3(2011) 105–116.

Jackson, S. "Happily never after: Young women's stories of abuse in heterosexual love relationships." *Feminism & Psychology* 11(2001) 305–321.

Jones, C., and A. Hosein. "Profiling university students' use of technology: Where is the net generation divide?" *International Journal of Technology, Knowledge and Society*, 6(2010) 43–58.

Kaufman, D. R. *Rachel's Daughters: Newly Orthodox Jewish Women*. New Brunswick, NJ: Rutgers University Press, 1991.

Laursen, B., and W.A. Collins. "Interpersonal conflict during adolescence," *Psychological Bulletin* 115 (1994) 197–209.

Liz Claiborne Inc./Teen Research Unlimited. (2007). *Study on Teen Dating Abuse*. http://www.loveisnotabuse.com.

McGuire, M. B. *Lived religion: Faith and Practice in Everyday Life*. New York, NY: Oxford University Press, 2008.

Molidor, C. and R.M. Tolman. "Gender and contextual factors in adolescent dating violence," *Violence Against Women* 4 (1998) 180–194.

Mulford, C. and P. Giordano. "Teen dating violence: A closer look at adolescent romantic relationships." www.nij.gov/journals/261/teen-dating-violence.htm. (2008).

National Institute of Justice. Teen Dating Violence. Journal. https://www.ncjrs.gov/pdffiles1/nij/224083.pdf. (2008)

O'Keefe, M. *In Brief: Teen Dating Violence: A Review of Risk Factors and Prevention Efforts*. http://www.vawnet.org/applied-research-papers/print-document.php?doc_id=409. (2005)

Overlien, C. and M. Hydén. Children's action when experiencing domestic violence. *Childhood* 16 (2009) 479.

Picard, P., *Tech Abuse in Teen Relationships Study*. Liz Claiborne Inc. http://loveisnotabuse.com/web/guest/search/-/journal_content/56/10123/83961 (2007).

Statistics Canada. *Children and Youth as Victims of Violent Crime.* (2005). www.statcan.gc.ca/daily-quotidien/050420/dq050420a-eng.htm. Accessed October 1, 2012.

Swahn M.H., et al., "Measuring sex differences in violence victimization and perpetration within date and same-sex peer relationships." *Journal of Interpersonal Violence.* 23(2008) 1120–1138.

Tanner, J. *Teenage Troubles: Youth and Deviance in Canada.* Don Mills, ON: Oxford University Press, 2010.

The Facts about Teen Dating Violence. www.vaw.umn.edu/documentgs/inbriefs/teendatingviolence. Accessed February 2, 2012.

Toth, M. J., et al. "Changing delivery methods, changing practices: Exploring instructional practices in face-to-face and hybrid courses." *MERLOT Journal of Online Learning and Teaching,* 6(2010) 617–633.

US Department of Justice, Bureau of Justice Statistics. *Special Report on Intimate Partner Violence.* http://bjs.ojp.usdoj.gov/content/pub/pdf/ipv.pdf. (2000).

Wekerle, C., and D.A. Wolfe, "Dating violence in mid-adolescence: Theory, significance, and emerging prevention initiatives," *Child Psychology Review* 19 (1999): 435–456.

19

Conclusion

Nancy Nason-Clark and Barbara Fisher-Townsend

Throughout this edited collection various chapters have explored why, when, and how strengthening families will help to end abuse.

Strengthening families of different varieties and ending abuse in the myriad of forms through which it surfaces, is God's way of bringing peace and safety to Christian homes across the world. We challenge congregations, their leaders, and the men, women, and youth who faithfully support them to consider their personal role in bringing this vision—inspired by the Scriptures—into reality.

Together our voices can be strong. We can be a heavenly chorus raising our voices for change, challenging our churches and our communities to live peacefully in accordance with the Scriptural mandate to treat others as we would like to be treated ourselves.

As a group of writers, we are united in our belief that every home should be a safe home, every home a shelter from the storms of life, every home a place where we are supported, treated with respect and dignity, and every home a place where men and women are encouraged to be all they can be. It is a tall order. It is a dream to guide our personal conduct and to measure our congregational and community life. We are far from reaching this goal—but toward it we strive.

This book—our third in the PASCH series—has been divided into several sections. The first part celebrates the life of Catherine Clark Kroeger. Following her desire to privilege the Scriptures in matters of condemning domestic abuse, we present the story of the Samaritan woman as retold by Amy Rasmussen Buckley. We then move into the book's three main sections: The Call to Strengthen Families and End Abuse; Working to Strengthen Individuals within Family Life; and Plan for Action.

In Part I, various chapters send forth the call for churches and those who lead and attend them to strengthen families and thereby help to bring an end to abuse. Juan Carlos Areán and Nancy Raines focus on children, Steve McMullin and Catherine Holtmann join us—Nancy and Barb—in a chapter that explores the story of men who act abusively. David Horita helps us all to see that how we frame our identities can serve as either a protective factor or a risk for unhealthy or abusive behavior. On that theme, Victoria Fahlberg has also written about risk and resilience as it relates to abuse.

In Part II, we focus on working to strengthen individuals within family life. Lorrie Wasyliw highlights the work of WINGS and their second stage housing initiative. Julie Owens and Rhonda Encinas consider both the lens of their own personal experience and that of women who reside in rural environs. Catherine Holtmann asks a very pertinent question: what would happen if our religious leaders, like the priests and bishops in the Roman Catholic Church, took seriously the issue of violence in the family and spoke out in unison in support of the abused and in condemnation of acts of aggression? Victoria Fahlberg, too, considers the role of religious leaders and focuses on pastors and other ordained leadership in the evangelical tradition.

The final section of the book, Part III, includes six chapters that demonstrate what a plan of action on the issue of abuse might look like. Steve McMullin considers how pastors might be prepared to respond to victims and their families using established best practices, Linda Peachey and Elsie Goerzen focus on one faith tradition, the Mennonites, and how the Central Mennonite Committee has prepared congregations for collaborative work on domestic violence. Another chapter examines the role of seminaries in preparing future leaders: here Steve McMullin and Nancy Nason-Clark document how some seminaries are responding at present to the issue of domestic violence and then consider ways that seminaries might be more proactive in the future.

Later chapters highlight two international initiatives, one in New Zealand, the other in England. Daphne Marsden shares some of her story of working in the prison system in Christchurch and the early days of The Esther Project, while Mandy Marshall and Peter Grant describe the origins and growth of Restored. Two chapters that grow out of data to understand domestic violence round out our discussion of the action plan: Irene Sevcik and her co-authors discuss the role of centred meditation amongst first responders to abuse, and members of the RAVE Project outline an emerging initiative of theirs called The Dating Game.

In our Introduction to this collection of essays, we described this phase of the work of PASCH as being in transition. PASCH began as a small group of therapists, domestic violence advocates, survivors, Biblical scholars, academics, and ordinary believers committed to understanding and responding to domestic violence *with the mind of Christ*. Increasingly we found many people who were committed to the same goals and we were able to join forces—to celebrate our strengths in proclaiming that domestic violence is a serious social problem within and beyond our congregational life and to recognize the diversity of talents to respond to those in need. There is a power in our words and there is an even greater power in our actions.

It is a time to celebrate the work that has been completed. It is also a time to recognize that there is much left to be done. The torch needs to be carried forward. As we look to the future—both as laypeople and as church leaders—we need to consider afresh our role in offering a cup of cold water to the thirsty, a bed for the night to those too frightened to go home, and a coordinated community response, which believes that victims need safety and abusers need accountability.

There is no place for abuse.